THE COUNTER-REVOLUTION OF SCIENCE

The Counter-Revolution of Science

STUDIES ON THE
ABUSE OF REASON

By F. A. Hayek

The Free Press of Glencoe
Collier-Macmillan Limited, London

PREFACE

THE STUDIES united in this volume, although in the first instance published separately in the course of a number of years, form part of a single comprehensive plan. For this republication the exposition has been slightly revised and a few gaps have been filled in, but the main argument is unchanged. Their arrangement is now systematic, in the order in which the argument develops, rather than the accidental one of their first appearance. The book thus begins with a theoretical discussion of the general issues and proceeds to an examination of the historical role played by the ideas in question. This is not mere pedantry or a device for avoiding unnecessary repetition but, it seems to me, essential in order to show the true significance of the particular development. But I am quite aware that as a result the opening sections of the book are relatively more difficult than the rest, and that it might have been more politic to put the more concrete matter in the forefront. I still believe that most readers who are interested in this kind of subject will find the present arrangement more convenient. But any reader who has little taste for abstract discussion may do well to read first the second part which has given the title to this volume. I hope he will then find the general discussion of the same problems in the first study more interesting.

These two major sections of the volume were first published in parts in *Economica* for 1942–1944 and for 1941 respectively. The third study, written more recently as a lecture appeared first in *Measure* for June 1951 but was prepared from notes collected at the same time as those for the first two essays. I have to thank the editors of both these journals and the London School of Economics and Political Science and the Henry Regnery Company of Chicago as their respective publishers for permission to reprint what first appeared under their auspices.

F. A. HAYEK

Contents

THE COUNTER-REVOLUTION OF SCIENCE

Part One

SCIENTISM
AND THE STUDY
OF SOCIETY

> *Systems which have universally owed their origin to the lucubrations of those who were acquainted with one art, but ignorant of the other; who therefore explained to themselves the phenomena, in that which was strange to them, by those in that which was familiar; and with whom, upon that account, the analogy, which in other writers gives occasion to a few ingenious similitudes, became the great hinge on which every thing turned.*
>
> ADAM SMITH (*Essay on the History of Astronomy*).

I

THE INFLUENCE OF THE NATURAL SCIENCES
ON THE SOCIAL SCIENCES

IN THE COURSE of its slow development in the eighteenth and early nineteenth centuries the study of economic and social phenomena was guided in the choice of its methods in the main by the nature of the problems it had to face.[1] It gradually developed a technique appropriate to these problems without much reflection on the character of the methods or on their relation to that of other disciplines of knowledge. Students of political economy could describe it alternatively as a branch of science or of moral or social philosophy without the least qualms whether their subject was scientific or philosophical. The term "science" had not yet assumed the special narrow meaning it has today,[2] nor was there any distinction made which singled out the physical or natural sciences and attributed to them a special dignity. Those who devoted themselves to those fields indeed readily chose the designation of philosophy when they were concerned with the more general aspects of their problems,[3] and occasionally we even find "natural philosophy" contrasted with "moral science."

During the first half of the nineteenth century a new attitude made its appearance. The term science came more and more to be confined to the physical and biological disciplines which at the same time began to claim for themselves a special rigorousness and certainty which distinguished them from all others. Their success was such that they soon came to exercise an extraordinary fascination on those working in other fields, who rapidly began to imitate their teaching and vocabulary. Thus the tyranny commenced which the methods and technique of the Sciences [4] in the narrow sense of the term have ever since exercised over the other subjects. These became increas-

13

ingly concerned to vindicate their equal status by showing that their methods were the same as those of their brilliantly successful sisters rather than by adapting their methods more and more to their own particular problems. And, although in the hundred and twenty years or so, during which this ambition to imitate Science in its methods rather than its spirit has now dominated social studies, it has contributed scarcely anything to our understanding of social phenomena, not only does it continue to confuse and discredit the work of the social disciplines, but demands for further attempts in this direction are still presented to us as the latest revolutionary innovations which, if adopted, will secure rapid undreamed of progress.

Let it be said at once, however, that those who were loudest in these demands were rarely themselves men who had noticeably enriched our knowledge of the Sciences. From Francis Bacon, the Lord Chancellor, who will forever remain the prototype of the "demagogue of science," as he has justly been called, to Auguste Comte and the "physicalists" of our own day, the claims for the exclusive virtues of the specific methods employed by the natural sciences were mostly advanced by men whose right to speak on behalf of the scientists were not above suspicion, and who indeed in many cases had shown in the Sciences themselves as much bigoted prejudice as in their attitude to other subjects. Just as Francis Bacon opposed Copernican Astronomy,[5] and as Comte taught that any too minute investigation of the phenomena by such instruments as the microscope was harmful and should be suppressed by the spiritual power of the positive society, because it tended to upset the laws of positive science, so this dogmatic attitude has so often misled men of this type in their own field that there should have been little reason to pay too much deference to their views about problems still more distant from the fields from which they derived their inspiration.

There is yet another qualification which the reader ought to keep in mind throughout the following discussion. The methods which scientists or men fascinated by the natural sciences have so often tried to force upon the social sciences were not always necessarily those which the scientists in fact followed in their own field, but rather those which they believed that they employed. This is not necessarily the same thing. The scientist reflecting and theorizing about his procedure is not always a reliable guide. The views about the character of the method of Science have undergone various fashions during the last few generations, while we must assume that the methods actually followed have remained essentially the same. But since it was what scientists believed that they did, and even the views which they had held some time before, which have influenced the social sciences, the following comments on the methods of the natural sciences also do not necessarily claim to be a true account of what the scientists in fact do, but an account of the views on the nature of scientific method which were dominant in recent times.

The history of this influence, the channels through which it operated, and the direction in which it affected social developments, will occupy us throughout the series of historical studies to which the present essay is designed to serve as an introduction. Before we trace the historical course of this influence and its effects, we shall here attempt to describe its general characteristics and the nature of the problems to which the unwarranted and unfortunate extensions of the habits of thought of the physical and biological sciences have given rise. There are certain typical elements of this attitude which we shall meet again and again and whose *prima facie* plausibility makes it necessary to examine them with some care. While in the particular historical instances it is not always possible to show how these characteristic views are connected with or derived from the habits of thought of the scientists, this is easier in a systematic survey.

It need scarcely be emphasized that nothing we shall have to say is aimed against the methods of Science in their proper sphere or is intended to throw the slightest doubt on their value. But to preclude any misunderstanding on this point we shall, wherever we are concerned, not with the general spirit of disinterested inquiry but with slavish imitation of the method and language of Science, speak of "scientism" or the "scientistic" prejudice. Although these terms are not completely unknown in English,[6] they are actually borrowed from the French, where in recent years they have come to be generally used in very much the same sense in which they will be used here.[7] It should be noted that, in the sense in which we shall use these terms, they describe, of course, an attitude which is decidedly unscientific in the true sense of the word, since it involves a mechanical and uncritical application of habits of thought to fields different from those in which they have been formed. The scientistic as distinguished from the scientific view is not an unprejudiced but a very prejudiced approach which, before it has considered its subject, claims to know what is the most appropriate way of investigating it.[8]

It would be convenient if a similar term were available to describe the characteristic mental attitude of the engineer which, although in many respects closely related to scientism, is yet distinct from it but which we intend to consider here in connection with the latter. No single word of equal expressiveness suggests itself, however, and we shall have to be content to describe this second element so characteristic of 19th and 20th century thought as the "engineering type of mind."

II

THE PROBLEM AND THE METHOD
OF THE NATURAL SCIENCES

BEFORE WE CAN understand the reasons for the trespasses of scientism we must try to understand the struggle which Science itself had to fight against concepts and ideas which were as injurious to its progress as the scientistic prejudice now threatens to become to the progress of the social studies. Although we live now in an atmosphere where the concepts and habits of thoughts of everyday life are to a high degree influenced by the ways of thinking of Science, we must not forget that the Sciences had in their beginning to fight their way in a world where most concepts had been formed from our relations to other men and in interpreting their actions. It is only natural that the momentum gained in that struggle should carry Science beyond the mark and create a situation where the danger is now the opposite one of the predominance of scientism impeding the progress of the understanding of society.[9] But even if the pendulum has now definitely swung in the opposite direction, only confusion could result if we failed to recognize the factors which have created this attitude and which justify it in its proper sphere.

There were three main obstacles to the advance of modern Science against which it has struggled ever since its birth during the Renaissance; and much of the history of its progress could be written in terms of its gradual overcoming of these difficulties. The first, although not the most important, was that for various reasons scholars had grown used to devoting most of their effort to analyzing other people's opinions: this was so not only because in the disciplines most developed at that time, like theology and law, this was the actual object, but even more because, during the decline of Science in the

17

Middle Ages, there seemed to be no better way of arriving at the truth about nature than to study the work of the great men of the past. More important was the second fact, the belief that the "ideas" of the things possessed some transcendental reality, and that by analyzing ideas we could learn something or everything about the attributes of the real things. The third and perhaps most important fact was that man had begun everywhere to interpret the events in the external world after his own image, as animated by a mind like his own, and that the natural sciences therefore met everywhere explanations by analogy with the working of the human mind, with "anthropomorphic" or "animistic" theories which searched for a purposive design and were satisfied if they had found in it the proof of the operation of a designing mind.

Against all this the persistent effort of modern Science has been to get down to "objective facts," to cease studying what men thought about nature or regarding the given concepts as true images of the real world, and, above all, to discard all theories which pretended to explain phenomena by imputing to them a directing mind like our own. Instead, its main task became to revise and reconstruct the concepts formed from ordinary experience on the basis of a systematic testing of the phenomena, so as to be better able to recognize the particular as an instance of a general rule. In the course of this process not only the provisional classification which the commonly used concepts provided, but also the first distinctions between the different perceptions which our senses convey to us, had to give way to a completely new and different way in which we learned to order or classify the events of the external world.

The tendency to abandon all anthropomorphic elements in the discussion of the external world has in its most extreme development even led to the belief that the demand for "explanation" itself is based on an anthropomorphic interpretation of events and that all Science ought to aim at is a complete description of nature.[10] There is, as we shall see, that element of truth in the first part of this contention that we can understand and explain human action in a way we cannot with physical phenomena, and that consequently the term "explain" tends to remain charged with a meaning not applicable to physical phenomena.[11] The actions of other men were probably the first experiences which made man ask the question "why?" and it took him a long time to learn, and he has not yet fully learned,[12] that with events other than human actions he could not expect the same kind of "explanation" as he can hope to obtain in the case of human behavior.

That the ordinary concepts of the kind of things that surround us do not provide an adequate classification which enables us to state general rules about their behavior in different circumstances, and that in order to do so we have to replace them by a different classification of events is familiar. It may, however, still sound surprising that what is true of these provisional abstractions should also be true of the very sense qualities which most of us are inclined to regard as the ultimate reality. But although it is less familiar that science breaks up and replaces the system of classification which our sense qualities represent, yet this is precisely what Science does. It begins with the realization that things which appear to us the same do not always behave in the same manner, and that things which appear different to us sometimes prove in all other respects to behave in the same way; and it proceeds from this experience to substitute for the classification of events which our senses provide a new one which groups together not what appears alike but what proves to behave in the same manner in similar circumstances.

While the naïve mind tends to assume that external events which our senses register in the same or in a different manner must be similar or different in more respects than merely in the way in which they affect our senses, the systematic testing of Science shows that this is frequently not true. It constantly shows that the "facts" are different from "appearances." We learn to regard as alike or unlike not simply what by itself looks, feels, smells, etc., alike or unlike, but what regularly appears in the same spatial and temporal context. And we learn that the same constellation of simultaneous sense perceptions may prove to proceed from different "facts," or that different combinations of sense qualities may stand for the same "fact." A white powder with a certain weight and "feel" and without taste or smell may prove to be any one of a number of different things according as it appears in different circumstances or after different combinations of other phenomena, or as it produces different results if combined in certain ways with other things. The systematic testing of behavior in different circumstances will thus often show that things which to our senses appear different behave in the same or at least a very similar manner. We may not only find that, e.g., a blue thing which we see in a certain light or after eating a certain drug is the same thing as the green thing which we see in different circumstances, or that what appears to have an elliptical shape may prove to be identical with what at a different angle appears to be circular, but we may also find that phenomena which appear as different as ice and water are "really" the same "thing."

This process of re-classifying "objects" which our senses have already classified in one way, of substituting for the "secondary" qualities in which our senses arrange external stimuli a new classification based on consciously established relations between classes of events is, perhaps, the most characteristic aspect of the procedure of the natural sciences. The whole history of modern Science proves to be a process of progressive emancipation from our innate classification of the external stimuli till in the end they completely disappear so that "physical science has now reached a stage of development that renders it impossible to express observable occurrences in language appropriate to what is perceived by our senses. The only appropriate language is that of mathematics," [13] i.e., the discipline developed to describe complexes of relationships between elements which have no attributes except these relations. While at first the new elements into which the physical world was "analyzed" were still endowed with "qualities," i.e., conceived as in principle visible or touchable, neither electrons nor waves, neither the atomic structure nor electromagnetic fields can be adequately represented by mechanical models.

The new world which man thus creates in his mind, and which consists entirely of entities which cannot be perceived by our senses, is yet in a definite way related to the world of our senses. It serves, indeed, to explain the world of our senses. The world of Science might in fact be described as no more than a set of rules which enables us to trace the connections between different complexes of sense perceptions. But the point is that the attempts to establish such uniform rules which the perceptible phenomena obey have been unsuccessful so long as we accepted as natural units, given entities, such constant complexes of sense qualities as we can simultaneously perceive. In their place new entities, "constructs," are created which can be defined only in terms of sense perceptions obtained of the "same" thing in different circumstances and at different times—a procedure which implies the postulate that the thing has in some sense remained the same although all its perceptible attributes may have changed.

In other words, although the theories of physical science at the stage which has now been reached can no longer be stated in terms of sense qualities, their significance is due to the fact that we possess rules, a "key," which enables us to translate them into statements about perceptible phenomena. One might compare the relation of modern physical theory to the world of our senses to that between the different ways in which one might "know" a dead language existing only in inscriptions in peculiar characters. The combinations of different characters of which these inscriptions are composed and which are the only form in which the language occurs correspond to the different combinations of sense qualities. As we come to know the language we gradually learn that different combinations of these characters may mean the same thing and that in different contexts the same group of characters may mean different things.[14] As we learn to recognize these new entities we penetrate into a new world where the units are different from the letters and obey in their relations definite laws not recognizable in the sequence of the individual letters. We can describe the laws of these new units, the laws of grammar, and all that can be expressed by combining the words according to these laws, without ever referring to the individual letters or the principle on which they are combined to make up the signs for whole words. It would be possible, e.g., to know all about the grammar of Chinese or Greek and the meaning of all the words in these languages without knowing Chinese or Greek characters (or the sounds of the Chinese or Greek words). Yet if Chinese or Greek occurred only written in their respective characters, all this knowledge would be of as little use as knowledge of the laws of nature in terms of abstract entities or constructs without knowledge of the rules by which these can be translated into statements about phenomena perceptible by our senses.

As in our description of the structure of the language there is no need for a description of the way in which the different units are made up from various combinations of letters (or sounds), so in our theoretical description of nature the different sense qualities through which we perceive nature disappear. They are no longer treated as part of the object and come to be regarded merely as ways in which we spontaneously perceive or classify external stimuli.[15]

The problem how man has come to classify external stimuli in the particular way which we know as sense qualities does not concern us here.[16] There are only two connected points which must be briefly mentioned now and to which we must return later. One is that, once we have learnt that the things in the external world show uniformity in their behavior towards each other only if we group them in a way different from that in which they appear to our senses, the question why they appear to us in that particular way, and especially why they appear in the same [17] way to different people becomes a genuine problem calling for an answer. The second is that the fact that different men do perceive different things in a similar manner which does not correspond to any known relation between these things in the external world, must be regarded as a significant datum of experience which must be the starting point in any discussion of human behavior.

We are not interested here in the methods of the Sciences for their own sake and we cannot follow up this topic further. The point which we mainly wanted to stress was that what men know or think about the external world or about themselves, their concepts and even the subjective qualities of their sense perceptions are to Science never ultimate reality, data to be accepted. Its concern is not what men think about the world and how they consequently behave, but what they ought to think. The concepts which men actually employ, the way in which they see nature, is to the scientist necessarily a provisional affair and his task is to change this picture, to change the concepts in use so as to be able to make more definite and more certain our statements about the new classes of events.

There is one consequence of all this which in view of what

follows requires a few more words. It is the special signficance which numerical statements and quantitative measurements have in the natural sciences. There is a widespread impression that the main importance of this quantitative nature of most natural sciences is their greater precision. This is not so. It is not merely adding precision to a procedure which would be possible also without the mathematical form of expression—it is of the essence of this process of breaking up our immediate sense data and of substituting for a description in terms of sense qualities one in terms of elements which possess no attributes but these relations to each other. It is a necessary part of the general effort of getting away from the picture of nature which man has now, of substituting for the classification of events which our senses provide another based on the relations established by systematic testing and experimenting.

To return to our more general conclusion: the world in which Science is interested is not that of our given concepts or even sensations. Its aim is to produce a new organization of all our experience of the external world, and in doing so it has not only to remodel our concepts but also to get away from the sense qualities and to replace them by a different classification of events. The picture which man has actually formed of the world and which guides him well enough in his daily life, his perceptions and concepts, are for Science not an object of study but an imperfect instrument to be improved. Nor is Science as such interested in the relation of man to things, in the way in which man's existing view of the world leads him to act. It *is* rather such a relation, or better a continuous process of changing these relationships. When the scientist stresses that he studies objective facts he means that he tries to study things independently of what men think or do about them. The views people hold about the external world is to him always a stage to be overcome.

But what are the consequences of the fact that people perceive the world and each other through sensations and concepts which are organized in a mental structure common to all of them? What can we say about the whole network of activities in which men are guided by the kind of knowledge they have and a great part of which at any time is common to most of them? While Science is all the time busy revising the picture of the external world that man possesses, and while to it this picture is always provisional, the fact that man has a definite picture, and that the picture of all beings whom we recognize as thinking men and whom we can understand is to some extent alike, is no less a reality of great consequence and the cause of certain events. Until Science had literally completed its work and not left the slightest unexplained residue in man's intellectual processes, the facts of our mind must remain not only data to be explained but also data on which the explanation of human action guided by those mental phenomena must be based. Here a new set of problems arises with which the scientist does not directly deal. Nor is it obvious that the particular methods to which he has become used would be appropriate for these problems. The question is here not how far man's picture of the external world fits the facts, but how by his actions, determined by the views and concepts he possesses, man builds up another world of which the individual becomes a part. And by "the views and concepts people hold" we do not mean merely their knowledge of external nature. We mean all they know and believe about themselves, about other people, and about the external world, in short everything which determines their actions, including science itself.

This is the field to which the social studies or the "moral sciences" address themselves.

III

THE SUBJECTIVE CHARACTER OF THE DATA
OF THE SOCIAL SCIENCES

BEFORE WE PROCEED to consider the effect of scientism on the study of society it will be expedient briefly to survey the peculiar object and the methods of the social studies. They deal, not with the relations between things, but with the relations between men and things or the relations between man and man. They are concerned with man's actions, and their aim is to explain the unintended or undesigned results of the actions of many men.

Not all the disciplines of knowledge which are concerned with the life of men in groups, however, raise problems which differ in any important respect from those of the natural sciences. The spread of contagious diseases is evidently a problem closely connected with the life of man in society and yet its study has none of the special characteristics of the social sciences in the narrower sense of the term. Similarly the study of heredity, or the study of nutrition, or the investigation of changes in the number or age composition of populations, do not differ significantly from similar studies of animals.[18] And the same applies to certain branches of anthropology, or ethnology, in so far as they are concerned with physical attributes of men. There are, in other words, natural sciences of man which do not necessarily raise problems with which we cannot cope with the methods of the natural sciences. Wherever we are concerned with unconscious reflexes or processes in the human body there is no obstacle to treating and investigating them "mechanically" as caused by objectively observable external events. They take place without the knowledge of the man concerned and without his having power to modify them; and the conditions under which they are produced can

25

be established by external observation without recourse to the assumption that the person observed classifies the external stimuli in any way differently from that in which they can be defined in purely physical terms.

The social sciences in the narrower sense, i.e., those which used to be described as the moral sciences,[19] are concerned with man's conscious or reflected action, actions where a person can be said to choose between various courses open to him, and here the situation is essentially different. The external stimulus which may be said to cause or occasion such actions can of course also be defined in purely physical terms. But if we tried to do so for the purposes of explaining human action, we would confine ourselves to less than we know about the situation. It is not because we have found two things to behave alike in relation to other things, but because they appear alike to us, that we expect them to appear alike to other people. We know that people will react in the same way to external stimuli which according to all objective tests are different, and perhaps also that they will react in a completely different manner to a physically identical stimulus if it affects their bodies in different circumstances or at a different point. We know, in other words, that in his conscious decisions man classifies external stimuli in a way which we know solely from our own subjective experience of this kind of classification. We take it for granted that other men treat various things as alike or unlike just as we do, although no objective test, no knowledge of the relations of these things to other parts of the external world justifies this. Our procedure is based on the experience that other people as a rule (though not always—e.g., not if they are colorblind or mad) classify their sense impressions as we do.

But we not only know this. It would be impossible to explain or understand human action without making use of this knowledge. People do behave in the same manner towards things, not because these things are identical in a physical sense, but because they have learnt to classify them as belonging to the same group, because they can put them to the same use or expect from them what to the people concerned is an equivalent effect. In fact, most of the objects of social or human action are not "objective facts" in the special narrow sense in which this term is used by the Sciences and contrasted to "opinions," and they cannot at all be defined in physical terms. So far as human actions are concerned the things *are* what the acting people think they are.

This is best shown by an example for which we can choose almost any object of human action. Take the concept of a "tool" or "instrument," or of any particular tool such as a hammer or a barometer. It is easily seen that these concepts cannot be interpreted to refer to "objective facts," i.e., to things irrespective of what people think about them. Careful logical analysis of these concepts will show that they all express relationships between several (at least three) terms, of which one is the acting or thinking person, the other some desired or imagined effect, and the third a thing in the ordinary sense. If the reader will attempt a definition he will soon find that he cannot give one without using some terms such as "suitable for" or "intended for" or some other expression referring to the use for which it is designed by somebody.[20] And a definition which is to comprise all instances of the class will not contain any reference to its substance, or shape, or other physical attribute. An ordinary hammer and a steam-hammer, or an aneroid barometer and a mercury barometer, have nothing in common except the purpose [21] for which men think they can be used.

It must not be objected that these are merely instances of abstractions to arrive at generic terms just as those used in the physical sciences. The point is that they are abstractions from *all* the physical attributes of the things in question and that their definitions must run entirely in terms of mental attitudes of men towards the things. The significant difference between the two views of the things stands out clearly if we think e.g. of the problem of the archæologist trying to determine whether what looks like a stone implement is in truth an "artifact," made by man, or merely a chance product of nature. There is no way of deciding this but by trying to understand the working of the mind of prehistoric man, of attempting to understand how he would have made such an implement. If we are not more aware that this is what we actually do in such cases and that we necessarily rely on our own knowledge of the working of a human mind, this is so mainly because of the impossibility of conceiving of an observer who does not possess a human mind and interprets what he sees in terms of the working of his own mind.

There are no better terms available to describe this difference between the approach of the natural and the social sciences than to call the former "objective" and the latter "subjective." Yet these terms are ambiguous and might prove misleading without further explanation. While for the natural scientist the contrast between objective facts and subjective opinions is a simple one, the distinction cannot as readily be applied to the object of the social sciences. The reason for this is that the object, the "facts" of the social sciences are also opinions—not opinions of the student of the social phenomena, of course, but opinions of those whose actions produce the object of the social scientist. In one sense his facts are thus as little "subjective" as those of the natural sciences, because they are independent of the particular observer; what he studies is not determined by his fancy or imagination but is in the same manner given to the observation by different people. But in another sense in which we distinguish facts from opinions, the facts of the social sciences are merely opinions, views held by the people whose actions we study. They differ from the facts of the physical sciences in being beliefs or opinions held by particular people, beliefs which as such are our data, irrespective of whether they are true or false, and which, moreover, we cannot directly observe in the minds of the people but which we can recognize from what they do and say merely because we have ourselves a mind similar to theirs.

In the sense in which we here use the contrast between the subjectivist approach of the social sciences and the objectivist approach of the natural sciences it says little more than what is commonly expressed by saying that the former deal in the first instance with the phenomena of individual minds, or mental phenomena, and not directly with material phenomena. They deal with phenomena which can be understood only because the object of our study has a mind of a structure similar to our own. That this is so is no less an empirical fact than our knowledge of the external world. It is shown not merely by the possibility of communicating with other people—we act on this knowledge every time we speak or write; it is confirmed by the very results of our study of the external world. So long as it was naïvely assumed that all the sense qualities (or their relations) which different men had in common were properties of the external world, it could be argued that our knowledge of other minds is no more than our common knowledge of the external world. But once we have learnt that our senses make things appear to us alike or different which prove to be alike or different in none of their relations between themselves, but only in the way in which they affect our senses, this fact that men classify external stimuli in a particular way becomes a significant fact of experience. While qualities disappear from our scientific picture of the external world they must remain part of our scientific picture of the human mind. In fact the elimination of qualities from our picture of the external world does not mean that these qualities do not "exist," but that when we study qualities we study not the physical world but the mind of man.

In some connections, for instance when we distinguish between the "objective" properties of things which manifest themselves in their relations to each other, and the properties merely attributed to them by men, it might be preferable to contrast "objective" with "attributed," instead of using the ambiguous term "subjective." The word "attributed" is, however, only of limited usefulness. The main reasons why it is expedient to retain the terms "subjective" and "objective" for the contrast with which we are concerned, although they inevitably carry with them some misleading connotations, are not only that most of the other available terms, such as "mental" and "material," carry with them an even worse burden of metaphysical associations, and that at least in economics [22] the term "subjective" has long been used precisely in the sense in which we use it here. What is more important is that the term "subjective" stresses another important fact to which we shall yet have to refer: that the knowledge and beliefs of different people, while possessing that common structure which makes communication possible, will yet be different and often conflicting in many respects. If we could assume that all the knowledge and beliefs of different people were identical, or if we were concerned with a single mind, it would not matter whether we described it as an "objective" fact or as a subjective phenomenon. But the concrete knowledge which guides the action of any group of people never exists as a consistent and coherent body. It only exists in the dispersed, incomplete, and inconsistent form in which it appears in many individual minds, and this dispersion and imperfection of all knowledge is one of the basic facts from which the social sciences have to start. What philosophers and logicians often contemptuously dismiss as "mere" imperfections of the human mind becomes in the social sciences a basic fact of crucial importance. We shall later see how the opposite "absolutist" view, as if knowledge, and particularly the concrete knowledge of particular circumstances, were given "objectively," i.e., as if it were the same for all people, is a source of constant errors in the social sciences.

The "tool" or "instrument" which we have before used as an illustration of the objects of human action can be matched by similar instances from any other branch of social study. A "word" or a "sentence," a "crime" or a "punishment," [23] are of course not objective facts in the sense that they can be defined without referring to our knowledge of people's conscious intentions with regard to them. And the same is quite generally true wherever we have to explain human behavior towards things; these things must then not be defined in terms of what we might find out about them by the objective methods of science, but in terms of what the person acting thinks about them. A medicine or a cosmetic, e.g., for the purposes of social study, are not what cures an ailment or improves a person's looks, but what people think will have that effect. Any knowledge which we may happen to possess about the true nature of the material thing, but which the people whose action we want to explain do not possess, is as little relevant to the explanation of their actions as our private disbelief in the efficacy of a magic charm will help us to understand the behavior of the savage who believes in it. If in investigating our contemporary society the "laws of nature" which we have to use as a datum because they affect people's actions are approximately the same as those which figure in the works of the natural scientists, this is for our purposes an accident which must not deceive us about the different character of these laws in the two fields. What is relevant in the study of society is not whether these laws of nature are true in any objective sense, but solely whether they are believed and acted upon by the people. If the current "scientific" knowledge of the society which we study included the belief that the soil will bear no fruit till certain rites or incantations are performed, this would be quite as important for us as any law of nature which we now believe to be correct. And all the "physical laws of production" which we meet, e.g., in economics, are not physical laws in the sense of the physical sciences but people's beliefs about what they can do.

What is true about the relations of men to things is, of course, even more true of the relations between men, which for the purposes of social study cannot be defined in the objective terms of the physical sciences but only in terms of human beliefs. Even such a seemingly purely biological relationship as that between parent and child is in social study not defined in physical terms and cannot be so defined for their purposes: it makes no difference with regard to people's actions whether their belief that a particular child is their natural offspring is mistaken or not.

All this stands out most clearly in that among the social sciences whose theory has been most highly developed, economics. And it is probably no exaggeration to say that every important advance in economic theory during the last hundred years was a further step in the consistent application of subjectivism.[24] That the objects of economic activity cannot be defined in objective terms but only with reference to a human purpose goes without saying. Neither a "commodity" or an "economic good," nor "food" or "money," can be defined in physical terms but only in terms of views people hold about things. Economic theory has nothing to say about the little round disks of metal as which an objective or materialist view might try to define money. It has nothing to say about iron or steel, timber or oil, or wheat or eggs as such. The history of any particular commodity indeed shows that as human knowledge changes the same material thing may represent quite different economic categories. Nor could we distinguish in physical terms whether two men barter or exchange or whether they are playing some game or performing some religious ritual. Unless we can understand what the acting people mean by their actions any attempt to explain them, i.e., to subsume them under rules which connect similar situations with similar actions, are bound to fail.[25]

This essentially subjective character of all economic theory, which it has developed much more clearly than most other branches of the social sciences,[26] but which I believe it has in common with all the social sciences in the narrower sense, is best shown by a closer consideration of one of its simplest theorems, e.g., the "law of rent." In its original form this was a proposition about changes in the value of a thing defined in physical terms, namely land. It stated, in effect,[27] that changes in the value of the commodities in the production of which land was required would cause much greater changes in the value of land than in the value of the other factors whose co-operation was required. In this form it is an empirical generalization which tells us neither why nor under what conditions it will be true. In modern economics its place is taken by two distinct propositions of different character which together lead to the same conclusion. One is part of pure economic theory and asserts that whenever in the production of one commodity different (scarce) factors are required in proportions which can be varied, and of which one can be used only for this (or only for comparatively few) purposes while the others are of a more general usefulness, a change in the value of the product will affect the value of the former more than that of the latter. The second proposition is the empirical statement that land is as a rule in the position of the first kind of factor, i.e. that people know of many more uses for their labor than they will know for a particular piece of land. The first of these propositions, like all propositions of pure economic theory, is a statement about the implications of certain human attitudes towards things and as such necessarily true irrespective of time and place. The second is an assertion that the conditions postulated in the first proposition prevail at a given time and with respect to a particular piece of land, because the people dealing with it hold certain beliefs about its usefulness and the usefulness of other things required in order to cultivate it. As an empirical generalization it can of course be disproved and frequently will be disproved. If, e.g., a piece of land is used to produce some special fruit the cultivation of which requires a certain rare skill, the effect of a fall in the demand for the fruit may fall exclusively on the wages of the men with the special skill, while the value of the land may remain practically unaffected. In such a situation it would be labor to which the "law of rent" applies. But when we ask: "why?" or: "how can I find out whether the law of rent will apply in any particular case?" no information about the physical attributes of the land, the labor, or the product can give us the answer. It depends on the subjective factors stated in the theoretical law of rent; and only in so far as we can find out what the knowledge and beliefs of the people concerned are in the relevant respects shall we be in a position to predict in what manner a change in the price of the product will affect the prices of the factors. What is true of the theory of rent is true of the theory of price generally: it has nothing to say about the behavior of the price of iron or wool, of things of such and such physical properties, but only about things about which people have certain beliefs and which they want to use in a certain manner. And our explanation of a particular price phenomenon can therefore also never be affected by any additional knowledge which we (the observers) acquire about the good concerned, but only by additional knowledge about what the people dealing with it think about it.

We cannot here enter into a similar discussion of the more complex phenomena with which economic theory is concerned and where in recent years progress has been particularly closely connected with the advance of subjectivism. We can only point to the new problems which these developments make appear more and more central, such as the problem of the compatibility of intentions and expectations of different people, of the division of knowledge between them, and the process by which the relevant knowledge is acquired and expectations formed.[28] We are not here concerned, however, with the specific problems of economics, but with the common character of all disciplines which deal with the results of conscious human action. The points which we want to stress are that in all such attempts we must start from what men think and mean to do: from the fact that the individuals which compose society are guided in their actions by a classification of things or events according to a system of sense qualities and of concepts which has a common structure and which we know because we, too, are men; and that the concrete knowledge which different individuals possess will differ in important respects. Not only man's action towards external objects but also all the relations between men and all the social institutions can be understood only in terms of what men think about them. Society as we know it is, as it were, built up from the concepts and ideas held by the people; and social phenomena can be recognized by us and have meaning to us only as they are reflected in the minds of men.

The structure of men's minds, the common principle on which they classify external events, provide us with the knowledge of the recurrent elements of which different social structures are built up and in terms of which we can alone describe and explain them.[29] While concepts or ideas can, of course, exist only in individual minds, and while, in particular, it is only in individual minds that different ideas can act upon another, it is not the whole of the individual minds in all their complexity, but the individual concepts, the views people have formed of each other and of the things, which form the true elements of the social structure. If the social structure can remain the same although different individuals succeed each other at particular points, this is not because the individuals which succeed each other are completely identical, but because they succeed each other in particular relations, in particular attitudes they take towards other people and as the objects of particular views held by other people about them. The individuals are merely the *foci* in the network of relationships and it is the various attitudes of the individuals towards each other (or their similar or different attitudes towards physical objects) which form the recurrent, recognizable and familiar elements of the structure. If one policeman succeeds another at a particular post, this does not mean that the new man will in all respects be identical with his predecessor, but merely that he succeeds him in certain attitudes towards his fellow man and as the object of certain attitudes of his fellow men which are relevant to his function as policeman. But this is sufficient to preserve a constant structural element which can be separated and studied in isolation.

While we can recognize these elements of human relationships only because they are known to us from the working of our own minds, this does not mean that the significance of their combination in a particular pattern relating different individuals must be immediately obvious to us. It is only by the systematic and patient following up of the implications of many people holding certain views that we can understand, and often even only learn to see, the unintended and often uncomprehended results of the separate and yet interrelated actions of men in society. That in this effort to reconstruct these different patterns of social relations we must relate the individual's action not to the objective qualities of the persons and things towards which he acts, but that our data must be man and the physical world as they appear to the men whose actions we try to explain, follows from the fact that only what people know or believe can enter as a motive into their conscious action.

IV

THE INDIVIDUALIST AND "COMPOSITIVE" METHOD OF THE SOCIAL SCIENCES

AT THIS POINT it becomes necessary briefly to interrupt the main argument in order to safeguard ourselves against a misconception which might arise from what has just been said. The stress which we have laid on the fact that in the social sciences our data or "facts" are themselves ideas or concepts must, of course, not be understood to mean that *all* the concepts with which we have to deal in the social sciences are of this character. There would be no room for any scientific work if this were so; and the social sciences no less than the natural sciences aim at revising the popular concepts which men have formed about the objects of their study, and at replacing them by more appropriate ones. The special difficulties of the social sciences, and much confusion about their character, derive precisely from the fact that in them ideas appear in two capacities, as it were, as part of their object and as ideas about that object. While in the natural sciences the contrast between the object of our study and our explanation of it coincides with the distinction between ideas and objective facts, in the social sciences it is necessary to draw a distinction between those ideas which are *constitutive* of the phenomena we want to explain and the ideas which either we ourselves or the very people whose actions we have to explain may have formed *about* these phenomena and which are not the cause of, but theories about, the social structures.

This special difficulty of the social sciences is a result, not merely of the fact that we have to distinguish between the views held by the people which are the object of our study and our views about them, but also of the fact that the people who are our object them-

36

selves not only are motivated by ideas but also form ideas about the undesigned results of their actions—popular theories about the various social structures or formations which we share with them and which our study has to revise and improve. The danger of substituting "concepts" (or "theories") for the "facts" is by no means absent in the social sciences and failure to avoid it has exercised as detrimental an effect here as in the natural sciences; [30] but it appears on a different plane and is very inadequately expressed by the contrast between "ideas" and "facts." The real contrast is between ideas which by being held by the people become the causes of a social phenomenon and the ideas which people form about that phenomenon. That these two classes of ideas are distinct (although in different contexts the distinction may have to be drawn differently [31]) can easily be shown. The changes in the opinions which people hold about a particular commodity and which we recognize as the cause of a change in the price of that commodity stand clearly in a different class from the ideas which the same people may have formed about the causes of the change in price or about the "nature of value" in general. Similarly, the beliefs and opinions which lead a number of people regularly to repeat certain acts, e.g. to produce, sell, or buy certain quantities of commodities, are entirely different from the ideas they may have formed about the whole of the "society," or the "economic system," to which they belong and which the aggregate of all their actions constitutes. The first kind of opinions and beliefs are a condition of the existence of the "wholes" which would not exist without them; they are, as we have said, "constitutive," essential for the existence of the phenomenon which the people refer to as "society" or the "economic system," but which will exist irrespectively of the concepts which the people have formed about these wholes.

It is very important that we should carefully distinguish between the motivating or constitutive opinions on the one hand and the speculative or explanatory views which people have formed about the wholes; confusion between the two is a source of constant danger. Is it the ideas which the popular mind has formed about such collectives as "society" or the "economic system," "capitalism" or "imperialism," and other such collective entities, which the social scientist must regard as no more than provisional theories, popular abstractions, and which he must not mistake for facts. That he consistently refrains from treating these pseudo-entities as "facts," and that he systematically starts from the concepts which guide individuals in their actions and not from the results of their theorizing about their actions, is the characteristic feature of that methodological individualism which is closely connected with the subjectivism of the social sciences. The scientistic approach, on the other hand, because it is afraid of starting from the subjective concepts determining individual actions, is, as we shall presently see, regularly led into the very mistake it attempts to avoid, namely of treating as facts those collectives which are no more than popular generalizations. Trying to avoid using as data the concepts held by individuals where they are clearly recognizable and explicitly introduced as what they are, people brought up in scientistic views frequently and naïvely accept the speculative concepts of popular usage as definite facts of the kind they are familiar with.

We shall have to discuss the nature of this collectivist prejudice inherent in the scientistic approach more fully in a later section.

A few more remarks must be added about the specific theoretical method which corresponds to the systematic subjectivism and individualism of the social sciences. From the fact that it is the concepts and views held by individuals which are directly known to us and which form the elements from which we must build up, as it were, the more complex phenomena, follows another important difference between the method of the social disciplines and the natural sciences. While in the former it is the attitudes of individuals which are the familiar elements and by the combination of which we try to reproduce the complex phenomena, the results of individual actions, which are much less known—a procedure which often leads to the *discovery* of principles of structural coherence of the complex phenomena which had not (and perhaps could not) be established by direct observation—the physical sciences necessarily begin with the complex phenomena of nature and work backwards to infer the elements from which they are composed. The place where the human individual stands in the order of things brings it about that in one direction what he perceives are the comparatively complex phenomena which he analyzes, while in the other direction what is given to him are elements from which those more complex phenomena are composed that he cannot observe as wholes.[32] While the method of the natural sciences is in this sense, analytic, the method of the social sciences is better described as compositive [33] or synthetic. It is the so-called wholes, the groups of elements which are structurally connected, which we learn to single out from the totality of observed phenomena only as a result to our systematic fitting together of the elements with familiar properties, and which we build up or reconstruct from the known properties of the elements.

It is important to observe that in all this the various types of individual beliefs or attitudes are not themselves the object of our explanation, but merely the elements from which we build up the structure of possible relationships between individuals. In so far as we analyze individual thought in the social sciences the purpose is not to explain that thought but merely to distinguish the possible types of elements with which we shall have to reckon in the construction of different patterns of social relationships. It is a mistake, to which careless expressions by social scientists often give countenance, to believe that their aim is to *explain* conscious action. This, if it can be done at all, is a different task, the task of psychology. For the social sciences the types of conscious action are data [34] and all they have to do with regard to these data is to arrange them in such orderly fashion that they can be effectively used for their task.[35] The problems which they try to answer arise only in so far as the conscious action of many men produce undesigned results, in so far as regularities are observed which are not the result of anybody's design. If social phenomena showed no order except in so far as they were consciously designed, there would indeed be no room for theoretical sciences of society and there would be, as is often argued, only problems of psychology. It is only in so far as some sort of order arises as a result of individual action but without being designed by any individual that a problem is raised which demands a theoretical explanation. But although people dominated by the scientistic prejudice are often inclined to deny the existence of any such order (and thereby the existence of an object for theoretical sciences of society), few if any would be prepared to do so consistently: that at least language shows a definite order which is not the result of any conscious design can scarcely be questioned.

The reason of the difficulty which the natural scientist experiences in admitting the existence of such an order in social phenomena is that these orders cannot be stated in physical terms, that if we define the elements in physical terms no such order is visible, and that the units which show an orderly arrangement do not (or at least need not) have any physical properties in common (except that men react to them in the "same" way—although the "sameness" of different people's reaction will again, as a rule, not be definable in physical terms). It is an order in which things behave in the same way because they mean the same thing to man. If, instead of regarding as alike and unlike what appears so to the acting man, we were to take for our units only what Science shows to be alike or unlike, we should probably find no recognizable order whatever in social phenomena—at least not till the natural sciences had completed their task of analysing all natural phenomena into their ultimate constituents and psychology had also fully achieved the reverse task of explaining in all detail how the ultimate units of physical science come to appear to man just as they do, i.e., how that apparatus of classification operates which our senses constitute.

It is only in the very simplest instances that it can be shown briefly and without any technical apparatus how the independent actions of individuals will produce an order which is no part of their intentions; and in those instances the explanation is usually so obvious that we never stop to examine the type of argument which leads us to it. The way in which footpaths are formed in a wild broken country is such an instance. At first everyone will seek for himself what seems to him the best path. But the fact that such a path has been used once is likely to make it easier to traverse and therefore more likely to be used again; and thus gradually more and more clearly defined tracks arise and come to be used to the exclusion of other possible ways. Human movements through the region come to conform to a definite pattern which, although the result of deliberate decisions of many people, has yet not been consciously designed by anyone. This explanation of how this happens is an elementary "theory" applicable to hundreds of particular historical instances; and it is not the observation of the actual growth of any particular track, and still less of many, from which this explanation derives its cogency, but from our general knowledge of how we and other people behave in the kind of situation in which the successive people find themselves who have to seek their way and who by the cumulative effect of their action create the path. It is the elements of the complex of events which are familiar to us from everyday experience, but it is only by a deliberate effort of directed thought that we come to see the necessary effects of the combination of such actions by many people. We "understand" the way in which the result we observe can be produced, although we may never be in a position to watch the whole process or to predict its precise course and result.

It makes no difference for our present purpose whether the process extends over a long period of time as it does in such cases as the evolution of money or the formation of language, or whether it is a process which is constantly repeated anew as in the case of the formation of prices or the direction of production under competition. The former instances raise theoretical (i.e. generic) problems (as distinguished from the specifically historical problems in the precise sense which we shall have to define later) which are fundamentally similar to the problems raised by such recurring phenomena as the determination of prices. Although in the study of any particular instance of the evolution of an "institution" like money or the language the theoretical problem will frequently be so overlaid by the consideration of the particular circumstances involved (the properly historical task), this does not alter the fact that any explanation of a historical process involves assumptions about the kind of circumstances that can produce certain kinds of effects—assumptions which, where we have to deal with results which were not directly willed by somebody, can only be stated in the form of a generic scheme, in other words a theory.

The physicist who wishes to understand the problems of the social sciences with the help of an analogy from his own field would have to imagine a world in which he knew by direct observation the inside of the atoms and had neither the possibility of making experiments with lumps of matter nor opportunity to observe more than the interactions of a comparatively few atoms during a limited period.

From his knowledge of the different kinds of atoms he could build up models of all the various ways in which they could combine into larger units and make these models more and more closely reproduce all the features of the few instances in which he was able to observe more complex phenomena. But the laws of the macrocosm which he could derive from his knowledge of the microcosm would always remain "deductive"; they would, because of his limited knowledge of the data of the complex situation, scarcely ever enable him to predict the precise outcome of a particular situation; and he could never confirm them by controlled experiment—although they might be disproved by the observation of events which according to his theory are impossible.

In a sense some problems of theoretical astronomy are more similar to those of the social sciences than those of any of the experimental sciences. Yet there remain important differences. While the astronomer aims at knowing all the elements of which his universe is composed, the student of social phenomena cannot hope to know more than the types of elements from which his universe is made up. He will scarcely ever know even of all the elements of which it consists and he will certainly never know all the relevant properties of each of them. The inevitable imperfection of the human mind becomes here not only a basic datum about the object of explanation but, since it applies no less to the observer, also a limitation on what he can hope to accomplish in his attempt to explain the observed facts. The number of separate variables which in any particular social phenomenon will determine the result of a given change will as a rule be far too large for any human mind to master and manipulate them effectively.[36] In consequence our knowledge of the principle by which these phenomena are produced will rarely if ever enable us to predict the precise result of any concrete situation. While we can explain the principle on which certain phenomena are produced and can from this knowledge exclude the possibility of certain results, e.g. of certain events occurring together, our knowledge will in a sense be only negative, i.e. it will merely enable us to preclude certain results but not enable us to narrow the range of possibilities sufficiently so that only one remains.

The distinction between an explanation merely of the principle on which a phenomenon is produced and an explanation which enables us to predict the precise result is of great importance for the understanding of the theoretical methods of the social sciences. It arises, I believe, also elsewhere, e.g. in biology, and certainly in psychology. It is, however, somewhat unfamiliar and I know no place where it is adequately explained. The best illustration in the field of the social sciences is probably the general theory of prices as represented, e.g., by the Walrasian or Paretian systems of equations. These systems show merely the principle of coherence between the prices of the various types of commodities of which the system is composed; but without knowledge of the numerical values of all the constants which occur in it and which we never do know, this does not enable us to predict the precise results which any particular change will have.[37] Apart from this particular case, a set of equations which shows merely the form of a system of relationships but does not give the values of the constants contained in it, is perhaps the best general illustration of an explanation merely of the principle on which any phenomenon is produced.

This must suffice as a positive description of the characteristic problems of the social sciences. It will become clearer as we contrast in the following sections the specific procedure of the social sciences with the most characteristic aspects of the attempts to treat their object after the fashion of the natural sciences.

V

THE OBJECTIVISM OF THE SCIENTISTIC APPROACH

THE GREAT DIFFERENCES between the characteristic methods of the physical sciences and those of the social sciences explain why the natural scientist who turns to the work of the professional students of social phenomena so often feels that he has got among a company of people who habitually commit all the mortal sins which he is most careful to avoid, and that a science of society conforming to his standards does not yet exist. From this to the attempt to create a new science of society which satisfies his conception of Science is but a step. During the last four generations attempts of this kind have been constantly made; and though they have never produced the results which had been expected, and though they did not even succeed in creating that continuous tradition which is the symptom of a healthy discipline, they are repeated almost every month by someone who hopes thereby to revolutionize social thought. Yet, though these efforts are mostly disconnected, they regularly show certain characteristic features which we must now consider. These methodological features can be conveniently treated under the headings of "objectivism," "collectivism," and "historicism," corresponding to the "subjectivism," the "individualism," and the theoretical character of the developed disciplines of social study.

The attitude which, for want of a better term, we shall call the "objectivism" of the scientistic approach to the study of man and society, has found its most characteristic expression in the various attempts to dispense with our subjective knowledge of the working of the human mind, attempts which in various forms have affected almost all branches of social study. From Auguste Comte's denial of the possibility of introspection, through various attempts to create an

44

"objective psychology," down to the behaviorism of J. B. Watson and the "physicalism" of O. Neurath, a long series of authors have attempted to do without the knowledge derived from "introspection." But, as can be easily shown, these attempts to avoid the use of knowledge which we possess are bound to break down.

A behaviorist or physicalist, to be consistent, ought not to begin by observing the reactions of people to what our senses tell us are similar objects; he ought to confine himself to studying the reactions to stimuli which are identical in a strictly physical sense. He ought, e.g., not to study the reactions of persons who are shown a red circle or made to hear a certain tune, but solely the effects of a light wave of a certain frequency on a particular point of the retina of the human eye, etc., etc. No behaviorist, however, seriously contemplates doing so. They all take it naïvely for granted that what appears alike to us will also appear alike to other people. Though they have no business to do so, they make constant use of the classification of external stimuli by our senses and our mind as alike or unlike, a classification which we know only from our personal experience of it and which is not based on any objective tests showing that these facts also behave similarly in relation to each other. This applies as much to what we commonly regard as simple sense qualities, such as color, the pitch of sound, smell, etc., as to our perception of configurations (*Gestalten*) by which we classify physically very different things as specimens of a particular "shape," e.g., as a circle or a certain tune. To the behaviorist or physicalist the fact that we recognize these things as similar is no problem.

This naïve attitude, however, is in no way justified by what the development of physical science itself teaches us. As we have seen before,[38] one of the main results of this development is that things that to us appear alike may not be alike in any objective sense, i.e., may have no other properties in common. Once we have to recognize, however, that things differ in their effects on our senses not necessarily in the same way in which they differ in their behavior towards each other, we are no longer entitled to take it for granted that what to us appears alike or different will also appear so to others. That this is so as a rule is an important empirical fact which, on the one hand, demands explanation (a task for psychology) and which, on the other hand, must be accepted as a basic datum in our study of people's conduct. That different objects mean the same thing to different people, or that different people mean the same thing by different acts, remain important facts though physical science may show that these objects or acts possess no other common properties.

It is true, of course, that we know nothing about other people's minds except through sense perceptions, i.e., the observation of physical facts. But this does not mean that we know nothing but physical facts. Of what kind the facts are with which we have to deal in any discipline is not determined by all the properties possessed by the concrete objects to which the discipline applies, but only by those properties by which we classify them for the purposes of the discipline in question. To take an example from the physical sciences: all levers or pendulums of which we can conceive have chemical and optical properties; but when we talk about levers or pendulums we do not talk about chemical or optical facts. What makes a number of individual phenomena facts of one kind are the attributes which we select in order to treat them as members of one class. And though all social phenomena with which we can possibly be concerned will possess physical attributes, this does not mean that they must be physical facts for our purpose.

The significant point about the objects of human activity with which we are concerned in the social sciences, and about these human activities themselves, is that in interpreting human activities we spontaneously and unconsciously class together as instances of the same object or the same act any one of a large number of physical facts which may have no physical property in common. We know that other people like ourselves regard any one of a large number of physically different things, $a, b, c, d, \ldots$ etc., as belonging to the same class; and we know this because other people, like ourselves, react to any one of these things by any one of the movements $\alpha, \beta, \gamma, \delta, \ldots$ which again may have no physical property in common. Yet this knowledge on which we constantly act, which must necessarily precede, and is pre-supposed by, any communication with other men, is not conscious knowledge in the sense that we are in a position exhaustively to enumerate all the different physical phenomena which we unhesitatingly recognize as members of the class: we do not know which of many possible combinations of physical properties we shall recognize as a certain word, or as a "friendly face" or a "threatening gesture." Probably in no single instance has experimental research yet succeeded in precisely determining the range of different phenomena which we unhesitatingly treat as meaning the same thing to us as well as to other people; yet we constantly and successfully act on the assumption that we do classify these things in the same manner as other people do. We are not in a position—and may never be in the position—to substitute objects defined in physical terms for the mental categories we employ in talking about other people's actions.[39] Whenever we do so the physical facts to which we refer are significant not as physical facts, i.e., not as members of a class all of which have certain physical properties in common, but as members of a class of what may be physically completely different things but which "mean" the same thing to us.

It becomes necessary here to state explicitly a consideration which is implied in the whole of our argument on this point and which, though it seems to follow from the modern conception of the character of physical research, is yet still somewhat unfamiliar. It is that not only those mental entities, such as "concepts" or "ideas," which are commonly recognized as "abstractions," but *all* mental phenomena, sense perceptions and images as well as the more abstract "concepts" and "ideas," must be regarded as acts of classification performed by the brain.[40] This is, of course, merely another way of saying that the qualities which we perceive are not properties of the objects but ways in which we (individually or as a race) have learnt to group or classify external stimuli. To perceive is to assign to a familiar category (or categories): we could not perceive anything completely different from everything else we have ever perceived before. This does not mean, however, that everything which we actually class together must possess common properties additional to the fact that we react in the same way to these things. It is a common but dangerous error to believe that things which our senses or our mind treat as members of the same class must have something else in common beyond being registered in the same manner by our mind. Although there will usually exist some objective justification why we regard certain things as similar, this need not always be the case. But while in our study of nature classifications which are not based on any similarity in the behavior of the objects towards each other must be treated as "deceptions" of which we must free ourselves, they are of positive significance in our attempts to understand human action. The important difference between the position of these mental categories in the two spheres is that when we study the working of external nature our sensations and thoughts are not links in the chain of observed events—they are merely about them; but in the mechanism of society they form an essential link, the forces here at work operate through these mental entities which are directly known to us: while the things in the external world do not behave alike or differently because they appear alike to us, we do behave in a similar or different manner because the things appear alike or different to us.

The behaviorist or physicalist who in studying human behavior wished really to avoid using the categories which we find ready in our mind, and who wanted to confine himself strictly to the study of man's reactions to objects defined in physical terms, would consistently have to refuse to say anything about human actions till he had experimentally established how our senses and our mind group external stimuli as alike or unlike. He would have to begin by asking which physical objects appear alike to us and which do not (and how it comes about that they do) before he could seriously undertake to study human behavior towards these things.

It is important to observe that our contention is not that such an attempt to explain the principle of how our mind or our brain transforms physical facts into mental entities is impossible. Once we recognize this as a process of classification there is no reason why we should not learn to understand the principle on which it operates. Classification is, after all, a mechanical process, i.e., a process which could be performed by a machine which "sorts out" and groups objects according to certain properties.[41] Our argument is, rather, in the first instance, that for the task of the social sciences such an explanation of the formation of mental entities and their relations to the physical facts which they represent is unnecessary, and that such an explanation would help us in no way in our task; and, secondly, that such an explanation, although conceivable, is not only not available at present and not likely to be available for a long time yet, but also unlikely to be ever more than an "explanation of the principle" [42] on which this apparatus of classification works. It would seem that any apparatus of classification would always have to possess a degree of complexity greater than any one of the different things which it classifies; and if this is correct it would follow that it is impossible that our brain should ever be able to produce a complete explanation (as distinguished from a mere explanation of the principle) of the particular ways in which it itself classifies external stimuli. We shall later have to consider the significance of the related paradox that to "explain" our own knowledge would require that we should know more than we actually do, which is, of course, a self-contradictory statement.

But let us assume for the moment that we had succeeded in fully reducing all mental phenomena to physical processes. Assume that we knew the mechanism by which our central nervous system groups any one of the (elementary or complex) stimuli, $a, b, c, \ldots$ or $l, m, n, \ldots$ or $r, s, t, \ldots$ into definite classes determined by the fact that to any member of one class we shall react by any one of the members of the corresponding classes or reactions $\alpha, \beta, \gamma, \ldots$ or $\nu \xi, o, \ldots$ or $\varphi, \chi, \psi \ldots$ This assumption implies both that this system is not merely familiar to us as the way in which our own mind acts, but that we explicitly know all the relations by which it is determined, and that we also know the mechanism by which the classification is actually effected. We should then be able strictly to correlate the mental entities with definite groups of physical facts. We should thus have "unified" science, but we should be in no better position with respect to the specific task of the social sciences than we are now. We should still have to use the old categories, though we should be able to explain their formation and though we should know the physical facts "behind" them. Although we should know that a different arrangement of the facts of nature is more appropriate for explaining external events, in interpreting human actions we should still have to use the classification in which these facts actually appear in the minds of the acting people. Thus, quite apart from the fact that we should probably have to wait forever till we were able to substitute physical facts for the mental entities, even if this were achieved we should be no better equipped for the task we have to solve in the social sciences.

The idea, implied in Comte's hierarchy of the sciences [43] and in many similar arguments, that the social sciences must in some sense be "based" on the physical sciences, that they can only hope for success after the physical sciences have advanced far enough to enable us to treat social phenomena in physical terms, in "physical language," is, therefore, entirely erroneous. The problem of explaining mental processes by physical ones is entirely distinct from the problems of the social sciences, it is a problem for physiological psychology. But whether it is solved or not, for the social sciences the given mental entities must provide the starting point, whether their formation has been explained or not.

We cannot discuss here all the other forms in which the characteristic "objectivism" of the scientistic approach has made itself felt and led to error in the social sciences. We shall, in the course of our historical survey, find this tendency to look for the "real" attributes of the objects of human activity which lie behind men's views about them, represented in a great many different ways. Only a brief survey can be attempted here.

Nearly as important as the various forms of behaviorism, and closely connected with them, is the common tendency in the study of social phenomena to attempt to disregard all the "merely" qualitative phenomena and to concentrate, on the model of the natural sciences, on the quantitative aspects, on what is measurable. We have seen before [44] how in the natural sciences this tendency is a necessary consequence of their specific task of replacing the picture of the world in terms of sense qualities by one in which the units are defined exclusively by their explicit relations. The success of this method in that field has brought it about that it is now generally regarded as the hall-mark of all genuinely scientific procedure. Yet its *raison d'être*, the need to replace the classification of events which our senses and our mind provide by a more appropriate one, is absent where we try to understand human beings, and where this understanding is made possible by the fact that we have a mind like theirs, and that from the mental categories we have in common with them we can reconstruct the social complexes which are our concern. The blind transfer of the striving for quantitative measurements [45] to a field in which the specific conditions are not present which give it its basic importance in the natural sciences, is the result of an entirely unfounded prejudice. It is probably responsible for the worst aberrations and absurdities produced by scientism in the social sciences. It not only leads frequently to the selection for study of the most irrelevant aspects of the phenomena because they happen to be measurable, but also to "measurements" and assignments of numerical values which are absolutely meaningless. What a distinguished philosopher recently wrote about psychology is at least equally true of the social sciences, namely that it is only too easy "to rush off to measure something without considering what it is we are measuring, or what measurement means. In this respect some recent measurements are of the same logical type as Plato's determination that a just ruler is 729 times as happy as an unjust one." [46]

Closely connected with the tendency to treat the objects of human activity in terms of their "real" attributes instead of as what they appear to the acting people is the propensity to conceive of the student of society as endowed with a kind of super-mind, with some sort of absolute knowledge, which makes it unnecessary for him to start from what is known by the people whose actions he studies. Among the most characteristic manifestations of this tendency are the various forms of social "energetics" which, from the earlier attempts of Ernest Solvay, Wilhelm Ostwald and F. Soddy down to our own day [47] have constantly reappeared among scientists and engineers when they turned to the problems of social organization. The idea underlying these theories is that, as science is supposed to teach that everything can be ultimately reduced to quantities of energy, man should in his plans treat the various things not according to the concrete usefulness they possess for the purposes for which he knows how to use them, but as the interchangeable units of abstract energy which they "really" are.

Another, hardly less crude and even more widespread, example of this tendency is the conception of the "objective" possibilities of production, of the quantity of social output which the physical facts are supposed to make possible, an idea which frequently finds expression in quantitative estimates of the supposed "productive capacity" of society as a whole. These estimates regularly refer, not to what men can produce by means of any stated organization, but to what in some undefined "objective" sense "could" be produced from the available resources. Most of these assertions have no ascertainable meaning whatever. They do not mean that x or y or any particular organization of people could achieve these things. What they amount to is that *if* all the knowledge dispersed among many people could be mastered by a single mind, and *if* this master-mind could make all the people act at all times as he wished, certain results could be achieved; but these results could, of course, not be known to anybody except to such a master-mind. It need hardly be pointed out that an assertion about a "possibility" which is dependent on such conditions has no relation to reality. There is no such thing as the productive capacity of society in the abstract—apart from particular forms of organization. The only fact which we can regard as given is that there are particular people who have certain concrete knowledge about the way in which particular things can be used for particular purposes. This knowledge never exists as an integrated whole or in one mind, and the only knowledge that can in any sense be said to exist are these separate and often inconsistent and even conflicting views of different people.

Of very similar nature are the frequent statements about the "objective" needs of the people, where "objective" is merely a name for somebody's views about what the people ought to want. We shall have to consider further manifestations of this "objectivism" towards the end of this part when we turn from the consideration of scientism proper to the effects of the characteristic outlook of the engineer, whose conceptions of "efficiency" have been one of the most powerful forces through which this attitude has affected current views on social problems.

VI

THE COLLECTIVISM
OF THE SCIENTISTIC APPROACH

CLOSELY CONNECTED WITH the "objectivism" of the scientistic approach is its methodological collectivism, its tendency to treat "wholes" like "society" or the "economy," "capitalism" (as a given historical "phase") or a particular "industry" or "class" or "country" as definitely given objects about which we can discover laws by observing their behavior as wholes. While the specific subjectivist approach of the social sciences starts, as we have seen, from our knowledge of the inside of these social complexes, the knowledge of the individual attitudes which form the elements of their structure, the objectivism of the natural sciences tries to view them from the outside [48]; it treats social phenomena not as something of which the human mind is a part and the principles of whose organization we can reconstruct from the familiar parts, but as if they were objects directly perceived by us as wholes.

There are several reasons why this tendency should so frequently show itself with natural scientists. They are used to seek first for empirical regularities in the relatively complex phenomena that are immediately given to observation, and only after they have found such regularities to try and explain them as the product of a combination of other, often purely hypothetical, elements (constructs) which are assumed to behave according to simpler and more general rules. They are therefore inclined to seek in the social field, too, first for empirical regularities in the behavior of the complexes before they feel that there is need for a theoretical explanation. This tendency is further strengthened by the experience that there are few regularities in the behavior of individuals which can be established

53

in a strictly objective manner; and they turn therefore to the wholes in the hope that they will show such regularities. Finally, there is the rather vague idea that since "social phenomena" are to be the object of study, the obvious procedure is to start from the direct observation of these "social phenomena," where the existence in popular usage of such terms as "society" or "economy" is naïvely taken as evidence that there must be definite "objects" corresponding to them. The fact that people all talk about "the nation" or "capitalism" leads to the belief that the first step in the study of these phenomena must be to go and see what they are like, just as we should if we heard about a particular stone or a particular animal.[49]

The error involved in this collectivist approach is that it mistakes for facts what are no more than provisional theories, models constructed by the popular mind to explain the connection between some of the individual phenomena which we observe. The paradoxical aspect of it, however, is, as we have seen before,[50] that those who by the scientistic prejudice are led to approach social phenomena in this manner are induced, by their very anxiety to avoid all merely subjective elements and to confine themselves to "objective facts," to commit the mistake they are most anxious to avoid, namely that of treating as facts what are no more than vague popular theories. They thus become, when they least suspect it, the victims of the fallacy of "conceptual realism" (made familiar by A. N. Whitehead as the "fallacy of misplaced concreteness").

The naïve realism which uncritically assumes that where there are commonly used concepts there must also be definite "given" things which they describe is so deeply embedded in current thought about social phenomena that it requires a deliberate effort of will to free oneselves from it. While most people will readily admit that in this field there may exist special difficulties in recognizing definite wholes because we have never many specimens of a kind before us and therefore cannot readily distinguish their constant from their merely accidental attributes, few are aware that there is a much more fundamental obstacle: that the wholes as such are never given to our observation but are without exception constructions of our mind. They are not "given facts," objective data of a similar kind which we spontaneously recognize as similar by their common physical attributes. They cannot be perceived at all apart from a mental scheme that shows the connection between some of the many individual facts which we can observe. Where we have to deal with such social wholes we cannot (as we do in the natural sciences) start from the observation of a number of instances which we recognize spontaneously by their common sense attributes as instances of "societies" or "economies," "capitalisms" or "nations," "languages" or "legal systems," and where only after we have collected a sufficient number of instances we begin to seek for common laws which they obey. Social wholes are not given to us as what we may call "natural units" which we recognize as similar with our senses, as we do with flowers or butterflies, minerals or light-rays, or even forests or ant-heaps. They are not given to us as similar things before we even begin to ask whether what looks alike to us also behaves in the same manner. The terms for collectives which we all readily use do not designate definite things in the sense of stable collections of sense attributes which we recognize as alike by inspection; they refer to certain structures of relationships between some of the many things which we can observe within given spatial and temporal limits and which we select because we think that we can discern connections between them—connections which may or may not exist in fact.

What we group together as instances of the same collective or whole are different complexes of individual events, by themselves perhaps quite dissimilar, but believed by us to be related to each other in a similar manner; they are selections of certain elements of a complex picture on the basis of a theory about their coherence. They do not stand for definite things or classes of things (if we understand the term "thing" in any material or concrete sense) but for a pattern or order in which different things may be related to each other—an order which is not a spatial or temporal order but can be defined only in terms of relations which are intelligible human attitudes. This order or pattern is as little perceptible as a physical fact as these relations themselves; and it can be studied only by following up the implications of the particular combination of relationships. In other words, the wholes about which we speak exist only if, and to the extent to which, the theory is correct which we have formed about the connection of the parts which they imply, and which we can explicitly state only in the form of a model built from those relationships.[51]

The social sciences, thus, do not deal with "given" wholes but their task is to *constitute* these wholes by constructing models from the familiar elements—models which reproduce the structure of relationships between some of the many phenomena which we always simultaneously observe in real life. This is no less true of the popular concepts of social wholes which are represented by the terms current in ordinary language; they too refer to mental models, but instead of a precise description they convey merely vague and indistinct suggestions of the way in which certain phenomena are connected. Sometimes the wholes constituted by the theoretical social sciences will roughly correspond with the wholes to which the popular concepts refer, because popular usage has succeeded in approximately separating the significant from the accidental; sometimes the wholes constituted by theory may refer to entirely new structural connections of which we did not know before systematic study commenced and for which ordinary language has not even a name. If we take current concepts like those of a "market" or of "capital," the popular meaning of these words corresponds at least in some measure to the similar concepts which we have to form for theoretical purposes, although even in these instances the popular meaning is far too vague to allow the use of these terms without first giving them a more precise meaning. If they can be retained in theoretical work at all it is, however, because in these instances even the popular concepts have long ceased to describe particular concrete things, definable in physical terms, and have come to cover a great variety of different things which are classed together solely because of a recognized similarity in the structure of the relationships between men and things. A "market," e.g., has long ceased to mean only the periodical meeting of men at a fixed place to which they bring their products to sell them from temporary wooden stalls. It now covers any arrangements for regular contacts between potential buyers and sellers of any thing that can be sold, whether by personal contact, by telephone or telegraph, by advertising, etc., etc.[52]

When, however, we speak of the behavior of, e.g., the "price system" as a whole and discuss the complex of connected changes which will correspond in certain conditions to a fall in the rate of interest, we are not concerned with a whole that obtrudes itself on popular notice or that is ever definitely given; we can only reconstruct it by following up the reactions of many individuals to the initial change and its immediate effects. That in this case certain changes "belong together"—that among the large number of other changes which in any concrete situation will always occur simultaneously with them and which will often swamp those which form part of the complex in which we are interested, a few form a more closely interrelated complex—we do not know from observing that these particular changes regularly occur together. That would indeed be impossible because what in different circumstances would have to be regarded as the same set of changes could not be determined by any of the physical attributes of the things but only by singling out certain relevant aspects in the attitudes of men towards the things; and this can be done only by the help of the models we have formed.

The mistake of treating as definite objects "wholes" that are no more than constructions, and that can have no properties except those which follow from the way in which we have constructed them from the elements, has probably appeared most frequently in the form of the various theories about a "social" or "collective" mind [63] and has in this connection raised all sorts of pseudo-problems. The same idea is frequently but imperfectly concealed under the attributes of "personality" or "individuality" which are ascribed to society. Whatever the name, these terms always mean that, instead of reconstructing the wholes from the relations between individual minds which we directly know, a vaguely apprehended whole is treated as something akin to the individual mind. It is in this form that in the social sciences an illegitimate use of anthropomorphic concepts has had as harmful an effect as the use of such concepts in the natural sciences. The remarkable thing here is, again, that it should so frequently be the empiricism of the positivists, the arch-enemies of any anthropomorphic concepts even where they are in place, which leads them to postulate such metaphysical entities and to treat humanity, as for instance Comte does, as one "social being," a kind of super-person. But as there is no other possibility than either to compose the whole from the individual minds or to postulate a super-mind in the image of the individual mind, and as positivists reject the first of these alternatives, they are necessarily driven to the second. We have here the root of that curious alliance between 19th century positivism and Hegelianism which will occupy us in a later study.

The collectivist approach to social phenomena has not often been so emphatically proclaimed as when the founder of sociology, Auguste Comte, asserted with respect to them that, as in biology, "the whole of the object is here certainly much better known and more immedately accessible" [54] than the constituent parts. This view has exercised a lasting influence on that scientistic study of society which he attempted to create. Yet the particular similarity between the objects of biology and those of sociology, which fitted so well in Comte's hierarchy of the sciences, does not in fact exist. In biology we do indeed first recognize as things of one kind natural units, stable combinations of sense properties, of which we find many instances which we spontaneously recognize as alike. We can, therefore, begin by asking why these definite sets of attributes regularly occur together. But where we have to deal with social wholes or structures it is not the observation of the regular coexistence of certain physical facts which teaches us that they belong together or form a whole. We do not first observe that the parts always occur together and afterwards ask what holds them together; but it is only because we know the ties that hold them together that we can select a few elements from the immensely complicated world around us as parts of a connected whole.

We shall presently see that Comte and many others regard social phenomena as given wholes in yet another, different, sense, contending that concrete social phenomena can be understood *only* by considering the totality of everything that can be found within certain spatio-temporal boundaries, and that any attempt to select parts or aspects as systematically connected is bound to fail. In this form the argument amounts to a denial of the possibility of a theory of social phenomena as developed, e.g., by economics, and leads directly to what has been misnamed the "historical method" with which, indeed, methodological collectivism is closely connected. We shall have to discuss this view below under the heading of "historicism."

The endeavor to grasp social phenomena as "wholes" finds its most characteristic expression in the desire to gain a distant and comprehensive view in the hope that thus regularities will reveal themselves which remain obscure at closer range. Whether it is the conception of an observer from a distant planet, which has always been a favorite with positivists from Condorcet to Mach,[55] or whether it is the survey of long stretches of time through which it is hoped that constant configurations or regularities will reveal themselves, it is always the same endeavor to get away from our inside knowledge of human affairs and to gain a view of the kind which, it is supposed, would be commanded by somebody who was not himself a man but stood to men in the same relation as that in which we stand to the external world.

This distant and comprehensive view of human events at which the scientistic approach aims is now often described as the "macroscopic view." It would probably be better called the telescopic view (meaning simply the distant view—unless it be the view through the inverted telescope!) since its aim is deliberately to ignore what we can see only from the inside. In the "macrocosm" which this approach attempts to see, and in the "macrodynamic" theories which it endeavors to produce, the elements would not be individual human beings but collectives, constant configurations which, it is presumed, could be defined and described in strictly objective terms.

In most instances this belief that the total view will enable us to distinguish wholes by objective criteria, however, proves to be just an illusion. This becomes evident as soon as we seriously try to imagine of what the macrocosm would consist if we were really to dispense with our knowledge of what things *mean* to the acting men, and if we merely observed the actions of men as we observe an ant-heap or a bee-hive. In the picture such a study could produce there could not appear such things as means or tools, commodities or money, crimes or punishments, or words or sentences; it could contain only physical objects defined either in terms of the sense attributes they present to the observer or even in purely relational terms. And since the human behavior towards the physical objects would show practically no regularities discernible to such an observer, since men would in a great many instances not appear to react alike to things which would to the observer seem to be the same, nor differently to what appeared to him to be different, he could not hope to achieve an explanation of their actions unless he had first succeeded in reconstructing in full detail the way in which men's senses and men's minds pictured the external world to them. The famous observer from Mars, in other words, before he could understand even as much of human affairs as the ordinary man does, would have to reconstruct from our behavior those immediate data of our mind which to us form the starting-point of any interpretation of human action.

If we are not more aware of the difficulties which would be encountered by an observer not possessed of a human mind, this is so because we never seriously imagine the possibility that any being with which we are familiar might command sense perceptions or knowledge denied to us. Rightly or wrongly we tend to assume that the other minds which we encounter can differ from ours only by being inferior, so that everything which they perceive or know can also be perceived or be known to us. The only way in which we can form an approximate idea of what our position would be if we had to deal with an organism as complicated as ours but organized on a different principle, so that we should not be able to reproduce its working on the analogy of our own mind, is to conceive that we had to study the behavior of people with a knowledge vastly superior to our own. If, e.g., we had developed our modern scientific technique while still confined to a part of our planet, and then had made contact with other parts inhabited by a race which had advanced knowledge much further, we clearly could not hope to understand many of their actions by merely observing what they did and without directly learning from them their knowledge. It would not be from observing them in action that we should acquire their knowledge, but it would be through being taught their knowledge that we should learn to understand their actions.

There is yet another argument which we must briefly consider which supports the tendency to look at social phenomena "from the outside," and which is easily confused with the methodological collectivism of which we have spoken though it is really distinct from it. Are not social phenomena, it may be asked, from their definition mass phenomena, and is it not obvious, therefore, that we can hope to discover regularities in them only if we investigate them by the method developed for the study of mass phenomena, i.e., statistics? Now this is certainly true of the study of certain phenomena, such as those which form the object of vital statistics and which, as has been mentioned before, are sometimes also described as social phenomena, although they are essentially distinct from those with which we are here concerned.

Nothing is more instructive than to compare the nature of these statistical wholes, to which the same word "collective" is sometimes also applied, with that of the wholes or collectives with which we have to deal in the theoretical social sciences. The statistical study is concerned with the attributes of individuals, though not with attributes of particular individuals, but with attributes of which we know only that they are possessed by a certain quantitatively determined proportion of all the individuals in our "collective" or "population." In order that any collection of individuals should form a true statistical collective it is even necessary that the attributes of the individuals whose frequency distribution we study should not be systematically connected or, at least, that in our selection of the individuals which form the "collective" we are not guided by any knowledge of such a connection. The "collectives" of statistics, on which we study the regularities produced by the "law of large numbers," are thus emphatically not wholes in the sense in which we describe social structures as wholes. This is best seen from the fact that the properties of the "collectives" with statistics studies must remain unaffected if from the total of elements we select at random a certain part. Far from dealing with structures of relationships, statistics deliberately and systematically disregard the relationships between the individual elements. It is, to repeat, concerned with the properties of the *elements* of the "collective," though not with the properties of particular elements, but with the frequency with which elements with certain properties occur among the total. And, what is more, it assumes that these properties are *not* systematically connected with the different ways in which the elements are related to each other.

The consequence of this is that in the statistical study of social phenomena the structures with which the theoretical social sciences are concerned actually disappear. Statistics may supply us with very interesting and important information about what is the raw material from which we have to reproduce these structures, but it can tell us nothing about these structures themselves. In some field this is immediately obvious as soon as it is stated. That the statistics of words can tell us nothing about the structure of a language will hardly be denied. But although the contrary is sometimes suggested, the same holds no less true of other systematically connected wholes such as, e.g., the price system. No statistical information about the elements can explain to us the properties of the connected wholes. Statistics could produce knowledge of the properties of the wholes only if it had information about statistical collectives the elements of which were wholes, i.e., if we had statistical information about the properties of many languages, many price systems, etc. But, quite apart from the practical limitations imposed on us by the limited number of instances which are known to us, there is an even more serious obstacle to the statistical study of these wholes: the fact which we have already discussed, that these wholes and their properties are not given to our observation but can only be formed or composed by us from their parts.

What we have said applies, however, by no means to all that goes by the name of statistics in the social sciences. Much that is thus described is not statistics in the strict modern sense of the term; it does not deal with mass phenomena at all, but is called statistics only in the older, wider sense of the word in which it is used for any descriptive information about the State or society. Though the term will to-day be used only where the descriptive data are of quantitative nature, this should not lead us to confuse it with the science of statistics in the narrower sense. Most of the economic statistics which we ordinarily meet, such as trade statistics, figures about price changes, and most "time series," or statistics of the "national income," are not data to which the technique appropriate to the investigation of mass phenomena can be applied. They are just "measurements" and frequently measurements of the type already discussed at the end of Section V above. If they refer to significant phenomena they may be very interesting as information about the conditions existing at a particular moment. But unlike statistics proper, which may indeed help us to discover important regularities in the social world (though regularities of an entirely different order from those with which the theoretical sciences of society deal), there is no reason to expect that these measurements will ever reveal anything to us which is of significance beyond the particular place and time at which they have been made. That they cannot produce generalizations does, of course, not mean that they may not be useful, even very useful; they will often provide us with the data to which our theoretical generalizations must be applied to be of any practical use. They are an instance of the historical information about a particular situation the significance of which we must further consider in the next sections.

VII

THE HISTORICISM OF THE SCIENTISTIC APPROACH

To SEE THE "historicism" to which we must now turn described as a product of the scientistic approach may cause surprise since it is usually represented as the opposite to the treatment of social phenomena on the model of the natural sciences. But the view for which this term is properly used (and which must not be confused with the true method of historical study) proves on closer consideration to be a result of the same prejudices as the other typical scientistic misconceptions of social phenomena. If the suggestion that historicism is a form rather than the opposite of scientism has still somewhat the appearance of a paradox, this is so because the term is used in two different and in some respect opposite and yet frequently confused senses: for the older view which justly contrasted the specific task of the historian with that of the scientist and which denied the possibility of a theoretical science of history, and for the later view which, on the contrary, affirms that history is the only road which can lead to a theoretical science of social phenomena. However great is the contrast between these two views sometimes called "historicism" if we take them in their extreme forms, they have yet enough in common to have made possible a gradual and almost unperceived transition from the historical method of the historian to the scientistic historicism which attempts to make history a "science" and the only science of social phenomena.

The older historical school, whose growth has recently been so well described by the German historian Meinecke, though under the misleading name of *Historismus*,[56] arose mainly in opposition to certain generalizing and "pragmatic" tendencies of some, particularly French, 18th century views. Its emphasis was on the singular or unique (*individuell*) character of all historical phenomena which could be understood only genetically as the joint result of many forces working through long stretches of time. Its strong opposition to the "pragmatic" interpretation, which regards social institutions as the product of conscious design, implies in fact the use of a "compositive" theory which explains how such institutions can arise as the unintended result of the separate actions of many individuals. It is significant that among the fathers of this view Edmund Burke is one of the most important and Adam Smith occupies an honorable place.

Yet, although this historical method implies theory, i.e., an understanding of the principles of structural coherence of the social wholes, the historians who employed it not only did not systematically develop such theories and were hardly aware that they used them; but their just dislike of any generalization about historical developments also tended to give their teaching an anti-theoretical bias which, although originally aimed only against the wrong kind of theory, yet created the impression that the main difference between the methods appropriate to the study of natural and to that of social phenomena was the same as that between theory and history. This opposition to theory of the largest body of students of social phenomena made it appear as if the difference between the theoretical and the historical treatment was a necessary consequence of the differences between the objects of the natural and the social sciences; and the belief that the search for general rules must be confined to the study of natural phenomena, while in the study of the social world the historical method must rule, became the foundation on which later historicism grew up. But while historicism retained the claim for the pre-eminence of historical research in this field, it almost reversed the attitude to history of the older historical school, and under the influence of the scientistic currents of the age came to represent history as the empirical study of society from which ultimately generalization would emerge. History was to be the source from which a new science of society would spring, a science which should at the same time be historical and yet produce what theoretical knowledge we could hope to gain about society.

We are here not concerned with the actual steps in that process of transition from the older historical school to the historicism of the younger. It may just be noticed that historicism in the sense in which the term is used here, was created not by historians but by students of the specialized social sciences, particularly economists, who hoped thereby to gain an empirical road to the theory of their subject. But to trace this development in detail and to show how the men responsible for it were actually guided by the scientistic views of their generation must be left to the later historical account.[57]

The first point we must briefly consider is the nature of the distinction between the historical and the theoretical treatment of any subject which in fact makes it a contradiction in terms to demand that history should become a theoretical science or that theory should ever be "historical." If we understand that distinction, it will become clear that it has no necessary connection with the difference of the concrete objects with which the two methods of approach deal, and that for the understanding of any concrete phenomenon, be it in nature or in society, both kinds of knowledge are equally required.

That human history deals with events or situations which are unique or singular when we consider all aspects which are relevant for the answer of a particular question which we may ask about them, is, of course, not peculiar to human history. It is equally true of any attempt to explain a concrete phenomenon if we only take into account a sufficient number of aspects—or, to put it differently, so long as we do not deliberately select only such aspects of reality as fall within the sphere of any one of the systems of connected propositions which we regard as distinct theoretical sciences. If I watch and record the process by which a plot in my garden that I leave untouched for months is gradually covered with weeds, I am describing a process which in all its detail is no less unique than any event in human history. If I want to explain any particular configuration of different plants which may appear at any stage of that process, I can do so only by giving an account of all the relevant influences which have affected different parts of my plot at different times. I shall have to consider what I can find out about the differences of the soil in different parts of the plot, about differences in the radiation of the sun, of moisture, of the air-currents, etc., etc.; and in order to explain the effects of all these factors I shall have to use, apart from the knowledge of all these particular facts, various parts of the theory of physics, of chemistry, biology, meteorology, and so on. The result of all this will be the explanation of a particular phenomenon, but not a theoretical science of how garden plots are covered with weeds.

In an instance like this the particular sequence of events, their causes and consequences, will probably not be of sufficient general interest to make it worth while to produce a written account of them or to develop their study into a distinct discipline. But there are large fields of natural knowledge, represented by recognized disciplines, which in their methodological character are no different from this. In geography, e.g., and at least in a large part of geology and astronomy, we are mainly concerned with particular situations, either of the earth or of the universe; we aim at explaining a unique situation by showing how it has been produced by the operation of many forces subject to the general laws studied by the theoretical sciences. In the specific sense of a body of general rules in which the term "science" is often used [58] these disciplines are not "sciences," i.e., they are not theoretical sciences but endeavors to apply the laws found by the theoretical sciences to the explanation of particular "historical" situations.

The distinction between the search for generic principles and the explanation of concrete phenomena has thus no necessary connection with the distinction between the study of nature and the study of society. In both fields we need generalizations in order to explain concrete and unique events. Whenever we attempt to explain or understand a particular phenomenon we can do so only by recognizing it or its parts as members of certain classes of phenomena, and the explanation of the particular phenomenon presupposes the existence of general rules.

There are very good reasons, however, for a marked difference in emphasis, reasons why, generally speaking, in the natural sciences the search for general laws has the pride of place, with their application to particular events usually little discussed and of small general interest, while with social phenomena the explanation of the particular and unique situation is as important and often of much greater interest than any generalization. In most natural sciences the particular situation or event is generally one of a very large number of similar events, which as particular events are only of local and temporary interest and scarcely worth public discussion (except as evidence of the truth of the general rule). The important thing for them is the general law applicable to all the recurrent events of a particular kind. In the social field, on the other hand, a particular or unique event is often of such general interest and at the same time so complex and so difficult to see in all its important aspects, that its explanation and discussion constitute a major task requiring the whole energy of a specialist. We study here particular events because they have contributed to create the particular environment in which we live or because they are part of that environment. The creation and dissolution of the Roman Empire or the Crusades, the French Revolution or the Growth of Modern Industry are such unique complexes of events, which have helped to produce the particular circumstances in which we live and whose explanation is therefore of great interest.

It is necessary, however, to consider briefly the logical nature of these singular or unique objects of study. Probably the majority of the numerous disputes and confusions which have arisen in this connection are due to the vagueness of the common notion of what can constitute *one* object of thought—and particularly to the misconception that the totality (i.e., all possible aspects) of a particular situation can ever constitute one single object of thought. We can touch here only on a very few of the logical problems which this belief raises.

The first point which we must remember is that, strictly speaking, *all* thought must be to some degree abstract. We have seen before that all perception of reality, including the simplest sensations, involves a classification of the object according to some property or properties. The same complex of phenomena which we may be able to discover within given temporal and spatial limits may in this sense be considered under many different aspects; and the principles according to which we classify or group the events may differ from each other not merely in one but in several different ways. The various theoretical sciences deal only with those aspects of the phenomena which can be fitted into a single body of connected propositions. It is necessary to emphasize that this is no less true of the theoretical sciences of nature than of the theoretical sciences of society, since an alleged tendency of the natural sciences to deal with the "whole" or the totality of the real things is often quoted by writers inclined to historicism as a justification for doing the same in the social field.[59] Any discipline of knowledge, whether theoretical or historical, however, can deal only with certain selected aspects of the real world; and in the theoretical sciences the principle of selection is the possibility of subsuming these aspects under a logically connected body of rules. The same thing may be for one science a pendulum, for another a lump of brass, and for a third a convex mirror. We have already seen that the fact that a pendulum possesses chemical and optical properties does not mean that in studying laws of pendulums we must study them by the methods of chemistry and optics—though when we apply these laws to a particular pendulum we may well have to take into account certain laws of chemistry or optics. Similarly, as has been pointed out, the fact that all social phenomena have physical properties does not mean that we must study them by the methods of the physical sciences.

The selection of the aspects of a complex of phenomena which can be explained by means of a connected body of rules is, however, not the only method of selection or abstraction which the scientist will have to use. Where investigation is directed, not at establishing rules of general applicability, but at answering a particular question raised by the events in the world about him, he will have to select those features that are relevant to the particular question. The important point, however, is that he still must select a limited number from the infinite variety of phenomena which he can find at the given time and place. We may, in such cases, sometimes speak as if he considered the "whole" situation as he finds it. But what we mean is not the inexhaustible totality of everything that can be observed within certain spatio-temporal limits, but certain features thought to be relevant to the question asked. If I ask why the weeds in my garden have grown in this particular pattern no single theoretical science will provide the answer. This, however, does not mean that to answer it we must know everything that can be known about the space-time interval in which the phenomenon occurred. While the question we ask designates the phenomena to be explained, it is only by means of the laws of the theoretical sciences that we are able to select the other phenomena which are relevant for its explanation. The object of scientific study is never the totality of all the phenomena observable at a given time and place, but always only certain selected aspects: and according to the question we ask the same spatio-temporal situation may contain any number of different objects of study. The human mind indeed can never grasp a "whole" in the sense of all the different aspects of a real situation.

The application of these considerations to the phenomena of human history leads to very important consequences. It means nothing less than that a historical process or period is never a single definite object of thought but becomes such only by the question we ask about it; and that, according to the question we ask, what we are accustomed to regard as a single historical event can become any number of different objects of thought.

It is confusion on this point which is mainly responsible for the doctrine now so much in vogue that all historical knowledge is necessarily relative, determined by our "standpoint" and bound to change with the lapse of time.[60] This view is a natural consequence of the belief that the commonly used names for historical periods or complexes of events, such as "the Napoleonic Wars," or "France during the Revolution," or "the Commonwealth Period," stand for definitely given objects, unique individuals [61] which are given to us in the same manner as the natural units in which biological specimens or planets present themselves. Those names of historical phenomena define in fact little more than a period and a place and there is scarcely a limit to the number of different questions which we can ask about events which occurred during the period and within the region to which they refer. It is only the question that we ask, however, which will define our object; and there are, of course, many reasons why at different times people will ask different questions about the same period.[62] But this does not mean that history will at different times and on the basis of the same information give different answers to the same question. Only this, however, would entitle us to assert that historical knowledge is relative. The kernel of truth in the assertion about the relativity of historical knowledge is that historians will at different times be interested in different objects, but not that they will necessarily hold different views about the same object.

We must dwell a little longer on the nature of the "wholes" which the historian studies, though much of what we have to say is merely an application of what has been said before about the "wholes" which some authors regard as objects of theoretical generalizations. What we said then is just as true of the wholes which the historian studies. They are never given to him as wholes, but always reconstructed by him from their elements which alone can be directly perceived. Whether he speaks about the government that existed or the trade that was carried on, the army that moved, or the knowledge that was preserved or disseminated, he is never referring to a constant collection of physical attributes that can be directly observed, but always to a system of relationships between some of the observed elements which can be merely inferred. Words like "government" or "trade" or "army" or "knowledge" do not stand for single observable things but for structures of relationships which can be described only in terms of a schematic representation or "theory" of the persistent system of relationships between the ever-changing elements.[63] These "wholes," in other words, do not exist for us apart from the theory by which we constitute them, apart from the mental technique by which we can reconstruct the connections between the observed elements and follow up the implications of this particular combination.

The place of theory in historical knowledge is thus in forming or constituting the wholes to which history refers; it is prior to these wholes which do not become visible except by following up the system of relations which connects the parts. The generalizations of theory, however, do not refer, and cannot refer, as has been mistakenly believed by the older historians (who for that reason opposed theory), to the concrete wholes, the particular constellations of the elements, with which history is concerned. The models of "wholes," of structural connections, which theory provides ready-made for the historian to use (though even these are not the given elements about which theory generalizes but the results of theoretical activity), are not identical with the "wholes" which the historian considers. The models provided by any one theoretical science of society consist necessarily of elements of one kind, elements which are selected because their connection can be explained by a coherent body of principles and not because they help to answer a particular question about concrete phenomena. For the latter purpose the historian will regularly have to use generalizations belonging to different theoretical spheres. His work, thus, as is true of all attempts to explain particular phenomena, presupposes theory; it is, as is all thinking about concrete phenomena, an application of generic concepts to the explanation of particular phenomena.

If the dependence of the historical study of social phenomena on theory is not always recognized, this is mainly due to the very simple nature of the majority of theoretical schemes which the historian will employ and which brings it about that there will be no dispute about the conclusions reached by their help, and little awareness that he has used theoretical reasoning at all. But this does not alter the fact that in their methodological character and validity the concepts of social phenomena which the historian has to employ are essentially of the same kind as the more elaborate models produced by the systematic social sciences. All the unique objects of history which he studies are in fact either constant patterns of relations, or repeatable processes in which the elements are of a generic character. When the historian speaks of a State or a battle, a town or a market, these words cover coherent structures of individual phenomena which we can comprehend only by understanding the intentions of the acting individuals. If the historian speaks of a certain system, say the feudal system, persisting over a period of time, he means that a certain pattern of relationships continued, a certain type of actions were regularly repeated, structures whose connection he can understand only by mental reproduction of the individual attitudes of which they were made up. The unique wholes which the historian studies, in short, are not given to him as individuals,[64] as natural units of which he can find out by observation which features belong to them, but constructions made by the kind of technique that is systematically developed by the theoretical sciences of society. Whether he endeavors to give a genetic account of how a particular institution arose, or a descriptive account of how it functioned, he cannot do so except by a combination of generic considerations applying to the elements from which the unique situation is composed. Though in this work of reconstruction he cannot use any elements except those he empirically finds, not observation but only the "theoretical" work of reconstruction can tell him which among those that he can find are part of a connected whole.

Theoretical and historical work are thus logically distinct but complementary activities. If their task is rightly understood, there can be no conflict between them. And though they have distinct tasks, neither is of much use without the other. But this does not alter the fact that neither can theory be historical nor history theoretical. Though the general is of interest only because it explains the particular, and though the particular can be explained only in generic terms, the particular can never be the general and the general never the particular. The unfortunate misunderstandings that have arisen between historians and theorists are largely due to the name "historical school" which has been usurped by the mongrel view better described as historicism and which is indeed neither history nor theory.

The naïve view which regards the complexes which history studies as given wholes naturally leads to the belief that their observation can reveal "laws" of the development of these wholes. This belief is one of the most characteristic features of that scientistic history which under the name of historicism was trying to find an empirical basis for a theory of history or (using the term philosophy in its old sense equivalent to "theory") a "philosophy of history," and to establish necessary successions of definite "stages" or "phases," "systems" or "styles," following each other in historical development. This view on the one hand endeavors to find laws where in the nature of the case they cannot be found, in the succession of the unique and singular historical phenomena, and on the other hand denies the possibility of the kind of theory which alone can help us to understand unique wholes, the theory which shows the different ways in which the familiar elements can be combined to produce the unique combinations we find in the real world. The empiricist prejudice thus led to an inversion of the only procedure by which we can comprehend historical wholes, their reconstruction from the parts; it induced scholars to treat as if they were objective facts vague conceptions of wholes which were merely intuitively comprehended; and it finally produced the view that the elements which are the only thing that we can directly comprehend and from which we must reconstruct the wholes, on the contrary, could be understood only from the whole, which had to be known before we could understand the elements.

The belief that human history, which is the result of the interaction of innumerable human minds, must yet be subject to simple laws accessible to human minds is now so widely held that few people are at all aware what an astonishing claim it really implies. Instead of working patiently at the humble task of rebuilding from the directly known elements the complex and unique structures which we find in the world, and of tracing from the changes in the relations between the elements the changes in the wholes, the authors of these pseudo-theories of history pretend to be able to arrive by a kind of mental short cut at a direct insight into the laws of succession of the immediately apprehended wholes. However doubtful their status, these theories of development have achieved a hold on public imagination much greater than any of the results of genuine systematic study. "Philosophies" or "theories" [65] of history (or "historical theories") have indeed become the characteristic feature, the "darling vice" [66] of the 19th century. From Hegel and Comte, and particularly Marx, down to Sombart and Spengler these spurious theories came to be regarded as representative results of social science; and through the belief that one kind of "system" must as a matter of historical necessity be superseded by a new and different "system," they have even exercised a profound influence on social evolution. This they achieved mainly because they looked like the kind of laws which the natural sciences produced; and in an age when these sciences set the standard by which all intellectual effort was measured, the claim of these theories of history to be able to predict future developments was regarded as evidence of their pre-eminently scientific character. Though merely one among many characteristic 19th century products of this kind, Marxism more than any of the others has become the vehicle through which this result of scientism has gained so wide an influence that many of the opponents of Marxism equally with its adherents are thinking in its terms.

Apart from setting up a new ideal this development had, however, also the negative effect of discrediting the existing theory on which past understanding of social phenomena had been based. Since it was supposed that we could directly observe the changes in the whole of society or of any particular changed social phenomenon, and that everything within the whole must necessarily change with it, it was concluded that there could be no timeless generalizations about the elements from which these wholes were built up, no universal theories about the ways in which they might be combined into wholes. All social theory, it was said, was necessarily historical, *zeitgebunden,* true only of particular historical "phases" or "systems."

All concepts of individual phenomena, according to this strict historicism, are to be regarded as merely historical categories, valid only in a particular historical context. A price in the 12th century or a monopoly in the Egypt of 400 B.C., it is argued, is not the same "thing" as a price or a monopoly today, and any attempt to explain that price or the policy of that monopolist by the same theory which we would use to explain a price or a monopoly of today is therefore vain and bound to fail. This argument is based on a complete misapprehension of the function of theory. Of course, if we ask why a particular price was charged at a particular date, or why a monopolist then acted in a particular manner, this is a historical question which cannot be fully answered by any one theoretical discipline; to answer it we must take into account the particular circumstances of time and place. But this does not mean that we must not, in selecting the factors relevant to the explanation of the particular price, etc., use precisely the same theoretical reasoning as we would with regard to a price of today.

What this contention overlooks is that "price" or "monopoly" are not names for definite "things," fixed collections of physical attributes which we recognize by some of these attributes as members of the same class and whose further attributes we ascertain by observation; but that they are objects which can be defined only in terms of certain relations between human beings and which cannot possess any attributes except those which follow from the relations by which they are defined. They can be recognized by us as prices or monopolies only because, and in so far as, we can recognize these individual attitudes, and from these as elements compose the structural pattern which we call a price or monopoly. Of course the "whole" situation, or even the "whole" of the men who act, will greatly differ from place to place and from time to time. But it is solely our capacity to recognize the familiar elements from which the unique situation is made up which enables us to attach any meaning to the phenomena. Either we cannot thus recognize the meaning of the individual actions, they are nothing but physical facts to us, the handing over of certain material things, etc., or we must place them in the mental categories familiar to us but not definable in physical terms. If the first contention were true this would mean that we could not know the facts of the past at all, because in that case we could not understand the documents from which we derive all knowledge of them.[67]

Consistently pursued historicism necessarily leads to the view that the human mind is itself variable and that not only are most or all manifestations of the human mind unintelligible to us apart from their historical setting, but that from our knowledge of how the whole situations succeed each other we can learn to recognize the laws according to which the human mind changes, and that it is the knowledge of these laws which alone puts us in a position to understand any particular manifestation of the human mind. Historicism, because of its refusal to recognize a compositive theory of universal applicability unable to see how different configurations of the same elements may produce altogether different complexes, and unable, for the same reason, to comprehend how the wholes can ever be anything but what the human mind consciously designed, was bound to seek the cause of the changes in the social structures in changes of the human mind itself—changes which it claims to understand and explain from changes in the directly apprehended wholes. From the extreme assertion of some sociologists that logic itself is variable, and the belief in the "pre-logical" character of the thinking of primitive people, to the more sophisticated contentions of the modern "sociology of knowledge," this approach has become one of the most characteristic features of modern sociology. It has raised the old question of the "constancy of the human mind" in a more radical form than has ever been done before.

This phrase is, of course, so vague that any dispute about it without giving it further precision is futile. That not only any human individual in its historically given complexity, but also certain types predominant in particular ages or localities, differ in significant respects from other individuals or types is, of course, beyond dispute. But this does not alter the fact that in order that we should be able to recognize or understand them at all as human beings or minds, there must be certain invariable features present. We cannot recognize "mind" in the abstract. When we speak of mind what we mean is that certain phenomena can be successfully interpreted on the analogy of our own mind, that the use of the familiar categories of our own thinking provides a satisfactory working explanation of what we observe. But this means that to recognize something as mind is to recognize it as something similar to our own mind, and that the possibility of recognizing mind is limited to what is similar to our own mind. To speak of a mind with a structure fundamentally different from our own, or to claim that we can observe changes in the basic structure of the human mind is not only to claim what is impossible: it is a meaningless statement. Whether the human mind is in this sense constant can never become a problem—because to recognize mind cannot mean anything but to recognize something as operating in the same way as our own thinking.

To recognize the existence of a mind always implies that we add something to what we perceive with our senses, that we interpret the phenomena in the light of our own mind, or find that they fit into the ready pattern of our own thinking. This kind of interpretation of human actions may not be always successful, and, what is even more embarrassing, we may never be absolutely certain that it is correct in any particular case; all we know is that it works in the overwhelming number of cases. Yet it is the only basis on which we ever understand what we call other people's intentions, or the meaning of their actions; and certainly the only basis of all our historical knowledge since this is all derived from the understanding of signs or documents. As we pass from men of our own kind to different types of beings we may, of course, find that what we can thus understand becomes less and less. And we cannot exclude the possibility that one day we may find beings who, though perhaps physically resembling men, behave in a way which is entirely unintelligible to us. With regard to them we should indeed be reduced to the "objective" study which the behaviorists want us to adopt towards men in general. But there would be no sense in ascribing to these beings a mind different from our own. We should know nothing of them which we could call mind, we should indeed know nothing about them but physical facts. Any interpretation of their actions in terms of such categories as intention or purpose, sensation or will, would be meaningless. A mind about which we can intelligibly speak must be like our own.

The whole idea of the variability of the human mind is a direct result of the erroneous belief that mind is an object which we observe as we observe physical facts. The sole difference between mind and physical objects, however, which entitles us to speak of mind at all, is precisely that wherever we speak of mind we interpret what we observe in terms of categories which we know only because they are the categories in which our own mind operates. There is nothing paradoxical in the claim that all mind must run in terms of certain universal categories of thought, because where we speak of mind this means that we can successfully interpret what we observe by arranging it in these categories. And anything which can be comprehended through our understanding of other minds, anything which we recognize as specifically human, must be comprehensible in terms of these categories.

Through the theory of the variability of the human mind, to which the consistent development of historicism leads, it cuts, in effect, the ground under its own feet: it is led to the self-contradictory position of generalizing about facts which, if the theory were true, could not be known. If the human mind were really variable so that, as the extreme adherents of historicism assert, we could not directly understand what people of other ages meant by a particular statement, history would be inaccessible to us. The wholes from which we are supposed to understand the elements would never become visible to us. And even if we disregard this fundamental difficulty created by the impossibility of understanding the documents from which we derive all historical knowledge, without first understanding the individual actions and intentions the historian could never combine them into wholes and never explicitly state what these wholes are. He would, as indeed is true of so many of the adherents of historicism, be reduced to talking about "wholes" which are intuitively comprehended, to making uncertain and vague generalizations about "styles" or "systems" whose character could not be precisely defined.

It follows indeed from the nature of the evidence on which all our historical knowledge is based that history can never carry us beyond the stage where we can understand the working of the minds of the acting people because they are similar to our own. Where we cease to understand, where we can no longer recognize categories of thought similar to those in terms of which we think, history ceases to be human history. And precisely at that point, and only at that point, do the general theories of the social sciences cease to be valid. Since history and social theory are based on the same knowledge of the working of the human mind, the same capacity to understand other people, their range and scope is necessarily co-terminous. Particular propositions of social theory may have no application at certain times, because the combination of elements to which they refer to do not occur.[68] But they remain nevertheless true. There can be no different theories for different ages, though at some times certain parts and at others different parts of the same body of theory may be required to explain the observed facts, just as, e.g., generalizations about the effect of very low temperatures on vegetation may be irrelevant in the tropics but still true. Any true theoretical statement of the social sciences will cease to be valid only where history ceases to be human history. If we conceive of somebody observing and recording the doings of another race, unintelligible to him and to us, his records would in a sense be history, such as, e.g., the history of an antheap. Such history would have to be written in purely objective, physical terms. It would be the sort of history which corresponds to the positivist ideal, such as the proverbial observer from another planet might write of the human race. But such history could not help us to understand any of the events recorded by it in the sense in which we understand human history.

When we speak of man we necessarily imply the presence of certain familiar mental categories. It is not the lumps of flesh of a certain shape which we mean, nor any units performing definite functions which we could define in physical terms. The completely insane, none of whose actions we can understand, is not a man to us—he could not figure in human history except as the object of other people's acting and thinking. When we speak of man we refer to one whose actions we can understand. As old Democritus said

$$\text{ἄνθρωπος ἔστιν ὃ πάντες ἴδμεν.}^{69}$$

VIII

"PURPOSIVE" SOCIAL FORMATIONS

IN THE CONCLUDING portions of this essay we have to consider certain practical attitudes which spring from the theoretical views already discussed. Their most characteristic common feature is a direct result of the inability, caused by the lack of a compositive theory of social phenomena, to grasp how the independent action of many men can produce coherent wholes, persistent structures of relationships which serve important human purposes without having been designed for that end. This produces a "pragmatic" [70] interpretation of social institutions which treats all social structures which serve human purposes as the result of deliberate design and which denies the possibility of an orderly or purposeful arrangement in anything which is not thus constructed.

This view receives strong support from the fear of employing any anthropomorphic conceptions which is so characteristic of the scientistic attitude. This fear has produced an almost complete ban on the use of the concept of "purpose" in the discussion of spontaneous social growths, and it often drives positivists into an error similar to that they wish to avoid: having learnt that it is erroneous to regard everything that behaves in an apparently purposive manner as created by a designing mind, they are led to believe that no result of the action of many men can show order or serve a useful purpose unless it is the result of deliberate design. They are thus driven back to a view which is essentially the same as that which, till the eighteenth century, made man think of language or the family as having been "invented," or the state as having been created by an explicit social contract, and in opposition to which the compositive theories of social structures were developed.

80

As the terms of ordinary language are somewhat misleading, it is necessary to move with great care in any discussion of the "purposive" character of spontaneous social formations. The risk of being lured into an illegitimate anthropomorphic use of the term purpose is as great as that of denying that the term purpose in this connection designates something of importance. In its strict original meaning "purpose" indeed presupposes an acting person deliberately aiming at a result. The same, however, as we have seen before,[71] is true of other concepts like "law" or "organization," which we have nevertheless been forced, by the lack of other suitable terms, to adopt for scientific use in a non-anthropomorphic sense. In the same way we may find the term "purpose" indispensable in a carefully defined sense.

The character of the problem may usefully be described first in the words of an eminent contemporary philosopher who, though elsewhere, in the strict positivist manner, he declares that "the concept of purpose must be entirely excluded from the scientific treatment of the phenomena of life," yet admits the existence of "a general principle which proves frequently valid in psychology and biology and also elsewhere: namely that the result of unconscious or instinctive processes is frequently exactly the same as would have arisen from rational calculation." [72] This states one aspect of the problem very clearly: namely, that a result which, if it were deliberately aimed at, could be achieved only in a limited number of ways, may actually be achieved by one of those methods, although nobody has consciously aimed at it. But it still leaves open the question why the particular result which is brought about in this manner should be regarded as distinguished above others and therefore deserve to be described as the "purpose."

If we survey the different fields in which we are constantly tempted to describe phenomena as "purposive" though they are not directed by a conscious mind, it becomes rapidly clear that the "end" or "purpose" they are said to serve is always the preservation of a "whole," of a persistent structure of relationships, whose existence we have come to take for granted before we understood the nature of the mechanism which holds the parts together. The most familiar instances of such wholes are the biological organisms. Here the conception of the "function" of an organ as an essential condition for the persistence of the whole has proved to be of the greatest heuristic value. It is easily seen how paralyzing an effect on research it would have had if the scientific prejudice had effectively banned the use of all teleological concepts in biology and, e.g., prevented the discoverer of a new organ from immediately asking what "purpose" or "function" it serves.[73]

Though in the social sphere we meet with phenomena which in this respect raise analogous problems, it is, of course, dangerous to describe them for that reason as organisms. The limited analogy provides as such no answer to the common problem, and the loan of an alien term tends to obscure the equally important differences. We need not labor further the now familiar fact that the social wholes, unlike the biological organisms, are not given to us as natural units, fixed complexes which ordinary experience shows us to belong together, but are recognizable only by a process of mental reconstruction; or that the parts of the social whole, unlike those of a true organism, can exist away from their particular place in the whole and are to a large extent mobile and exchangeable. Yet, though we must avoid overworking the analogy, certain general considerations apply in both cases. As in the biological organisms we often observe in spontaneous social formations that the parts move as if their purpose were the preservation of the wholes. We find again and again that if it were somebody's deliberate aim to preserve the structure of those wholes, and if he had knowledge and the power to do so, he would have to do it by causing precisely those movements which in fact are taking place without any such conscious direction.

In the social sphere these spontaneous movements which preserve a certain structural connection between the parts are, moreover, connected in a special way with our individual purposes: the social wholes which are thus maintained are the condition for the achievement of many of the things at which we as individuals aim, the environment which makes it possible even to conceive of most of our individual desires and which gives us the power to achieve them.

There is nothing more mysterious in the fact that, e.g., money or the price system enable man to achieve things which he desires, although they were not designed for that purpose, and hardly could have been consciously designed before that growth of civilization which they made possible, than that, unless man had tumbled upon these devices, he would not have achieved the powers he has gained. The facts to which we refer when we speak of "purposive" forces being at work here, are the same as those which create the persistent social structures which we have come to take for granted and which form the conditions of our existence. The spontaneously grown institutions are "useful" because they were the conditions on which the further development of man was based—which gave him the powers which he used. If, in the form in which Adam Smith put it, the phrase that man in society "constantly promotes ends which are no part of his intention" has become the constant source of irritation of the scientistically-minded, it describes nevertheless the central problem of the social sciences. As it was put a hundred years after Smith by Carl Menger, who did more than any other writer to carry beyond Smith the elucidation of the meaning of this phrase, the question "how it is possible that institutions which serve the common welfare and are most important for its advancement can arise without a common will aiming at their creation" is still "the significant, perhaps the most significant, problem of the social sciences." [74]

That the nature and even the existence of this problem is still so little recognized [75] is closely connected with a common confusion about what we mean when we say that human institutions are made by man. Though in a sense man-made, i.e., entirely the result of human actions, they may yet not be designed, not be the intended product of these actions. The term institution itself is rather misleading in this respect, as it suggests something deliberately instituted. It would probably be better if this term were confined to particular contrivances, like particular laws and organizations, which have been created for a specific purpose, and if a more neutral term like "formations" (in a sense similar to that in which the geologists use it, and corresponding to the German *Gebilde*) could be used for those phenomena, which, like money or language, have not been so created.

From the belief that nothing which has not been consciously designed can be useful or even essential to the achievement of human purposes, it is an easy transition to the belief that since all "institutions" have been made by man, we must have complete power to refashion them in any way we desire.[76] But, though this conclusion at first sounds like a self-evident commonplace, it is, in fact, a complete *non sequitur,* based on the equivocal use of the term "institution." It would be valid only if all the "purposive" formations were the result of design. But phenomena like language or the market, money or morals, are not real artifacts, products of deliberate creation.[77] Not only have they not been designed by any mind, but they are also preserved by, and depend for their functioning on, the actions of people who are not guided by the desire to keep them in existence. And, as they are not due to design but rest on individual actions which we do not now control, we at least can not take it for granted that we can improve upon, or even equal, their performance by any organization which relies on the deliberate control of the movements of its parts. In so far as we learn to understand the spontaneous forces, we may hope to use them and modify their operations by proper adjustment of the institutions which form part of the larger process. But there is all the difference between thus utilizing and influencing spontaneous processes and an attempt to replace them by an organization which relies on conscious control.

We flatter ourselves undeservedly if we represent human civilization as entirely the product of conscious reason or as the product of human design, or when we assume that it is necessarily in our power deliberately to re-create or to maintain what we have built without knowing what we were doing. Though our civilization is the result of a cumulation of individual knowledge, it is not by the explicit or conscious combination of all this knowledge in any individual brain, but by its embodiment in symbols which we use without understanding them, in habits and institutions, tools and concepts,[78] that man in society is constantly able to profit from a body of knowledge neither he nor any other man completely possesses. Many of the greatest things man has achieved are not the result of consciously directed thought, and still less the product of a deliberately co-ordinated effort of many individuals, but of a process in which the individual plays a part which he can never fully understand. They are greater than any individual precisely because they result from the combination of knowledge more extensive than a single mind can master.

It has been unfortunate that those who have recognized this so often draw the conclusion that the problems it raises are purely historical problems, and thereby deprive themselves of the means of effectively refuting the views they try to combat. In fact, as we have seen,[79] much of the older "historical school" was essentially a reaction against the type of erroneous rationalism we are discussing. If it failed it was because it treated the problem of explaining these phenomena as entirely one of the accidents of time and place and refused systematically to elaborate the logical process by which alone we can provide an explanation. We need not return here to this point already discussed.[80] Though the explanation of the way in which the parts of the social whole depend upon each other will often take the form of a genetic account, this will be at most "schematic history" which the true historian will rightly refuse to recognize as real history. It will deal, not with the particular circumstances of an individual process, but only with those steps which are essential to produce a particular result, with a process which, at least in principle, may be repeated elsewhere or at different times. As is true of all explanations, it must run in generic terms, it will deal with what is sometimes called the "logic of events," neglect much that is important in the unique historical instance, and be concerned with a dependence of the parts of the phenomenon upon each other which is not even necessarily the same as the chronological order in which they appeared. In short, it is not history, but compositive social theory.

One curious aspect of this problem which is rarely appreciated is that it is only by the individualist or compositive method that we can give a definite meaning to the much abused phrases about the social processes and formations being in any sense "more" than "merely the sum" of their parts, and that we are enabled to understand how structures of interpersonal relationships emerge, which make it possible for the joint efforts of individuals to achieve desirable results which no individual could have planned or foreseen. The collectivist, on the other hand, who refuses to account for the wholes by systematically following up the interactions of individual efforts, and who claims to be able directly to comprehend social wholes as such, is never able to define the precise character of these wholes or their mode of operation, and is regularly driven to conceive of these wholes on the model of an individual mind.

Even more significant of the inherent weakness of the collectivist theories is the extraordinary paradox that from the assertion that society is in some sense "more" than merely the aggregate of all individuals their adherents regularly pass by a sort of intellectual somersault to the thesis that in order that the coherence of this larger entity be safeguarded it must be subjected to conscious control, i.e., to the control of what in the last resort must be an individual mind. It thus comes about that in practice it is regularly the theoretical collectivist who extols individual reason and demands that all forces of society be made subject to the direction of a single mastermind, while it is the individualist who recognizes the limitations of the powers of individual reason and consequently advocates freedom as a means for the fullest development of the powers of the inter-individual process.

IX

"CONSCIOUS" DIRECTION AND THE GROWTH OF REASON

THE UNIVERSAL DEMAND for "conscious" control or direction of social processes is one of the most characteristic features of our generation. It expresses perhaps more clearly than any of its other clichés the peculiar spirit of the age. That anything is not consciously directed as a whole is regarded as itself a blemish, a proof of its irrationality and of the need completely to replace it by a deliberately designed mechanism. Yet few of the people who use the term "conscious" so freely seem to be aware precisely what it means; most people seem to forget that "conscious" and "deliberate" are terms which have meaning only when applied to individuals, and that the demand for conscious control is therefore equivalent to the demand for control by a single mind.

This belief that processes which are consciously directed are necessarily superior to any spontaneous process is an unfounded superstition. It would be truer to say, as A. N. Whitehead has argued in another connection, that on the contrary "civilization advances by extending the number of important operations we can perform without thinking about them." [81] If it is true that the spontaneous interplay of social forces sometimes solves problems no individual mind could consciously solve, or perhaps even perceives, and if they thereby create an ordered structure which increases the power of the individuals without having been designed by any one of them, they are superior to conscious action. Indeed, any social processes which deserve to be called "social" in distinction to the action of individuals are almost *ex definitione* not conscious. In so far as such processes are capable of producing a useful order which could not have been

87

produced by conscious direction, any attempt to make them subject to such direction would necessarily mean that we restrict what social activity can achieve to the inferior capacity of the individual mind.[82]

The full significance of this demand for universal conscious control will be seen most clearly if we consider it first in its most ambitious manifestation, even though this is as yet merely a vague aspiration and important mainly as a symptom: this is the application of the demand for conscious control to the growth of the human mind itself. This audacious idea is the most extreme result to which man has yet been led by the success of reason in the conquest of external nature. It has become a characteristic feature of contemporary thought and appears in what on a first view seem to be altogether different and even opposite systems of ideas. Whether it is the late L. T. Hobhouse who holds up to us "the ideal of a collective humanity self-determining in its progress as the supreme object of human activity and the final standard by which the laws of conduct should be judged," [83] or Dr. Joseph Needham who argues that "the more control consciousness has over human affairs, the more truly human and hence super-human man will become," [84] whether it is the strict followers of Hegel who adumbrate the master's view of Reason becoming conscious of itself and taking control of its fate, or Dr. Karl Mannheim who thinks that "man's thought has become more spontaneous and absolute than it ever was, since it now perceives the possibility of determining itself," [85] the basic attitude is the same. Though, according as these doctrines spring from Hegelian or positivist views, those who hold them form distinct groups who mutually regard themselves as completely different from and greatly superior to the other, the common idea that the human mind is, as it were, to pull itself up by its own boot-straps, springs from the same general approach: the belief that by studying human Reason from the outside and as a whole we can grasp the laws of its motion in a more complete and comprehensive manner than by its patient exploration from the inside, by actually following up the processes in which individual minds interact.

This pretension to be able to increase the powers of the human mind by consciously controlling its growth is thus based on the same theoretical view which claims to be able fully to explain this growth, a claim which implies the possession of a kind of super-mind on the part of those who make it; and it is no accident that those who hold these theoretical views should also wish to see the growth of mind thus directed.

It is important to understand the precise sense in which the claim to be able to "explain" existing knowledge and beliefs must be interpreted in order to justify the aspirations based on it. For this purpose it would not be sufficient if we possessed an adequate theory which explained the *principles* on which the processes operate to which the growth of mind is due. Such knowledge of the mere principles (either a theory of knowledge or a theory of the social processes involved) will assist in creating conditions favorable to that growth, but could never provide a justification for the claim that it should be deliberately directed. This claim presupposes that we are able to arrive at a substantive explanation of why we hold the particular views we hold, of how our actual knowledge is determined by specific conditions. It is this which the "sociology of knowledge" and the various other derivatives of the "materialist interpretation of history" undertake when, e.g., they "explain" the Kantian philosophy as the product of the material interests of the German bourgeoisie in the late 18th century, or whatever other similar theses they present.

We cannot enter here into a discussion of the reasons why even with respect to views now regarded as errors, and which on the basis of our better present knowledge we may in a sense be able to explain, that method does not really provide an explanation. The crucial point is that to attempt this with respect to our present knowledge involves a contradiction: if we knew how our present knowledge is conditioned or determined, it would no longer be our present knowledge. To assert that we can explain our own knowledge is to assert that we know more than we do know, a statement which is non-sense in the strict meaning of that term.[86] There may, perhaps, be sense in the statement that to a greatly superior mind our present knowledge would appear as "relative," or as conditioned in a certain manner by assignable circumstances. But the only conclusion *we* should be entitled to draw from this would be one opposite to that of the "boot-strap theory of mental evolution": it would be that on the basis of our present knowledge we are not in a position successfully to direct its growth. To draw any other conclusion than this, to derive from the thesis that human beliefs are determined by circumstances the claim that somebody should be given power to determine these beliefs, involves the claim that those who are to assume that power possess some sort of super-mind. Those who hold these views have indeed regularly some special theory which exempts their own views from the same sort of explanation and which credits them, as a specially favored class, or simply as the "free-floating intelligentsia," with the possession of absolute knowledge.

While in a sense this movement represents thus a sort of super-rationalism, a demand for the direction of everything by a super-mind, it prepares at the same time the ground for a thorough irrationalism. If truth is no longer discovered by observation, reasoning and argument, but by uncovering hidden causes which, unknown to the thinker, have determined his conclusions, if whether a statement is true or false is no longer decided by logical argument and empirical tests, but by examining the social position of the person who made it, when in consequence it becomes the membership of a class or race which secures or prevents the achievement of truth, and when in the end it is claimed that the sure instinct of a particular class or a people is always right, reason has been finally driven out.[87] This is no more than the natural result of a doctrine which starts out with the claim that it can intuitively recognize wholes in a manner superior to the rational reconstruction attempted by compositive social theory.

If it is true, moreover, as in their different ways both individualists and collectivists contend, that social processes can achieve things which it is beyond the power of the individual mind to achieve and plan, and that it is from those social processes that the individual mind derives what power it possesses, the attempt to impose conscious control on these processes must have even more fatal consequences. The presumptuous aspiration that "reason" should direct its own growth could in practice only have the effect that it would set limits to its own growth, that it would confine itself to the results which the directing individual mind can already foresee. Though this aspiration is a direct outcome of a certain brand of rationalism, it is, of course, the result of a misunderstood or misapplied rationalism which fails to recognize the extent to which individual reason is a product of inter-individual relationships. Indeed, the demand that everything, including the growth of the human mind, should be consciously controlled is itself a sign of the inadequate understanding of the general character of the forces which constitutes the life of the human mind and of human society. It is the extreme stage of these self-destructive forces of our modern "scientific" civilization, of that abuse of reason whose development and consequences will be the central theme of the following historical studies.

It is because the growth of the human mind presents in its most general form the common problem of all the social sciences that it is here that minds most sharply divide, and that two fundamentally different and irreconcilable attitudes manifest themselves: on the one hand the essential humility of individualism, which endeavors to understand as well as possible the principles by which the efforts of individual men have in fact been combined to produce our civilization, and which from this understanding hopes to derive the power to create conditions favorable to further growth; and, on the other hand, the hubris of collectivism which aims at conscious direction of all forces of society.

The individualist approach, in awareness of the constitutional limitations of the individual mind,[88] attempts to show how man in society is able, by the use of various resultants of the social process, to increase his powers with the help of the knowledge implicit in them and of which he is never aware; it makes us understand that the only "reason" which can in any sense be regarded as superior to individual reason does not exist apart from the inter-individual process in which, by means of impersonal media, the knowledge of successive generations and of millions of people living simultaneously is combined and mutually adjusted, and that this process is the only form in which the totality of human knowledge ever exists.

The collectivist method, on the other hand, not satisfied with the partial knowledge of this process from the inside, which is all the individual can gain, bases its demands for conscious control on the assumption that it can comprehend this process as a whole and make use of all knowledge in a systematically integrated form. It leads thus directly to political collectivism; and though logically methodological and political collectivism are distinct, it is not difficult to see how the former leads to the latter and how, indeed, without methodological collectivism political collectivism would be deprived of its intellectual basis: without the pretension that conscious individual reason can grasp all the aims and all the knowledge of "society" or "humanity," the belief that these aims are best achieved by conscious central direction loses its foundation. Consistently pursued it must lead to a system in which all members of society become merely instruments of the single directing mind and in which all the spontaneous social forces to which the growth of the mind is due are destroyed.[89]

It may indeed prove to be far the most difficult and not the least important task for human reason rationally to comprehend its own limitations. It is essential for the growth of reason that as individuals we should bow to forces and obey principles which we cannot hope fully to understand, yet on which the advance and even the preservation of civilization depends.[90] Historically this has been achieved by the influence of the various religious creeds and by traditions and superstitions which made men submit to those forces by an appeal to his emotions rather than to his reason. The most dangerous stage in the growth of civilization may well be that in which man has come to regard all these beliefs as superstitions and refuses to accept or to submit to anything which he does not rationally understand. The rationalist whose reason is not sufficient to teach him those limitations of the powers of conscious reason, and who despises all the institutions and customs which have not been consciously designed, would thus become the destroyer of the civilization built upon them. This may well prove a hurdle which man will repeatedly reach, only to be thrown back into barbarism.

It would lead too far here to refer more than briefly to another field in which this same characteristic tendency of our age shows itself: that of morals. Here it is against the observance of any general and formal rules whose *rationale* is not explicitly demonstrated that the same kind of objections are raised. But the demand that every action should be judged after full consideration of all its consequences and not by any general rules is due to a failure to see that the submission to general rules, couched in terms of immediately ascertainable circumstances, is the only way in which for man with his limited knowledge freedom can be combined with the essential minimum degree of order. Common acceptance of formal rules is indeed the only alternative to direction by a single will man has yet discovered. The general acceptance of such a body of rules is no less important because they have not been rationally constructed. It is at least doubtful whether it would be possible in this way to construct a new moral code that would have any chance of acceptance. But so long as we have not succeeded in doing so, any general refusal to accept existing moral rules merely because their expediency has not been rationally demonstrated (as distinguished from the case when the critic believes he has discovered a better moral rule in a particular instance and is willing to brave public disapproval in testing it) is to destroy one of the roots of our civilization.[91]

X

ENGINEERS AND PLANNERS

THE IDEAL OF conscious control of social phenomena has made its greatest influence felt in the economic field. The present popularity of "economic planning" is directly traceable to the prevalence of the scientistic ideas we have been discussing. As in this field the scientistic ideals manifest themselves in the particular forms which they take in the hands of the applied scientist and especially the engineer, it will be convenient to combine the discussion of this influence with some examination of the characteristic ideals of the engineers. We shall see that the influence on current views about problems of social organization of his technological approach, or the engineering point of view, is much greater than is generally realized. Most of the schemes for a complete remodelling of society, from the earlier utopias to modern socialism, bear indeed the distinct mark of this influence. In recent years this desire to apply engineering technique to the solution of social problems has become very explicit; [93] "political engineering" and "social engineering" have become fashionable catchwords which are quite as characteristic of the outlook of the present generation as its predilection for "conscious" control; in Russia even the artists appear to pride themselves on the name of "engineers of the soul," bestowed upon them by Stalin. These phrases suggest a confusion about the fundamental differences between the task of the engineer and that of social organizations on a larger scale which make it desirable to consider their character somewhat more fully.

We must confine ourselves here to a few salient features of the specific problems which the professional experience of the engineer constantly bring up and which determine his outlook. The first is that his characteristic tasks are usually in themselves complete: he will be concerned with a single end, control all the efforts directed towards this end, and dispose for this purpose over a definitely given supply of resources. It is as a result of this that the most characteristic feature of his procedure becomes possible, namely that, at least in principle, all the parts of the complex of operations are preformed in the engineer's mind before they start, that all the "data" on which the work is based have explicitly entered his preliminary calculations and been condensed into the "blue-print" that governs the execution of the whole scheme.[94, 95] The engineer, in other words, has complete control of the particular little world with which he is concerned, surveys it in all its relevant aspects and has to deal only with "known quantities." So far as the solution of his engineering problem is concerned, he is not taking part in a social process in which others may take independent decisions, but lives in a separate world of his own. The application of the technique which he has mastered, of the generic rules he has been taught, indeed presupposes such complete knowledge of the objective facts; those rules refer to objective properties of the things and can be applied only after all the particular circumstances of time and place have been assembled and brought under the control of a single brain. His technique, in other words, refers to typical situations defined in terms of objective facts, not to the problem of how to find out what resources are available or what is the relative importance of different needs. He has been trained in objective possibilities, irrespective of the particular conditions of time and place, in the knowledge of those properties of things which remain the same everywhere and at all times and which they possess irrespective of a particular human situation.

It is important, however, to observe that the engineer's view of his job as complete in itself is, in some measure, a delusion. He is in a position in a competitive society to treat it as such because he can regard that assistance from society at large on which he counts as one of his data, as given to him without having to bother about it. That he can buy at given prices the materials and the services of the men he needs, that if he pays his men they will be able to procure their food and other necessities, he will usually take for granted. It is through basing his plans on the data offered to him by the market that they are fitted into the larger complex of social activities; and it is because he need not concern himself how the market provides him with what he needs that he can treat his job as self-contained. So long as market prices do not change unexpectedly he uses them as a guide in his calculations without much reflection about their significance. But, though he is compelled to take them into account, they are not properties of things of the same kind as those which he understands. They are not objective attributes of things but reflections of a particular human situation at a given time and place. And as his knowledge does not explain why those changes in prices occur which often interfere with his plans, any such interference appears to him due to irrational (i.e., not consciously directed) forces, and he resents the necessity of paying attention to magnitudes which appear meaningless to him. Hence the characteristic and ever-recurrent demand for the substitution of *in natura* [96] calculation for the "artificial" calculation in terms of price or value, i.e., of a calculation which takes explicit account of the objective properties of things.

The engineer's ideal which he feels the "irrational" economic forces prevent him from achieving, based on his study of the objective properties of the things, is usually some purely technical optimum of universal validity. He rarely sees that his preference for these particular methods is merely a result of the type of problem he has most frequently to solve, and justified only in particular social positions. Since the most common problem the builder of machines meets is to extract from given resources the maximum of power, with the machinery to be used as the variable under his control, this maximum utilization of power is set up as an absolute ideal, a value in itself.[97] But there is, of course, no special merit economizing one of the many factors which limit the possible achievement, at the expense of others. The engineer's "technical optimum" proves frequently to be simply that method which it would be desirable to adopt if the supply of capital were unlimited, or the rate of interest were zero, which would indeed be a position in which we would aim at the highest possible rate of transformation of current input into current output. But to treat this as an immediate goal is to forget that such a state can be reached only by diverting for a long time resources which are wanted to serve current needs to the production of equipment. In other words, the engineer's ideal is based on the disregard of the most fundamental economic fact which determines our position here and now, the scarcity of capital.

The rate of interest is, of course, only one, though the least understood and therefore the most disliked, of those prices which act as impersonal guides to which the engineer must submit if his plans are to fit into the pattern of activity of society as a whole, and against the restraint of which he chafes because they represent forces whose *rationale* he does not understand. It is one of those symbols in which the whole complex of human knowledge and wants is automatically (though by no means faultlessly) recorded, and to which the individual must pay attention if he wants to keep in step with the rest of the system. If, instead of using this information in the abridged form in which it is conveyed to him through the price system, he were to try in every instance to go back to the objective facts and take them consciously into consideration, this would be to dispense with the method which makes it possible for him to confine himself to the immediate circumstances and to substitute for it a method which requires that all this knowledge be collected in one center and explicitly and consciously embodied in a unitary plan. The application of engineering technique to the whole of society requires indeed that the director possess the same complete knowledge of the whole society that the engineer possesses of his limited world. Central economic planning is nothing but such an application of engineering principles to the whole of society based on the assumption that such a complete concentration of all relevant knowledge is possible.[98]

Before we proceed to consider the significance of this conception of a rational organization of society, it will be useful to supplement the sketch of the typical outlook of the engineer by an even briefer sketch of the functions of the merchant or trader. This will not only further elucidate the nature of the problem of the utilization of knowledge dispersed among many people, but also help to explain the dislike which not only the engineer but our whole generation shows for all commercial activities, and the general preference that is now accorded to "production" compared to the activities which, somewhat misleadingly, are referred to as "distribution."

Compared with the work of the engineer that of the merchant is in a sense much more "social," i.e., interwoven with the free activities of other people. He contributes a step towards the achievement now of one end, now of another, and hardly ever is concerned with the complete process that serves a final need. What concerns him is not the achievement of a particular final result of the complete process in which he takes part, but the best use of the particular means of which he knows. His special knowledge is almost entirely knowledge of particular circumstances of time or place, or, perhaps, a technique of ascertaining those circumstances in a given field. But though this knowledge is not of a kind which can be formulated in generic propositions, or acquired once and for all, and though in an age of Science it is for that reason regarded as knowledge of an inferior kind, it is for all practical purposes no less important than scientific knowledge. And while it is perhaps conceivable that all theoretical knowledge might be combined in the heads of a few experts and thus made available to a single central authority, it is this knowledge of the particular, of the fleeting circumstances of the moment and of local conditions, which will never exist otherwise than dispersed among many people. The knowledge of when a particular material or machine can be used most effectively or where they can be obtained most quickly or cheaply is quite as important for the solution of a particular task as the knowledge of what is the best material or machine for the purpose. The former kind of knowledge has little to do with the permanent properties of classes of things which the engineer studies, but is knowledge of a particular human situation. And it is as the person whose task is to take account of these facts that the merchant will constantly come into conflict with the ideals of the engineer, with whose plans he interferes and whose dislike he thereby contracts.[99]

The problem of securing an efficient use of our resources is thus very largely one of how that knowledge of the particular circumstances of the moment can be most effectively utilized; and the task which faces the designer of a rational order of society is to find a method whereby this widely dispersed knowledge may best be drawn upon. It is begging the question to describe this task, as is usually done, as one of effectively using the "available" resources to satisfy "existing" needs. Neither the "available" resources nor the "existing" needs are objective facts in the sense of those with which the engineer deals in his limited field: they can never be directly known in all relevant detail to a single planning body. Resources and needs exist for practical purposes only through somebody knowing about them, and there will always be infinitely more known to all the people together than can be known to the most competent authority.[100] A successful solution can therefore not be based on the authority dealing directly with the objective facts, but must be based on a method of utilizing the knowledge dispersed among all members of society, knowledge of which in any particular instance the central authority will usually know neither who possesses it nor whether it exists at all. It can therefore not be utilized by consciously integrating it into a coherent whole, but only through some mechanism which will delegate the particular decisions to those who possess it, and for that purpose supply them with such information about the general situation as will enable them to make the best use of the particular circumstances of which only they know.

This is precisely the function which the various "markets" perform. Though every party in them will know only a small sector of all the possible sources of supply, or of the uses of, a commodity, yet, directly or indirectly, the parties are so interconnected that the prices register the relevant net results of all changes affecting demand or supply.[101] It is as such an instrument for communicating to all those interested in a particular commodity the relevant information in an abridged and condensed form that markets and prices must be seen if we are to understand their function. They help to utilize the knowledge of many people without the need of first collecting it in a single body, and thereby make possible that combination of decentralization of decisions and mutual adjustment of these decisions which we find in a competitive system.

In aiming at a result which must be based, not on a single body of integrated knowledge or of connected reasoning which the designer possesses, but on the separate knowledge of many people, the task of social organization differs fundamentally from that of organizing given material resources. The fact that no single mind can know more than a fraction of what is known to all individual minds sets limits to the extent to which conscious direction can improve upon the results of unconscious social processes. Man has not deliberately designed this process and has begun to understand it only long after it had grown up. But that something which not only does not rely on deliberate control for its working, but which has not even been deliberately designed, should bring about desirable results, which we might not be able to bring about otherwise, is a conclusion the natural scientist seems to find difficult to accept.

It is because the moral sciences tend to show us such limits to our conscious control, while the progress of the natural sciences constantly extends the range of conscious control, that the natural scientist finds himself so frequently in revolt against the teaching of the moral sciences. Economics, in particular, after being condemned for employing methods different from those of the natural scientist, stands doubly condemned because it claims to show limits to the technique by which the natural scientists continuously extend our conquest and mastery of nature.

It is this conflict with a strong human instinct, greatly strengthened in the person of the scientist and engineer, that makes the teaching of the moral sciences so very unwelcome. As Bertrand Russell has well described the position, "the pleasure of planned construction is one of the most powerful motives in men who combine intelligence with energy; whatever can be constructed according to a plan, such man will endeavor to construct . . . the desire to create is not in itself idealistic since it is a form of the love of power, and while the power to create exists there will be men desirous of using this power even if unaided nature would produce a better result than any that can be brought about by deliberate intention." [102] This statement occurs, however, at the beginning of a chapter, significantly headed "Artificially Created Societies," in which Russell himself seems to support these tendencies by arguing that "no society can be regarded as fully scientific unless it has been created deliberately with a certain structure to fulfill certain purposes." [103] As this statement will be understood by most readers, it expresses concisely that scientistic philosophy which through its popularizers has done more to create the present trend towards socialism than all the conflicts between economic interests which, though they raise a problem, do not necessarily indicate a particular solution. Of the majority of the intellectual leaders of the socialist movement, at least, it is probably true to say that they are socialists because socialism appears to them, as A. Bebel, the leader of the German Social Democratic movement defined it sixty years ago, as "science applied in clear awareness and with full insight to all fields of human activity." [104] The proof that the program of socialism actually derives from this kind of scientistic philosophy must be reserved for the detailed historical studies. At present our concern is mainly to show to what extent sheer intellectual error in this field may profoundly affect all prospects of humanity.

What the people who are so unwilling to renounce any of the powers of conscious control seem to be unable to comprehend is that this renunciation of conscious power, power which must always be power by men over other men, is for society as a whole only an apparent resignation, a self-denial individuals are called upon to exercise in order to increase the powers of the race, to release the knowledge and energies of the countless individuals that could never be utilized in a society consciously directed from the top. The great misfortune of our generation is that the direction which by the amazing progress of the natural sciences has been given to its interests is not one which assists us in comprehending the larger process of which as individuals we form merely a part or in appreciating how we constantly contribute to a common effort without either directing it or submitting to orders of others. To see this requires a kind of intellectual effort different in character from that necessary for the control of material things, an effort in which the traditional education in the "humanities" gave at least some practice, but for which the now predominant types of education seem less and less to prepare. The more our technical civilization advances and the more, therefore, the study of things as distinct from the study of men and their ideas qualifies for the more important and influential positions, the more significant becomes the gulf that separates two different types of mind: the one represented by the man whose supreme ambition is to turn the world round him into an enormous machine, every part of which, on his pressing a button, moves according to his design; and the other represented by the man whose main interest is the growth of the human mind in all its aspects, who in the study of history or literature, the arts or the law, has learned to see the individuals as part of a process in which his contribution is not directed but spontaneous, and where he assists in the creation of something greater than he or any other single mind can ever plan for. It is this awareness of being part of a social process, and of the manner in which individual efforts interact, which the education solely in the Sciences or in technology seems so lamentably to fail to convey. It is not surprising that many of the more active minds among those so trained sooner or later react violently against the deficiencies of their education and develop a passion for imposing on society the order which they are unable to detect by the means with which they are familiar.

In conclusion it is, perhaps, desirable to remind the reader once more that all we have said here is directed solely against a misuse of Science, not against the scientist in the special field where he is competent, but against the application of his mental habits in fields where he is not competent. There is no conflict between our conclusions and those of legitimate science. The main lesson at which we have arrived is indeed the same as that which one of the acutest students of scientific method has drawn from a survey of all fields of knowledge: it is that "the great lesson of humility which science teaches us, that we can never be omnipotent or omniscient, is the same as that of all great religions: man is not and never will be the god before whom he must bow down." [105]

Part Two

THE
COUNTER-REVOLUTION
OF SCIENCE

The age preferred the reign of intellect to the reign of liberty.
LORD ACTON.

I

THE SOURCE OF THE SCIENTISTIC HUBRIS: L'ECOLE POLYTECHNIQUE

§ 1. NEVER WILL MAN penetrate deeper into error than when he is continuing on a road which has led him to great success. And never can pride in the achievements of the natural sciences and confidence in the omnipotence of their methods have been more justified than at the turn of the eighteenth and nineteenth centuries, and nowhere more so than at Paris where almost all the great scientists of the age congregated. If it is true, therefore, that the new attitude of man towards social affairs in the nineteenth century is due to the new mental habits acquired in the intellectual and material conquest of nature, we should expect it to appear where modern science celebrated its greatest triumphs. In this we shall not be disappointed. Both the two great intellectual forces which in the course of the nineteenth century transformed social thought—modern socialism and that species of modern positivism, which we prefer to call scientism, spring directly from this body of professional scientists and engineers which grew up in Paris, and more particularly from the new institution which embodied the new spirit as no other, the *Ecole polytechnique*.

It is well known that French Enlightenment was characterized by a general enthusiasm for the natural sciences as never yet known before. Voltaire is the father of that cult of Newton which later was to be carried to ridiculous heights by Saint-Simon. And the new passion soon began to bear great fruits. At first the interest concentrated on the subjects connected with Newton's great name. In Clairault and d'Alembert, with Euler the greatest mathematicians of the period, Newton soon found worthy successors who in turn were followed by Lagrange and Laplace, no less giants. And with Lavoisier, not

105

only the founder of modern chemistry but also a great physiologist, and, to a lesser degree, with Buffon in biological science, France began to take the lead in all important fields of natural knowledge.

The great *Encyclopædie* was a gigantic attempt to unify and popularize the achievements of the new science, and d'Alembert's "Discours préliminaire" (1754) to the great work, in which he attempted to trace the rise, progress and affinities of the various sciences, may be regarded as the Introduction not only to the work but to a whole period. This great mathematician and physicist did much to prepare the way for the revolution in mechanics by which towards the end of the century his pupil Lagrange finally freed it from all metaphysical concepts and restated the whole subject without any reference to ultimate causes or hidden forces, merely describing the laws by which the effects were connected.[1] No other single step in any science expresses more clearly the tendency of the scientific movement of the age or had greater influence or symbolic significance.[2]

Yet while this step was still gradually preparing in the field where it was to take its most conspicuous form, the general tendency which it expressed was already recognized and described by d'Alembert's contemporary Turgot. In the amazing and masterly discourses which as a young man of 23 he delivered at the opening and the closing of the session of the Sorbonne in 1750, and in the sketch of a *Discourse on Universal History* of the same period, he outlined how the advance of our knowledge of nature was accompanied throughout by a gradual emancipation from those anthropomorphic concepts which first led man to interpret natural phenomena after his own image as animated by a mind like his own. This idea, which was later to become the leading theme of positivism and was ultimately misapplied to the science of man himself, was soon afterwards widely popularized by President C. de Brosses under the name of fetishism,[3] the name under which it remained known till it was much later replaced by the expressions anthropomorphism and animism. But Turgot went even further and, completely anticipating Comte on this point, described how this process of emancipation passed through three stages where, after supposing that natural phenomena were produced by intelligent beings, invisible but resembling ourselves, they began to be explained by abstract expressions such as essences and faculties, till at last "by observing reciprocal mechanical action of bodies hypotheses were formed which could be developed by mathematics and verified by experience." [4]

It has often been pointed out [5] that most of the leading ideas of French Positivism had already been formulated by d'Alembert and Turgot and their friends and pupils Lagrange and Condorcet. For most of what is valid and valuable in that doctrine this is unquestionably true, although their positivism differed from that of Hume by a strong tinge of French rationalism. And, as there will be no opportunity to go into this aspect more fully, it should perhaps be specially stressed at this stage that throughout the development of French positivism this rationalist element, probably due to the influence of Descartes, continued to play an important role.[6]

It must be pointed out however that these great French thinkers of the eighteenth century showed scarcely any trace yet of that illegitimate extension to the phenomena of society of scientistic methods of thought which later became so characteristic of that School—excepting perhaps certain ideas of Turgot about the philosophy of history and still more so some of Condorcet's last suggestions. But none of them had any doubt about the legitimacy of the abstract and theoretical method in the study of social phenomena, and they were all staunch individualists. It is particularly interesting to observe that Turgot, and the same is true of David Hume, was at the same time one of the founders of positivism and of abstract economic theory, against which positivism was later to be employed. But in some respects most of these men unwittingly started trains of thought which produced views on social matters very different from their own.

This is particularly true of Condorcet. A mathematician like d'Alembert and Lagrange, he definitely turned to the theory as well as to the practice of politics. And although to the last he understood that "meditation alone may lead us to general truths in the science of man," [7] he was not merely anxious to supplement this by extensive observation but occasionally expressed himself as if the method of the natural sciences were the only legitimate one in the treatment of the problems of society. It was particularly his desire to apply his beloved mathematics, especially the newly developed calculus of probability, to his second sphere of interest, which led him to stress more and more the study of those social phenomena which would be objectively observed and measured.[8] As early as 1783, in the oration at his reception into the *Académie,* he gave expression to what was to become a favorite idea of positivist sociology, that of an observer to whom physical and social phenomena would appear in the same light, because, "a stranger to our race, he would study human society as we study those of the beavers and bees." [9] And although he admits that this is an unattainable ideal because "the observer is himself a part of human society," he repeatedly exhorts the scholars "to introduce into the moral sciences the philosophy and the method of the natural sciences." [10]

The most seminal of his suggestions however occurs in his *Sketch of a Historical Picture of the Progress of the Human Mind,* the famous Testament of the Eighteenth Century, as it has been called, in which the unbounded optimism of the age found its last and greatest expression. Tracing human progress in a great outline through all history, he conceives of a science which might foresee the future progress of the human race, accelerate and direct it.[11] But to establish laws which will enable us to predict the future, history must cease to be a history of individuals and must become a history of the masses, must at the same time cease to be a record of individual facts but must become based on systematic observation.[12] Why should the attempt to base on the results of the history of the human race a picture of its future destiny be regarded as chimerical? "The only foundation for the knowledge of the natural sciences is the idea that the general laws, known or unknown, which regulate the phenomena of the Universe, are necessary and constant; and why should that principle be less true for the intellectual and moral faculties of man than for the other actions of nature?" [13] The idea of natural laws of historical development and the collectivist view of history were born, merely as bold suggestions, it is true, but to remain with us in a continuous tradition to the present day.[14]

§ 2.   Condorcet himself became a victim of the Revolution. But his work guided to a large extent that same Revolution, particularly its educational reforms, and it was only as a result of these that towards the beginning of the new century the great institutionalized and centralized organization of science arose which created one of the most glorious periods of scientific advance, became not only the birthplace of that scientism which is more particularly our concern but was probably also largely responsible for the relative decline of the position of French science in the course of the century from indubitably the first place in the world to one not only behind Germany but also behind other nations. As is so often the case with similar movements, it was only on the second or third generation that the mischief was done by the pupils of the great men who exaggerated the ideas of their masters and misapplied them beyond their proper limits.

In three respects the direct consequences of the Revolution are of special interest to us. In the first place, the very collapse of the existing institutions called for immediate application of all the knowledge which appeared as the concrete manifestation of that Reason which was the Goddess of the Revolution. As one of the new scientific journals which sprang up at the end of the Terror expressed it: "The Revolution has razed everything to the ground. Government, morals, habits, everything has to be rebuilt. What a magnificent site for the architects! What a grand opportunity of making use of all the fine and excellent ideas that had remained speculative, of employing so many materials that could not be used before, of rejecting so many others that had been obstructions for centuries and which one had been forced to use." [15]

The second consequence of the Revolution which we must briefly consider is the complete destruction of the old and the creation of an entirely new educational system which had profound effects on the outlook and general views of the whole next generation. The third is more particularly the foundation of the *Ecole Polytechnique*.

The Revolution had swept away the old system of *collèges* and *universités* which was based largely on classical education, and after some short-lived experiments replaced them in 1795 by the new *écoles centrales* which became the sole centers of secondary education.[16] In conformity with the ruling spirit and by an over-violent reaction against the older schools, the teaching in the new institutions was for some years confined almost exclusively to the scientific subjects. Not only the ancient languages were reduced to a minimum and in practice almost entirely neglected, even the instruction in literature, grammar, and history was very inferior, and moral and religious instruction, of course, completely absent.[17] Although after some years a new reform endeavored to make good some of the gravest deficiencies,[18] the interruption for a series of years of the instruction in those subjects was sufficient to change the whole intellectual atmosphere. Saint-Simon described this change in 1812 or 1813: "Such is the difference in this respect between the state of . . . even thirty years ago and that of today that while in those not distant days, if one wanted to know whether a person had received a distinguished education, one asked: "Does he know his Greek and Latin authors well?,' today one asks: 'Is he good at mathematics? Is he familiar with the achievements of physics, of chemistry, of natural history, in short, of the positive sciences and those of observation?' " [19]

Thus a whole generation grew up to whom that great storehouse of social wisdom, the only form indeed in which an understanding of the social processes achieved by the greatest minds is transmitted, the great literature of all ages, was a closed book. For the first time in history that new type appeared which as the product of the German *Realschule* and of similar institutions was to become so important and influential in the later nineteenth and the twentieth century: the technical specialist who was regarded as educated because he had passed through difficult schools but who had little or no knowledge of society, its life, growth, problems and its values, which only the study of history, literature and languages can give.

§ 3.   Not only in secondary education but still more so in higher education the Revolutionary Convention had created a new type of institution which was to become permanently established and a model imitated by the whole world: the *Ecole Polytechnique*. The wars of the Revolution and the help which some of the scientists had been able to render in the production of essential supplies [20] had led to a new appreciation of the need of trained engineers, in the first instance for military purposes. But industrial advance also created a new interest in machines. Scientific and technological progress created a widespread enthusiasm for technological studies, which expressed itself in the foundation of such societies as the *Association philo-technique* and the *Société polytechnique*.[21] Higher technical education had till then been confined to specialized schools such as the *Ecole des Ponts et Chaussés* and the various military schools. It was at one of the latter that G. Monge, the founder of descriptive geometry, Minister of Marine during the Revolution and later friend of Napoleon, taught. He sponsored the idea of a single great school in which all classes of engineers should receive their training in the subjects they had in common.[22] He communicated that idea to Lazare Carnot, the "organizer of victory," his old pupil and himself no mean physicist and engineer.[23] These two men impressed their stamp on the new institution which was created in 1794. The new *Ecole Polytechnique* was (against the advice of Laplace [24]) to be devoted mainly to the applied sciences—in contrast to the *Ecole Normale,* created at the same time and devoted to theory—and remained so during the first ten or twenty years of its existence. The whole teaching centered, to a much higher degree than is still true of similar institutions, around Monge's subject, descriptive geometry, or the art of blue-print making, as we may call it to show its special significance for engineers.[25] First organized on essentially civilian lines, the School was later given a purely military organization by Napoleon who also, however much he favored it otherwise, resisted any attempt to liberalize its curriculum, and conceded even the provision of a course in so harmless a subject as literature only with reluctance.[26]

Yet in spite of the limitations as to the subjects taught, and the even more serious limitations of the previous education of the students in its early years, the *Ecole* commanded from the very beginning a teaching staff probably more illustrious than any other institution in Europe has had before or since. Lagrange was among its first professors, and although Laplace was not a regular teacher there, he was connected with the school in many ways, including the office of chairman of its council. Monge, Fourier, Prony, and Poinsot were among the first generation of teachers of mathematical and physical subjects; Berthollet, who continued the work of Lavoisier, and several others hardly less distinguished,[27] taught chemistry. The second generation which began to take over early in the new century included such names as Poisson, Ampère, Gay-Lussac, Thénard, Arago, Cauchy, Fresnel, Malus, to mention only the best known, incidentally nearly all ex-students of the *Ecole*. The institution had only existed for a few years when it had become famous all over Europe, and the first interval of peace in 1801–2 brought Volta, Count Rumford and Alexander von Humboldt [28] on pilgrimage to the new temple of science.

§ 4.   This is not the place to speak at length of the conquests of nature associated with these names. We are only concerned with the general spirit of exuberance which they engendered, with the feeling which they created that there were no limits to the powers of the human mind and to the extent to which man could hope to harness and control all the forces which so far had threatened and intimidated him. Nothing perhaps expresses more clearly this spirit than Laplace's bold idea of a world formula which he expressed in a famous passage of his *Essai philosophique sur les Probabilités:* "A mind that in a given instance knew all the forces by which nature is animated and the position of all the bodies of which it is composed, if it were vast enough to include all these data within his analysis, could embrace in one single formula the movements of the largest bodies of the Universe and of the smallest atoms; nothing would be uncertain for him; the future and the past would be equally before his eyes." [29] This idea, which exercised so profound a fascination [30] on generations of scientistically-minded people is, as is now becoming apparent, not only a conception which describes an unattainable ideal, but in fact a quite illegitimate deduction from the principles by which we establish laws for particular physical events. It is now itself regarded by modern positivists as a "metaphysical fiction." [31]

It has been well described how the whole of the teaching at the *Ecole Polytechnique* was penetrated with the positivist spirit of Lagrange and all the courses and the textbooks used were modelled on his example.[32] Perhaps even more important, however, for the general outlook of the polytechnicians was the definite practical bent inherent in all its teaching, the fact that all the sciences were taught mainly in their practical applications and that all the pupils looked forward to using their knowledge as military or civil engineers. The very type of the engineer with his characteristic outlook, ambitions, and limitations was here created. That synthetic spirit which would not recognize sense in anything that had not been deliberately constructed, that love of organization that springs from the twin sources of military and engineering practices,[33] the æsthetic predilection for everything that had been consciously constructed over anything that had "just grown," was a strong new element which was added to— and in the course of time even began to replace—the revolutionary ardor of the young polytechnicians. The peculiar characteristics of this new type who, as it has been said, "prided themselves on having more precise and more satisfactory solutions than anyone else for all political, religious and social questions,"[34] and who "ventured to create a religion as one learns at the *Ecole* to build a bridge or a road"[35] was early noticed, and their propensity to become socialists has often been pointed out.[36] Here we must confine ourselves to point out that it was in this atmosphere that Saint-Simon conceived some of the earliest and most fantastic plans for the reorganization of society, and that it was at the *Ecole Polytechnique* where, during the first twenty years of its existence, Auguste Comte, Prosper Enfantin, Victor Considérant and some hundreds of later Saint-Simonians and Fourierists received their training, followed by a succession of social reformers throughout the century down to Georges Sorel.[37]

But, whatever the tendencies among the pupils of the institution, it must again be pointed out that the great scientists who built the fame of the *Ecole Polytechnique* were not guilty of illegitimate extensions of their technique and habits of thought to fields which were not their own. They little concerned themselves with problems of man and society.[38] This was the province of another group of men, in their time no less influential and admired, but whose efforts to continue the eighteenth century traditions in the social sciences were in the end to be swamped by the tide of scientism and silenced by political persecution. It was the misfortune of the *idéologues,* as they called themselves, that their very name should be perverted into a catchword describing the very opposite from what they stood for, and that their ideas should fall into the hands of the young engineers who distorted and changed them beyond recognition.

5. It is a curious fact that the French scholars of the time of which we are speaking should have been divided into two "distinct societies which had only one single trait in common, the celebrity of their names." [39] The first were the professors and examiners at the *Ecole Polytechnique* which we already know and those at the *Collège de France*. The second was the group of physiologists, biologists and psychologists, mostly connected with the *Ecole de Médecine* and known as the Ideologues.

Not all of the great biologists of which France could boast at the time belonged to this second group. At the *Collège de France,* Cuvier, the founder of comparative anatomy and probably the most famous of them, stood close to the pure scientists. The advances of the biological sciences as expounded by him contributed perhaps as much as anything else to create the belief in the omnipotence of the methods of pure science. More and more problems that had seemed to evade the powers of exact treatment were shown to be conquerable by the same methods.[40] The two other biologists whose names are now even better known than his, Lamarck and Geoffroy St. Hilaire, remained at the periphery of the ideologist group and did not concern themselves much with the study of man as a thinking being. But Cabanis and Main de Biran, with their friends Destutt de Tracy and Degérando, made the latter the central problem of their labors.

Ideology,[41] in the sense in which the term was used by that group, meant simply the analysis of human ideas and of human action, including the relation between man's physical and mental constitution.[42][43] The inspiration of the group came mainly from Condillac and the field of their studies was outlined by Cabanis, one of the founders of physiological psychology, in his *Rapports du physique et du moral de l'homme* (1802). And although there was much talk among them about applying the methods of natural science to man, this meant no more than that they proposed to study man without prejudices and without nebulous speculations about his end and destiny. But this prevented neither Cabanis nor his friends from devoting a large part of their life work to that analysis of human ideas which gave ideology its name. Nor did it occur to them to doubt the legitimacy of introspection. If the second head of the group, Destutt de

Tracy, proposed to regard the whole of ideology as part of zoology,[44] this did not preclude his confining himself entirely to that part of it which he called *idéologie rationelle,* in contrast to the *idéologie physiologique,* and which consisted of logic, grammar and economics.[45]

It cannot be denied that in all this, out of their enthusiasm for the pure sciences, they used many misleading expressions which were grossly misunderstood by Saint-Simon and Comte. Cabanis in particular stressed repeatedly that physics must be the basis of the moral sciences; [46] but with him too this meant no more than that account must be taken of the physiological bases of mental activities, and he always recognized the three seperate parts of the "science de l'homme," physiology, analysis of ideas, and morals.[47] But, in so far as the problems of society are concerned, while Cabanis' work remained mainly programatic in character, Destutt de Tracy made very important contributions. We need mention here only one: his analysis of value and its relation to utility, where, proceeding from the foundations laid by Condillac, he went very far in providing what classical English political economy lacked and what might have saved it from the impasse into which it got—a correct theory of value. Destutt de Tracy (and Louis Say, who later continued his work) may indeed be said to have anticipated by more than half a century what was to become one of the most important advances of social theory, the subjective (or marginal utility) theory of value.[48]

It is true that others outside their circle went much further in the application of the technique of the natural sciences to social phenomena, particularly the *Société des Observateurs de l'Homme,* which, largely under Cuvier's influence, went some way in confining social study to a mere recording of observations reminiscent of similar organizations of our own day.[49] But on the whole there can be no doubt that the ideologues preserved the best tradition of the eighteenth century *philosophes.* And while their colleagues at the *Ecole Polytechnique* became the admirers and friends of Napoleon and recieved from him all possible support, the ideologues remained staunch defenders of individual freedom and consequently incurred the wrath of the despot.

§ 6. It was Napoleon who gave currency to the word ideologue in its new sense by using it as a favorite expression of contempt for all those who ventured to defend freedom against him.[50] And he did not content himself with abuse. The man who understood better than any of his imitators that "in the long run the sword is always beaten by the spirit" did not hesitate to carry his "repugnance for all discussion and the teaching of political matters" [51] into practice. The economist J. B. Say, a member of the ideologist group and for some years editor of its journal, the *Décade philosophique,* was one of the first to feel the strong hand. When he refused to change a chapter in his *Traité d'économie politique* to suit the wishes of the dictator, the second edition was prohibited and the author removed from the *tribunat.*[52] In 1806 Destutt de Tracy had to appeal to President Jefferson to secure the publication of at least an English translation of his *Commentaire sur l'Esprit des lois* which he was not allowed to publish in his own country.[53] A little earlier (1803) the whole of the second class of the *Institut,* that of the moral and political science, had been suppressed.[54] In consequence, these subjects remained excluded from the great *Tableau de l'état et des progrès des sciences et des arts depuis 1789* which the three classes of the *Institut* had been ordered to furnish in 1802. This was symbolic of the whole position of these subjects under the Empire. The teaching of them was prevented and the whole younger generation grew up in ignorance of the achievements of the past. The door was thus opened to a new start unencumbered by the accumulated results of earlier study. Social problems were to be approached from a new angle. The methods, which since d'Alembert had so successfully been used in physics, whose character had now become explicit, and which more recently had been equally successful in chemistry and biology, were now to be applied to the science of man. With what results we shall gradually see.

II

THE "ACCOUCHEUR D'IDEES":
HENRI DE SAINT-SIMON

§ 1. Early training and experience can hardly be said to have qualified the count Henri de Saint-Simon for the rôle of a scientific reformer. But it must be admitted that when in 1798, at the age of 38,[55] he took up his abode opposite the *Ecole Polytechnique,* henceforth to interpret to the world the significance of scientific progress for the study of society, he was already a man of rich and varied experience; but scientific study had scarcely been included. The facts of his earlier life, only quite recently brought to light,[56] are considerably less elevating than the numerous anecdotes which he himself and his pupils have transmitted to us and which until lately formed almost our sole information about his youth. The legends tell us that he descended from Charlemagne, that d'Alembert supervised his education, and that his valet had orders to wake the ambitious young man daily with the words: *Levez-vous, Monsieur le Comte, vous avez de grandes choses à faire.* All this is not altogether impossible. It is certain, however, that for the first twenty years of his adult life he lived the life of an adventurer, as many sons of aristocratic families must have done during the period, but on a scale and with an intensity that can have been equalled by few of his contemporaries.

Almost as soon as he obtained a commission in the French Army he followed Lafayette to America and when, after four years, fighting ceased, he bade farewell to his profession. Even before this we find him dreaming of piercing the Isthmus of Panama. A little later he offered his services in Holland for an expedition against the British Indies and was also concerned more concretely with projects for building canals in Spain. The Revolution found him back in Paris, as the citoyen Bonhomme, forswearing his title and acting the extreme Sansculotte. But soon more profitable ventures offered themselves. In the sale of the church lands we find him as one of the most active intermediaries, speculating with borrowed money on a colossal scale, one of the great profiteers of inflation, who did not scorn any business that came his way, such as an attempted sale of the lead from the roofs of Notre Dame. It is not surprising to find him in prison during the terror. It was during the time he spent there that according to his own account he decided on the career of a philosopher. But, released, he once more preferred financial to metaphysical speculation. So long as the source of his funds (a Saxon diplomatist) continued to provide him with sufficient capital, he tried his hand at all sorts of commercial ventures, such as organizing a stage coach service, selling wine retail, manufacturing textiles and even "republican" playing cards in which the obnoxious kings and queens were replaced by *le génie* and *la liberté*. His plans were even more ambitious. He seems to have begun the construction of some large industrial plant and he at least contemplated a combined commercial and banking enterprise that "should be unique in the world." He also acted as spokesman for French financial interests at the Anglo-French discussions at Lille in 1797.

All these activities, however, came to a sudden end when in 1798 his partner returned to Paris and asked to be shown the accounts. Saint-Simon certainly knew what high living meant, and his house, run by the former *maître d'hôtel* of the Duc de Choiseul, and his kitchen, presided over by an equally reputed *chef,* were famous. But that all the costs of this should have gone down as expenses on the joint account rather upset the good Saxon count. He withdrew his funds, and Saint-Simon, still in possession of a fortune, substantial but no longer adequate to support further grandiose ventures, found it advisable to withdraw from commercial activity and henceforth to seek glory in the intellectual sphere.

We need not doubt that in the mind of the disappointed *faiseur* vague plans for the reorganization of society were already forming; and it is not surprising that he should soon find that all his experiences had not provided him with the knowledge which would enable him to elaborate these ideas. He therefore decided "to employ his money to acquire scientific knowledge." [57] It was at this time that he spent three years in close contact with the teachers and students of the *Ecole Polytechnique* as a kind of Maecenas-pupil, feasting the professors and assisting the students, one of whom, the great mathematician Poisson, he entirely supported for years and treated as his adopted son.

The method of study which Saint-Simon chose for himself was not of the ordinary. Feeling that his brain was no longer elastic enough to pursue a systematic course, he preferred to learn what he could in the more pleasant form of dinner-table conversation. He asked the scholars from whose knowledge he hoped to profit to his house, and appears even to have married for the sole purpose of keeping a house where he could properly entertain the great savants. Lagrange, Monge, Berthollet, and, probably after 1801, when he felt he had completed his education in the mechanical sciences and moved to the neighborhood of the *Ecole de Médecine,* Gall, Cabanis, and Bichat, are reported to have partaken of his hospitality. Yet this method of study seems to have proved to be of questionable value. At any rate in later life our hero complained to a friend that his "scholars and artists ate much but talked little. After dinner I went to sit in an easy chair in a corner of the salon and fell asleep. Fortunately Madame de Saint-Simon did the *honneurs* with much grace and *esprit.*" [58]

Whether it was merely that he became aware that this had been a bad investment and decided to cut the losses, or whether it was that another marriage appeared to him a more attractive method of instruction, yet not only the dinners but also the marriage came to an end soon after he had moved to the new place. He explained to his wife that "the first man of the world ought to be married to the first woman" and that, therefore, with much regret he had to ask her to be released. Was it an accident that the divorce was effected in the month after Madame de Staël had become a widow, the Madame de Staël who, in a book that had fired Saint-Simon's imagination, had only just celebrated the "positive sciences" and emphasized that the "science of politics was yet to be created?" [59] It is alleged that as soon as he was free he hurried to Le Coppet on the Lake of Geneva and proposed in the following words: "Madame, you are the most extraordinary woman on earth and I am the most extraordinary man; together we shall undoubtedly produce a still more extraordinary child." Legend adds that he also proposed that they should celebrate their nuptials in a balloon. About the terms in which the refusal was couched the versions vary.

§ 2.   The visit to Switzerland was also the occasion of Saint-Simon's first publication. In 1803 there appeared in Geneva the *Lettres d'un habitant de Genève à ses contemporains*,[60] a little tract in which the Voltairean cult of Newton was revived in a fantastically exaggerated form. It begins by proposing that a subscription should be opened before the tomb of Newton to finance the project of a great "Council of Newton" for which each subscriber is to have the right of nominating three mathematicians, three physicists, three chemists, three physiologists, three *littérateurs,* three painters and three musicians.[61] The twenty-one scholars and artists thus elected by the whole of mankind, and presided over by the mathematician who received the largest number of votes,[62] should become in their collective capacity the representatives of God on earth,[63] who would deprive the Pope, the cardinals, bishops and the priests of their office because they do not understand the divine science which God has entrusted to them and which some day will again turn earth into paradise.[64] In the divisions and sections into which the supreme Council of Newton will divide the world, similar local Councils of Newton will be created which will have to organize worship, research and instruction in and around the temples of Newton which will be built everywhere.[65]

Why this new "social organization," as Saint-Simon calls it for the first time in an unpublished manuscript of the same period? [66] Because we are still governed by people who do not understand the general laws that rule the universe. "It is necessary that the physiologists chase from their company the philosophers, moralists and metaphysicians just as the astronomers have chased out the astrologers and the chemists have chased out the alchemists." [67] The physiologists are competent in the first instance because "we are organized bodies; and it is by regarding our social relationships as physiological phenomena that I have conceived the project which I present to you." [68]

But the physiologists themselves are not yet quite scientific enough. They have yet to discover how their science can reach the perfection of astronomy by basing itself on the single law to which God has subjected the universe, the law of universal gravitation.[69] It will be the task of the Council of Newton by exercising its spiritual power to make people understand this law. Its tasks, however, go far beyond that. It will not only have to vindicate the rights of the men of genius, the scientists, the artists and all the people with liberal views;[70] it will also have to reconcile the second class of people, the proprietors, and the third, the people without property, to whom Saint-Simon addresses himself specially as his friends and whom he exhorts to accept this proposal which is the only way to prevent that "struggle which, from the nature of things, necessarily always exists between" the two classes.[71]

All this is revealed to Saint-Simon by the Lord himself, who announces to His prophet that He has placed Newton at His side and entrusted him with the enlightenment of the inhabitants of all planets. The instruction culminates in the famous passage from which much of later Saint-Simonian doctrine springs: "All men will work; they will regard themselves as laborers attached to one workshop whose efforts will be directed to guide human intelligence according to my divine foresight. The supreme Council of Newton will direct their works."[72] Saint-Simon has no qualms about the means that will be employed to enforce the instructions of his central planning body: "Anybody who does not obey the orders will be treated by the others as a quadruped."[73]

In condensing we had to try and bring some order into the incoherent and rambling jumble of ideas which this first pamphlet of Saint-Simon represents. It is the outpouring of a megalomaniac visionary who sprouts half-digested ideas, who all the time is trying to attract the attention of the world to his unappreciated genius and to the necessity of financing his works, and who does not forget to provide for himself as the founder of the new religion great power and the chairmanship of all the Councils for life.[74]

§ 3.   Soon after the publication of this first work, Saint-Simon found that his funds were entirely exhausted and the next few years he spent in increasing misery, importuning his old friends and associates with demands for money and, it appears, not stopping short of blackmail. Even his appeals to now powerful friends of the past, such as the Comte de Ségur, Napoleon's *grand maître des cérémonies,* procured him in the end no more than the miserable and humiliating position of copyist in a pawnbroking institution. After six months of this, weakened and ill, he met his former valet, who took him into his house. For four years (1806–1810) until his death that devoted servant provided for all the needs of his ex-master and even defrayed the cost of printing Saint-Simon's next work.

It seems that during this period Saint-Simon read more extensively than ever before; at least the *Introduction aux travaux scientifiques du XIXe siècle* [75] shows a wide although still very superficial and ill-digested knowledge of the scientific literature of the period. The main theme is still the same, but the methods proposed have somewhat changed. Before science can organize society, science itself must be organized.[76] The Council of Newton therefore now becomes the editorial committee of a great new Encyclopædia which is to systematize and unify all knowledge: "We must examine and co-ordinate it all from the point of view of Physicism." [77] This physicism is not merely a new general scientific method; it is to be a new religion, even if at first only for the educated classes.[78] It is to be the third great stage in the evolution of religion from Polytheism through "Deism" [79] to Physicism. But although the growth of Physicism has now been under way for eleven hundred years,[80] the victory is not yet complete. The reason is that the work of the past, particularly that of the French Encyclopedists, was merely critical and destructive.[81] It is for the great Emperor Napoleon, "the scientific chief of humanity as he is its political chief," "the most positive man of the age," to organize the scientific system in a new encyclopedia worthy of his name.[82] Under his direction the "physicist clergy" in the *atelier scientifique* will create a work that will organize physicism and found, on reasoning and observation, the principles which for ever will serve as guides to humanity.[83] The greatest man after the Emperor, and that is "undoubtedly the man who admires him most profoundly," offers himself for the task as his "scientific lieutenant, as a second Descartes, under whose leadership the works of the new school will be prodigious." [84]

It need hardly be said that this work is no more systematic than the first. After a vain attempt at coherent exposition it soon becomes admittedly a collection of disjointed notes from Saint-Simon's *portefeuille*. He abandoned the ambitious plan outlined at the beginning, as he himself explains in the sketch of his autobiography, because of lack of funds, or as he admits elsewhere, because he was not yet ripe for the task.[85] Yet, with all its defects, the work is a remarkable document. It combines, for the first time, nearly all the characteristics of the modern scientistic organizer. The enthusiasm for physicism (it is now called physicalism) and the use of "physical language," [86] the attempt to "unify science" and to make it the basis of morals, the contempt for all "theological," that is anthropomorphic, reasoning,[87] the desire to organize the work of others, particularly by editing a great encyclopedia, and the wish to plan life in general on scientific lines are all present. One could sometimes believe that one is reading a contemporary work of an H. G. Wells, a Lewis Mumford, or an Otto Neurath. Nor is the complaint missing about the intellectual crisis, the moral chaos, which must be overcome by the imposition of a new scientific creed. The book is indeed, more than the *Lettres d'un habitant de Genève,* the first and most important document of that "counter-revolution of science," as their fellow-reactionary Bonald called the movement,[88] which later found more open expression in Saint-Simon's avowed desire to "terminate the revolution" by conscious re-organization of society. It is the beginning of both modern positivism and modern socialism, which, thus, both began as definitely reactionary and authoritarian movements.

The *Introduction,* addressed to his fellow scientists, was not published but merely printed in a small number of copies for distribution among the members of the *Institut.* But although the great scientists to whom he sent it took no notice, he continued to appeal to them for assistance in a number of smaller tracts of a similar character. We can pass over the various minor writings of the next few years, which were mainly concerned with the project of an encyclopedia; during this time we find, gradually added to the megalomania of the prophet, the characteristic persecution mania of the *verkannte Genie* which expressed itself in violent abuse of the formerly so admired Laplace, whom he suspected of being responsible for his neglect.[89]

§ 4.   There are no further important developments in Saint-Simon's writings till 1813. Once more plunged into abject poverty by the death of his faithful valet, he starved and in the end fell dangerously ill. He was rescued by an old acquaintance, a *notaire,* who negotiated a settlement with his family under which, in return for giving up all expectations of future inheritance, he received a small annual pension. Once again settled in tolerable comfort, his work entered a new phase. Finally disillusioned in his hope of obtaining the collaboration of the physicists, he turned away from the *brutiers, infinitésimaux, algébristes et arithméticiens,*[90] whom he no longer conceded the right to regard themselves as the scientific advance guard of humanity, and taking up the second strand of though from his first work, he turned again to the biologists.

In his *Mémoire sur la science de l'homme* (part of which, however, still bears the separate title *Travail sur la gravitation universelle*), his problem is again how physiology, of which the science of man is a part, can be treated by the methods adopted by the physical sciences [91] and thus follow those sciences in the progress from the "conjectural" to the "positive" stage.[92] With the science of man, as part and summit of physiology, morals and politics must also become positive sciences,[93] and thus "the passage from the idea of many particular laws regulating the phenomena of the divers branches of physics to the idea of a single and unique law regulating them all" must become completed.[94] When this is achieved and all the particular sciences have become positive, the general science, i.e., philosophy, will also become positive.[95] It will then at last be able to become the new spiritual power, which must remain separate from the temporal power, since this is a division incapable of improvement.[96] With this organization of the "positive system" we shall have definitely entered into the third great epoch of human history of which the first, or preliminary, was ended with Socrates while the second or conjectural has lasted to the present.[97]

This development of ideas which we can observe enables us to predict their future movement.[98] Since "the cause which acts strongest on society is a change, a perfectioning of the ideas, the general beliefs," [99] we can do even more, we can develop a theory of history, a general history of mankind, which will deal not merely with the past and present but also with the future. Such an abridged history of the past, future and present of the human mind Saint-Simon proposed in the programme for the third memoir on the science of man. It is "the happiest idea which has ever presented itself to his mind" and he is "enchanted by the conception," [100] but for the moment he develops it no further. As with most of his works before 1814, the idea remained a promise of future things to come, a prospectus of work he would like to do, but the *Mémoire* itself is still an unorganized mass full of irrelevant detail and bizarre conceits from which one can extract the fertile ideas only because one knows their later development.

§ 5.   All this changed suddenly with Saint-Simon's next work, the *Réorganization de la société européenne,*[101] published in 1814. From that date onwards there issued under his name a stream of books and pamphlets in which ideas were systematically expounded and which sometimes were even well written. It is true that after a new period of abject misery, during which he underwent a cure in what looks suspiciously like a mental home, he was enabled to make a new start. But the man of fifty-five was hardly likely to have suddenly acquired the gift of lucid exposition. It is difficult to resist the belief that the change had something to do with the fact that from that date onwards he was able to secure the help of young collaborators and that the influence of these young men went beyond matters of mere exposition.

The first of these young helpers, who even appeared on the title page of the *Réorganization* as his co-author and pupil, was the future historian Augustin Thierry, then 19 years of age—the same Thierry who was later to become the leader of the new schools of historians who developed history as a history of the masses and of a struggle of class interests and, in this, profoundly influencced Karl Marx.[102]

The pamphlet on which he first collaborated with Saint-Simon is not of great interest to us, although it has achieved a certain celebrity for its advocacy of an Anglo-French Federation which, after the adherence of Germany, was to develop into a sort of European Federation with a common parliament. The fall of the French Empire and the negotiations going on at Vienna made Saint-Simon then apply his dominant idea of a reorganization of society to the whole of Europe; but in the execution of the idea there was little of the old Saint-Simon, except for occasional flights of fancy of which the phrase "the golden age that is not behind us but in front of us and that will be realized by the perfection of the social order" has by its later use as a motto by the Saint-Simonians become widely known.[103]

The collaboration of Saint-Simon and Thierry lasted about two years. During the hundred days, they wrote first against Napoleon and then against the Allies. The great Carnot, always one of Saint-Simon's admirers and then temporarily returned to power, procured for Saint-Simon a sub-librarianship at the *Arsenal,* equally temporary.[104] After Waterloo he fell for a brief period back into poverty. But he had now young friends among the new generation of bankers and industrialists whose fortunes were rising, and it was to them that he attached himself. The enthusiasm for industry was henceforth to replace the enthusiasm for science; or, at least, as the old love was not quite forgotten, he found a new force worthy to exercise the temporal power at the side of science which was to wield the spiritual power. And he found that the praise of industry was better rewarded than the appeals to the scientists or the adulation of the Emperor. Lafitte, governor of the Banque de France, was the first to help. He procured for Saint-Simon the considerable sum of 10,000 francs per month, to start a new journal to be called *l'Industrie littéraire et scientifique ligué avec l'industrie commerciale et manufacturière.*

Around the new editor a number of young men collected, and he began his career as the head of a school. At first the group consisted largely of artists, bankers, and industrialists—among them some very distinguished and influential men. There was even an economist among the contributors to the first volume of *l'Industrie,* St. Aubin, although one whom J. B. Say unkindly described as the "clown of political economy." He and Thierry appeared as the authors of the discussions of Finance and Politics which filled the first volume of *l'Industrie.* To the second volume, which appeared in 1817 under a slightly changed title,[105] Saint-Simon himself contributed some considerations on the relations between France and America.

This essay is on the whole in the spirit of the liberal group for whom Saint-Simon was then writing.[106] "The sole purpose towards which all our thoughts and all our efforts ought to be directed, the organization of society most favourable to industry in the widest sense of the term" is still best achieved by a political power which does nothing except to see that "the workers are not disturbed" and which arranges everything in such a way that all workers, whose combined force forms the true society, are able to exchange directly, and in complete freedom, the products of their various labors.[107] But his attempt to base all politics on economic considerations as he understands them, that is in fact on technological considerations, began soon to lead him outside the views of his liberal friends. We need only quote two of the "most general and most important truths" to which his considerations lead: "1st The production of useful things is the only reasonable and positive end which politics can set itself and the principle *respect for production and the producers* is infinitely more fruitful than the principle respect for property and the proprietors," and "7th. As the whole of mankind has a common purpose and common interests each man ought to regard himself in his social relations as engaged in a company of workers." "Politics, therefore, to sum up in two words, is the science of production, that is, the science which has for its object the order of things most favorable to all sorts of production." [108] We are back at the ideas of the *Habitant de Genève*—and at the same time at the end of what can be regarded as the independent development of Saint-Simon's thought.

The beginning defection of liberalism soon cost Saint-Simon his first assistant. "I cannot conceive of association without government of someone" are reported to have been Saint-Simon's words in the final quarrel, to which Thierry replied that he "could not conceive of association without liberty." [109] Soon this desertion by his assistant was to be followed by a mass flight of his liberal friends. But this came only after a new assistant of great intellectual force began to push Saint-Simon further along the road which he had only indicated but had not had the power to follow. In the summer of 1817 the young polytechnician Auguste Comte, the first and greatest of the host of engineers who were to recognize Saint-Simon as their master, joined him as secretary. Henceforth, to the death of Saint-Simon eight years later, the intellectual history of the two men is indissolubly fused. As we shall see in the next section, much of what is commonly regarded as Saint-Simonian doctrine, and what through the Saint-Simonians exercised a profound influence before Comte's public career as a philosopher began, was due to Auguste Comte.

III

SOCIAL PHYSICS: SAINT-SIMON AND COMTE

§ 1. MORE SURPRISING than anything else in Saint-Simon's career is the great fascination which towards the end of his life he exercised on younger men, some of them intellectually his superiors, who yet for years were satisfied to devil for him, to recognize him as their leader and to bring coherence and order into the thoughts thrown out by him, and whose whole intellectual careers were determind by his influence. Of no one is this more true than of Auguste Comte, whatever in later life he may have said about "the unfortunate personal influence that overshadowed my earliest efforts" or the "depraved juggler," as whom he had come to regard Saint-Simon.[110]

It is a vain attempt to distinguish precisely what part of the work of the period of seven years during which they collaborated is Saint-Simon's and what is Comte's—particularly as it seems likely that in conversation Saint-Simon was much more stimulating and inspiring than in his writings. Yet so much confusion has been caused about the actual relationships by some historians constantly attributing to Saint-Simon thoughts which occur first in works which appeared under his name but are known to have been written by Comte, while others have tried to vindicate Comte's complete independence of thought, that we must exercise some care about what in itself may not be a matter of great consequence.

Auguste Comte was nineteen years of age when in August, 1817, Saint-Simon offered him the position of secretary. The young man had little more than a year before been sent down from the *Ecole polytechnique,* after a brilliant career and just before the final examination, as the ring-leader in an insubordination. Since then he had earned his living as a mathematical coach, at the same time preparing himself for an appointment in America which did not materialize, and had translated a textbook on geometry from the English. During the same period he had steeped himself in the writings of Lagrange and Monge, of Montesquieu and Condorcet, and more recently had taken some interest in political economy.

This seems to have been the qualification on which Saint-Simon, anxious to develop his "science of production," engaged him to write the further parts of *L'Industrie*.[111] In any case, the new disciple was able to write in the three months or so during which he remained Saint-Simon's paid secretary the whole of the four parts of the third and the first and only part of the fourth volume of that publication.[112]

On the whole his contribution is merely a development of the doctrines of his new master which the disciple pushes somewhat further to their logical conclusions. The third volume is largely devoted to problems of the philosophy of history, the gradual transition from polytheism to the positive era, from the absolute monarchy through the transitory stage of the parliamentary liberal state to the new positive organization, and, above all, from the old "celestial" to the new terrestrial and positive morals.[113] Only now are we able to watch these transitions because we have learned to understand the laws to which they are subject.[114] All the institutions existing at any time, being an application of the ruling social philosophy, have their relative justification.[115] And anticipating one of the main features of his later philosophy, Comte sums up in the only sentence of this early work which he would later acknowledge: "There is nothing good and nothing bad absolutely speaking; everything is relative, this is the only absolute statement." [116]

No less alarming to Saint-Simon's supporters than the praise of "terrestrial morals" were the "Views on property and legislation" contained in volume four of *L'Industrie*. Although in general still mainly utilitarian (and consciously Benthamite [117]) in its insistence on the variability of the contents of property rights and the need to adapt them to the conditions of the time,[118] it strikes a new note in emphasizing that, while parliamentary government is merely a form, it is the constitution of property which is the fundamental thing, and that it is therefore "this Constitution which is the real basis of the social edifice" [119]—implying that with the revision of the law of property the whole social order can be changed.[120]

The third volume of *L'Industrie* was hardly completed when most of its liberal supporters withdrew from it after a public protest against the incursion of the journal into a field outside its professed program and against its advocacy of principles "which were destructive of all social order and incompatible with liberty." [121] Although Saint-Simon attempted a lame apology in the introduction of the fourth volume and promised to return to the original plan, the first issue of the new volume was also the last. The funds were exhausted and *L'Industrie,* and with it Comte's paid position, came to an end.

§ 2.   Comte continued, however, to collaborate with Saint-Simon in the various journalistic enterprises which the latter undertook during the next few years. His enthusiasm for his master was still undiminished. Saint-Simon is "the most excellent man he knows," the "most estimable and lovable of men," to whom he has sworn eternal friendship.[122] At the next attempt at a journalistic enterprise, the *Politique,* Comte becomes a partner and shareholder with Saint-Simon.[123] It is just one of the numerous liberal journals which in these years sprung up and died like mushrooms; but even its strongly liberal views, the advocacy by Comte of economy and the freedom of the press, did not secure it a life of more than five months. But three months after its death, in September, 1819, Saint-Simon, again with Comte's support, started another and more characteristic organ,[124] which contains perhaps the most remarkable of Saint-Simon's writings, the *Organisateur,* whose very name was a program. It was certainly the first of his publications which attracted wide attention inside and outside France and which made him generally known as a social reformer.

This is probably due more than anything else to the prosecution which he drew on himself by the celebrated *Parable* with which the new publication opens. In it Saint-Simon first shows that if France were suddenly deprived of the fifty chief scientists in each field, of the fifty chief engineers, artists, poets, industrialists, bankers and artisans of various kinds, her very life and civilization would be destroyed. He then contrasts this with the case of a similar misfortune befalling a corresponding number of persons of the aristocracy, of dignitaries of state, of courties and of members of the high clergy, and points out how little difference this would really make to the prosperity of France.[125] But although the best known, the parable is by no means the most interesting part of the *Organisateur*. To do justice to its title, he presents for the first time in a series of letters a real plan for the reorganization of society, or at least a plan for a reorganization of the political system which would give all social activity the scientific direction which it needs.[126] While his starting-point is now the English parliamentary system, which is the best system yet invented, his problem is how this system can be transformed into something resembling his Council of Newton of sixteen years before. The direction must be placed in the hands of the "industrialists," [127] that is, all those who do productive work. They are to be organized in three separate bodies. The first, the *chambre d'invention*,[128] is to consist of 200 engineers and 100 "artists" (poets, writers, painters, sculptors, architects and musicians) and would have to draw up the plans for public undertakings. The *chambre d'examination,* consisting of 100 each of biologists, physicists and mathematicians, would have to scrutinize and approve these plans. The *chambre d'exécution,* consisting entirely of the richest and most successful entrepreneurs, would watch over the execution of these works. Among the first tasks of the new parliament would be the reconstitution of the law of property, which "must be founded on a basis most favorable to production." [129]

The new system will come not only because its inherent advantages will be generally recognized, but, even more important, because it is the necessary outcome of the course which the advance of civilization has taken during the last seven hundred years.[130] This proves that his plan is not a utopia [131] but the result of the scientific treatment of history, of a true history of the whole of civilization, as Condorcet conceived it, which will enable us to continue on the predestined route with open eyes.[132]

As an "example of how industry ought to be conceived" [133] Saint-Simon then inserts two letters (the 8th and 9th) which, as we now know, were written by Comte, who later republished them under his own name.[134] The most important parts of these are the brief passages elucidating Saint-Simon's suggestion that the rise of the new system is the necessary result of the law of progress: "At no period has the progress of society been regulated by a system conceived by a man of genius and adopted by the masses. This would, from the nature of things, be impossible, for the law of human progress guides and dominates all; men are only its instruments." Therefore, "all we can do is consciously to obey this law, which constitutes our true providence, ascertaining the course it marks out for us, instead of being blindly impelled by it. Here in truth lies the goal of the grand philosophic revolution for our own times." [135] For the rest, and although Comte's contribution still contains few ideas which cannot be found in Saint-Simon's earlier work, these are now presented with a terseness and force of which the latter was never capable. We find now even more stress placed on the need for the "scientific and positive capacity" to replace the old spiritual power,[136] the same exposition of the successive advances of science towards the positive stage till at last philosophy, morals and politics also reach it and thereby make the new scientifically directed social system possible,[137] and the same impatience with the freedom of thought which is the denial of a spiritual power.[138] New is the special emphasis on the role of the new "class which occupies an intermediate position between the men of science, the artists, and the artisans, that of Engineers," which symbolizes the new union between the spiritual and temporal capacities; a union which "prepares the way for this joint direction of society." [139] Under their direction the whole of society will be organized to "act upon nature" as it is now organized in its separate parts.[140] In this joint enterprise the people will no longer be subjects but associates or partners,[141] and for the first time we find the suggestion that there will then no longer be any need of "government" but merely of "administration." [142]

To Comte's contribution Saint-Simon merely added at the end of the second letter a characteristic appeal to the scientists and in particular to the artists, who, as the true "engineers of the soul" as Lenin later described them, are to use all the forces of imagination "to exercise on the common mass sufficient action to determine them to follow irrevocably in the direction indicated and to assist their natural leaders in that great co-operation"—a first indication of the later Saint-Simonian theories about the social function of art.[143]

In the further description of the working of his new organization, Saint-Simon rises to an eloquence unknown to him before. "In the new political order the social organization will have for its sole and permanent purpose the best possible use for the satisfaction of human needs of all the knowledge acquired in the sciences, the fine arts, and industry" [144] and the increase of that knowledge. He does not stop to describe in detail "the astonishing degree of prosperity to which society can aspire with such an organization." [145] While, so far, men have applied to nature only their isolated forces and even mutually counteracted their efforts in consequence of the division of mankind into unequal parts of which the smaller has always used all its power to dominate the other, men will cease to command each other and will organize to apply to nature their combined efforts. All that is required is that in the place of the vague ends which our social system now serves a positive social purpose should be decided upon:

"In a society which is organised for the positive purpose of increasing its prosperity by means of science, art, and craftsmanship, the most important political act, that of determining the direction in which the community is to move, is no longer performed by men invested with social functions but by the body politic itself; . . . the aim and purpose of such an organisation are so clear and determined that there is no longer any room for arbitrariness of men or even of laws, because both can exist only in the vague, which is, so to speak, their natural, element. The actions of government that consist in commands will be reduced to nil or practically nil. All the questions that will have to be solved in such a political system, namely: By what enterprises can the community increase its present prosperity, making use of a given knowledge in science, in art, and in industry? By what measures can such knowledge be dispersed and brought to the furthest possible perfection? And finally by what means can these enterprises be carried out at a minimum cost and in minimum time?—all these questions, I contend, and all those to which they can give rise, are eminently positive and soluble. The decisions must be the result of scientific demonstrations totally independent of human will, and they will be subject to discussion by all those sufficiently educated to understand them. . . . Just as every question of social importance will necessarily be solved as well as the existing state of knowledge permits, so will all social functions necessarily be entrusted to those men who are most capable of exercising them in conformity with the general aims of the community. Under such an order we shall then see the disappearance of the three main disadvantages of the present political system, that is, arbitrariness, incapacity and intrigue." [146]

How perfectly this describes the beautiful illusions that ever since Saint-Simon's times have seduced scientifically trained minds! And yet how obvious it is to us now, even in this first formulation, that it is a delusion; that the idea is based on an extension of the scientific and enigneering technique far beyond the field to which they are appropriate. Saint-Simon is fully conscious of the significance of his ambitions; he knows that his way of treating the problem of social organization "exactly in the same manner as one treats other scientific questions" is new.[147] And how well has he succeeded in his intention *d'imprimer au XIXe siècle le caractère organisateur!* [148]

Yet at first he again fails with his appeals. It is the Bourbon King that he hopes will place himself at the head of the new movement and thereby not only meet all the dangers which threaten his house at the time, but also place France in the front of the march of civilization. Beside the glory which the Bourbons can acquire by social reforms even the fame of Bonaparte will pale.[149] But the only response is a prosecution as a moral accomplice in the assassination of the Duc de Berry,[150] since in his *Parable* he had incited the people to do away with the nobility. Although in the end he was acquitted, the proceedings serving only to stimulate interest in the editor of the *Organisateur,* the journal did not survive this crisis. Saint-Simon's funds were once again exhausted, and after a new appeal to all those who feel in themselves the vocation to develop the philosophy of the nineteenth century and to subscribe as *fondateurs de la politique positive,* also failed, this enterprise too came to an end.

§ 3.   Saint-Simon's next two major publications, although his most substantial works, are in the main only elaborations of the ideas sketched in the *Organisateur.* We can watch, however, how he moves more and more in the direction of that authoritarian socialism which was to take definite form only after his death in the hands of his pupils. In the exposition of his *Système industriel* (1821) [151]—really more systematic than anything that had yet come from his pen—his main theme is the "measures finally to terminate the revolution." He no longer attempts to conceal his dislike for the principles of liberty and for all those who by defending it stand in the way of the realization of his plans. "The vague and metaphysical idea of liberty" "impedes the action of the masses on the individual" [152] and is "contrary to the development of civilization and to the organization of a well-ordered system." [153] The theory of the rights of men [154] and the critical work of the lawyers and metaphysicians have served well enough to destroy the feudal and theological system and to prepare the industrial and scientific one. Saint-Simon sees more clearly than most socialists after him that the organization of society for a common purpose,[155] which is fundamental to all socialist systems, is incompatible with individual freedom and requires the existence of a spiritual power which can "choose the direction to which the national forces are to be applied." [156] The existing "constitutional, representative, or parliamentary system" is a mongrel system that uselessly prolongs the existence of anti-scientific and anti-industrial tendencies [156] because it allows different ends to compete. The philosophy that studies the march of civilization,[158] and the positive scientists [159] who are able to base scientific policy on co-ordinated series of historical facts,[160] are still to provide the spiritual power. Much more space, however, is now given to the organization of the temporal power by the industrialists—a theme which is further developed in the *Caté-chisme des Industriels* (1823).[161]

To entrust the entrepreneurs with the task of preparing the national budget and therefore with the direction of the national administration is the best means of securing for the mass of the people the maximum of employment and the best livelihood.[162] The industrialists, by the nature of their various works, form a natural hierarchy and they ought to organize into one big corporation which will enable them to act in concert for the achievement of their political interests.[163] In this hierarchy the bankers, who from their occupations know the relations between the different industries, are in the best position to co-ordinate the efforts of the different industries, and the biggest banking houses in Paris, by their central position, are called upon to exercise the central direction of the activities of all industrialists.[163] But while the direction of the work of all productive workers is to be in the hands of the entrepreneurs as their natural leaders, they are to use their powers in the interests of the poorest and most numerous classes; [164] the subsistence of the proletarians must be secured by the provision of work for the fit and by the support of the invalids.[165] In the one great factory which France will become, a new kind of freedom will exist: with the formula which Friedrich Engels was later to make famous, we are promised that under the new and definite organization, which is the final destiny of mankind,[166] the governmental or military organization will be replaced by the administrative or industrial.[167] The obstacle to this re-organization are the nobles and the clergy, the lawyers and the metaphysicians, and the military and the proprietors who represent the two past eras. The bourgeois, who have made the revolution and destroyed the exclusive privilege of the nobility to exploit the wealth of the nation, have now merged into one class with the latter, and there are now only two classes left.[168] In the political struggle for the right to exploit, which has continued since the revolution, the industrialists, that is, all those who work, have not yet really taken part. But

"the producers are not interested in whether they are pillaged by one class or another. It is clear that the struggle must in the end become one between the whole mass of the parasites and the whole mass of the producers till it is decided whether the latter will continue to be the prey of the former or whether they will obtain the supreme direction of a society of which they form already by far the largest part. This question must be decided as soon as it is put directly and plainly, considering the immense superiority of power of the producers over the non-producers.

The moment when this struggle must assume its true character has actually arrived. The party of the producers will not hesitate to show itself. And even among the men whom birth has placed in the class of parasites, those who excel by the width of their views and the greatness of their souls begin to feel that the only honorable rôle which they can play is to stimulate the producers to enter into political life, and to help them to obtain in the direction of the common affairs the preponderance they have already obtained in society." [169]

§ 4.   To the *Catéchisme des Industriels,* which was to spread these doctrines further, Auguste Comte contributed the third part, a substantial volume called a *Plan for the Scientific Operations necessary for Re-organizing Society,*[170] and two years later (1824) republished by its author under the even more anmbitious title *System of Posi-*

tive Policy—"a title premature indeed, but rightly indicating the scope" of his labors, as Comte said thirty years later.[171] It is the most significant single tract of the whole body of literature with which we are here concerned.

In this first form the "positive system" is little more than a brilliant restatement of Saint-Simon's doctrine.[172] Comte here carries still further his hatred of the dogma of the liberty of conscience, which is the great obstacle to reorganization.[173] Just as in astronomy, physics, chemistry, and physiology there is no such thing as liberty of conscience,[174] so this transitory fact will disappear once politics has been elevated to the rank of a natural science and the true and final doctrine has been definitely established.[175] This new science of *Social Physics,* that is to say, the study of the collective development of the human race, is really a branch of physiology, or the study of man conceived in its entire extension. In other words, the history of civilization is nothing but the indispensable result and complement of of the natural history of man." [176] Politics is thus on the point of becoming a positive science in accordance with the law of the three stages, which is now pronounced in its final form: "Each branch of knowledge is necessarily obliged to pass through three different theoretical states: the Theological or fictitious state; the Metaphysical or abstract state; lastly the Scientific or positive state," the definite state of all knowledge whatsoever.[177]

The object of social physics is to discover the natural and unavoidable laws of the progress of civilization which are as necessary as that of gravitation.[178] By civilization Comte means "the development of the human mind and its result, the increasing power of man over nature," the ways in which he has learned to act upon nature to modify it to his own advantage.[179] It is civilization in this sense, that is the state of Science, Fine Arts, and Industry, which determines and regulates the course of Social Organization.[180] Social physics, which, like all science, aims at prevision, enables us by observing the past to determine the social system which the progress of civilization tends to realize in our own day.[181] The superiority of positive politics consists in the fact that it *discovers* what is made necessary by these natural laws while other systems *invent*.[182] All that remains for us to do is to help into life the positive system which the course of civilization tends to produce, and we are certain to secure the best system now obtainable if we discover that which is most in harmony with the present state of civilization.[183]

It will be noticed how close Comte's view on the philosophy of history, which is commonly regarded as the opposite of a "materialist" interpretation, comes to that view—particularly if we remember the exact meaning which he gives to the term civilization. In fact, what anticipation of the materialist interpretation of history can be found in the Saint-Simonian writings—and we believe that they are the main source of that doctrine—can be traced directly to this and some of the earlier works of Comte.[184]

Although soon after the publication of the *Catéchisme des Industriels* Comte was finally to break with Saint-Simon when the latter began to turn his doctrine into a religion, the next two works which Comte published shortly after Saint-Simon's death in the Saint-Simonian *Producteur* [185] still continue the common line of thought. The first of these is of interest mainly for the more careful analysis of the progress towards the positive method. He shows how man "necessarily begins by regarding all the bodies which attract his attention as so many beings animated with a life resembling his own," [186] and it is interesting that at this stage Comte, who only a few years later was to deny the possibility of all introspection,[187] was still explaining this by the fact that "the personal action exerted by man on other beings is the only kind of which he comprehends the *modus operandi* through his consciousness of it." [188] But already he is on the way to denying the legitimacy of the disciplines which are based precisely on this knowledge. His attacks now aim not merely at the "revolting monstrosity," the anti-social dogma of the liberty of conscience,[189] and the anarchy of unregulated individualism generally,[190] but are already more specifically directed against the teachings of political economy.[191] Only by historical considerations can it be explained how that "strange phenomenon," the idea that a society ought not to be consciously organized, could ever have arisen.[192] But as "everything that develops spontaneously is necessarily legitimate during a certain period," [193] so the Critical Doctrine has had a relative justification during the past. But a perfect social order can be established only if we can in all cases "assign to every individual or nation that precise kind of activity for which they are respectively fitted." [194] But this presupposes a spiritual power, a moral code, of which again Comte cannot conceive except as deliberately constructed.[195] The necessary moral order can therefore be created only by a Government of Opinion which determines "the entire system of ideas and habits necessary for initiating individuals into the social order under which they must live." [196] The ideas, which, after he had allowed himself for twenty years to be deeply influenced by Comte, finally so revolted J. S. Mill that he described them as "the completest system of spiritual and temporal despotism which ever yet emanated from a human brain, unless possibly that of Ignatius Loyola," [197] were present in Comte's thoughts from the beginning. They are a necessary consequence of the whole system of thought which not only J. S. Mill, but the whole world, has taken over from Comte.

§ 5.   There is little more to say about the last phase of Saint-Simon's life. While the *Catéchisme des Industriels* was in the process of publication, a new financial crisis in his affairs threatened him again with starvation, and early in 1823 the old man, now really discouraged, tried to blow out his brains. He recovered, however, from the self-inflicted wound with the loss of one eye, and soon assistance came from a new, enthusiastic, and this time wealthy pupil. The young banker and former instructor at the *Ecole Polytechnique,* Olinde Rodrigues, not only provided for Saint-Simon's necessities during the last two years of his life, but also became the center of the little group which after his death developed into the *Ecole Saint-Simonien.* He was soon joined by the poet Léon Halévy, the physiologist Dr. Bailly, the lawyer Duveyrier and others. With them Saint-Simon prepared the *Opinions littéraires, philosophiques et industrielles* (1825) in which the banker, the poet and the physiologist each elaborated the parts of the doctrine of the master for which they possessed special competence. Only a little later in the same year appeared the last work of Saint-Simon, marking the final phase of his work, the *Nouveau Christianisme.*

Already for some time Saint-Simon had shown an increasing tendency away from the narrowly "scientific" and towards a more mystical and religious form of his doctrine. This had indeed been the final cause of the estrangement between him and Comte, who, however, was to undergo a similar change towards the end of his own career. In Saint-Simon's case this development is partly a return to his first ideas.

Since the great schism at the time of the reformation, he argues, none of the Christian churches represents true Christianity. They have all neglected the fundamental precept that men should behave as brothers towards each other. The main object of true Christianity must be "the speediest improvement of the moral and the physical existence of the poorest class"—a phrase which appears on almost every page of the brochure and which became the watchword of the Saint-Simonian group. Since the churches have made no use of their opportunity to improve the lot of the poor by the teaching and encouragement of the arts and the organization of industry, the Lord is now addressing the people and the princes through His new prophet. He undertakes to reconstruct theology, which from time to time needs to be renewed, just as physics, chemistry and physiology must be periodically re-written.[198] The new theology will pay more attention to the terrestrial interests of man. All that is required is an organization of industry that will assure a great amount of work of the kind which will secure the quickest advance of human intelligence. "You can create such conditions; now that the extent of our planet is known, let the scholars, the artists and the industrialists draw up a general plan of the works which must be carried out in order that the terrestrial possessions of the human race be put to the most productive use and made the most agreeable to inhabit in all respects." [199]

Saint-Simon survived the appearance of the *Nouveau Christianisme* by only a few weeks. He died in May, 1825, at the age of 65, calmly expecting his death while discussing future projects with the group of pupils that now surrounded him. The life that had been an example of the precepts he had laid down for all future sociologists, "passing through all classes of society, putting oneself personally in the greatest number of different social positions, and even creating for oneself and others relationships which have never existed before," [200] ended in peace, tolerable comfort and even in possession of a considerable reputation.

The funeral re-united the older pupils like Thierry and Comte with the new ones. The old Saint-Simon had just seen the beginnings of the school that under his name was to spread far and wide a body of ideas derived from his work. It is due to them that he has become a figure of considerable importance in the history of social ideas. While he was certainly an *original*, he was scarcely an original or profound thinker. The ideas which he bequeathed to his pupils were unquestionably held by many people at the time. But by his persistence and enthusiasm he gained adherents for them among men who were capable of developing them and in whom he inspired sufficient enthusiasm to act as a body in spreading them. As one of his French biographers has said, his rôle was *de faire flamboyer les idées comme des réclames lumineuses.*[201] He has performed it to perfection.

IV

THE RELIGION OF THE ENGINEERS:
ENFANTIN AND THE SAINT SIMONIANS

§ 1. Less than a month after Saint-Simon's death his friends and disciples constituted themselves into a formal association in order to realize the project of another journal which he still had discussed with them. The *Producteur,* which appeared in six volumes in 1825 and 1826, was edited by the group under the leadership of Olinde Rodrigues, with the collaboration of Auguste Comte and some others who were not strictly members. Soon another young engineer, who had seen Saint-Simon only once when Rodrigues introduced him, was to become the outstanding figure of the group and the editor of its journal.

Barthélemy-Prosper Enfantin was the son of a banker. He had entered the *Ecole Polytechnique* but had left it in 1814, two years before Comte, and, like him, without completing the course. He had since entered business, spent some years traveling and working in Germany and Russia, and had recently devoted some time to the study of political economy and particularly to the works of Jeremy Bentham. Although his education as an engineer had remained incomplete, or perhaps because of this, his belief in the unlimited powers of the mathematical and technical sciences remained one of the most characteristic features of his intellectual make-up. As he explained on one occasion, "when I have found the words *probabilities, logarithm, asymptote,* I am happy, because I have regained the road which leads me to formulas and forms." [202] An uncommonly handsome man according to the views of his contemporaries, he seems to have possessed great personal charm, which made it possible for him gradually to swing the entire Saint-Simonian movement in the direction into which his sentimental and mystical bent led him. But he also commanded considerable powers of intellect which enabled him to make important contributions before Saint-Simonism passed from its philosophical to its religious phase.[203]

It has been said, with some truth, that Saint-Simonism was born after Saint-Simon's death.[204] However pregnant in suggestions Saint-Simon's writings were, he never achieved a coherent system. It is probably also true that the very obscurity of his writings was one of the greatest incentives for his disciples to develop his doctrines further. It also explains why the importance of the joint efforts of Saint-Simon and his pupils has rarely been properly appreciated. The natural tendency of those who have recognized it has been to ascribe too much to Saint-Simon himself. Others, who have been led by this to study Saint-Simon's own writings, have been bound to turn away disappointed. Although almost all ideas of the School can be found somewhere in the works that have appeared in Saint-Simon's name,[205] the real force which decisively influenced European thought were the Saint-Simonians and not Saint-Simon himself. And we must never forget that the greatest of the Saint-Simonians in their early years, and the medium through whom many of them had received the doctrine of the master,[206] was Auguste Comte, who, as we know, still contributed to the *Producteur,* although he was no longer a member of the group and soon broke off all relations with it.

§ 2.　The new journal had for its expressed purpose "to develop and expand the principles of a philosophy of human nature based on the recognition that the destiny of our race is to exploit and modify external nature to its greatest advantage," and it believed that this could best be done by "incessantly extending association, one of the most powerful means at its command." [207] In order to attract the general public the programmatic articles were interspersed with others on technological or statistical subjects, which were often written by outsiders. But most of the journal was written by the little group of disciples. There can also be little doubt that, even during the year when the *Producteur* was the center of their activities, Enfantin had already the largest share in the development of the doctrines of the school, although for some time his position was equaled or even overshadowed by the powerful personality of another new recruit, Saint-Amand Bazard.[208] Slightly older than Rodrigues or Enfantin, and, as a former member of the French Carbonari movement, an experienced revolutionary, he joined the collaborators of the *Producteur,* who already had attracted some old Babouvists and Carbonaris. But although these, and Bazard in particular, played an important part in leading the Saint-Simonians towards more radical views, it is probable that the latter's doctrinal contributions are usually overrated and that his rôle is more appropriately described by a contemporary who said that "M. Enfantin found the ideas, M. Bazard formulated them.[209] Bazard's articles in the *Producteur,* apart from an even fiercer hatred of the liberty of conscience [210] than had been shown by Saint-Simon or even Comte, add little that is new. The same is true of most of the other contributors except Enfantin and, of course, Comte, although the elaboration of the Saint-Simonian doctrine of the social function of art by Léon Halévy must not be overlooked. He sees the time approaching when the "art of moving the masses" will be so perfectly developed that the painter, the musician, and the poet "will possess the power to please and to move with the same certainty as the mathematician solves a geometrical problem or the chemist analyzes some substance. Then only will the moral side of society be firmly established." [211] The word propaganda was not yet used in this connection, but the art of the modern Ministries of Propaganda would have been fully appreciated and these institutions were even foreseen by the Saint-Simonians.

Important developments occur in the economic articles which Enfantin contributed to the *Producteur.* The growth of nearly all the new elements of the social doctrine of the Saint-Simonians, which we shall meet presently in their final form in the celebrated *Exposition,* can be traced in these articles. The general interest in the problems of industrial *organization,* the enthusiasm for the new growth of joint-stock companies, the doctrine of general association, the increasing doubts about the usefulness of private property and of interest, the plans for the direction of all economic activity by the banks—all these ideas were gradually worked out and were more and more strongly emphasized. We must here be content to quote two sentences particularly characteristic of his approach to the problems. One ridicules the idea that "a human society could exist without an intelligence which directs it." [212] The other describes the concepts which have so far formed the preoccupation of political economy, namely "value, price, and production, which do not contain any constructive idea for the composition or organisation of society," as "irrelevant details." [213]

§ 3.   The *Producteur,* which had appeared first weekly, and then monthly, came to an end in October, 1826. While this meant the cessation for three years of all public activity of the group, there had already been created a common doctrine which could serve as the basis for intensive propaganda by word of mouth. It was at this time that they had their first great successes among the students of the *Ecole Polytechnique,* to which they specially directed their efforts. As Enfantin later expressed it: "The *Ecole Polytechnique* must be the channel through which our ideas will spread through society. It is the milk which we have sucked at our beloved School which must nourish the generations to come. It is there that we have learnt the positive language and the methods of research and demonstration which today secure the advance of the political sciences." [214] The success of these efforts was such that within a few years the group consisted of some hundred engineers with only a sprinkling of doctors and a few artists and bankers, who were mostly left over from Saint-Simon's immediate disciples, or, like the brothers Pereire, the cousins of Rodrigues, or his friend Gustave d'Eichthal, were personally related to them.

Among the first of the young engineers to join the movement were the two friends Abel Transon and Jules Lechevalier,[215] who through their knowledge of German philosophy helped to give the Saint-Simonian doctrines a certain Hegelian veneer which later proved so important in helping their success in Germany. A short time after followed Michel Chevalier, later famous as an economist, and Henri Fournel, who, to join the movement, resigned a position as director of the Creuzot works and later became Saint-Simon's biographer. Hippolyte Carnot, although himself never a pupil of the *Ecole Polytechnique,* since he had spent his youth with his father in exile, must also be counted with this group, not only as the son of Lazare, but still more as the brother of the polytechnician Sadi Carnot, the "founder of the science of energy," discoverer of the "Carnot cycle," the ideal of technical efficiency, with whom he lived in these years while the latter developed his famous theories and at the same time preserved a lively although never active interest in the political and social discussions of his friends.[216] At least by tradition and connections, if not by training, Hippolyte Carnot was as much an engineer as the others.

For a time the apartment of the Carnots was the place where Enfantin and Bazard taught an ever increasing number of young enthusiasts.[217] But towards the end of 1828 they had outgrown that accommodation and it was decided that a more formal oral exposition of their views should be given to a larger audience. It is probable that this was suggested by the success of a similar experiment by Comte, who in 1826 had begun to expound his *Positive Philosophy* to a distinguished audience, including, besides such scholars as Alexander von Humboldt and Poinsot, also Carnot, who had been sent there by Enfantin to receive his first instruction in Saint-Simonism.[218] Although Comte's attempt had soon been cut short by the mental affliction which interrupted his work for three years, it had attracted sufficient attention to invite imitation.

The course of lectures which the Saint-Simonians arranged in 1829 and 1830, in the form in which it has come down to us as the two parts of the *Doctrine de Saint-Simon, Exposition,*[219] is by far the most important document produced by Saint-Simon or his pupils and one of the great landmarks in the history of socialism which deserves to be much better known than it is outside France. If it is not the Bible of Socialism, as it has been called by a French scholar,[220] it deserves at least to be regarded as its Old Testament. And in some respects it did indeed carry socialist thought further than was done for nearly a hundred years after its publication.

§ 4. As befits one of the foundations of collectivist thought, the *Exposition* is the product of no single man. Although Bazard, as the most skillful speaker, delivered the majority of the lectures, their content was the result of discussion among the group. The published texts were actually written by H. Carnot from notes taken by him and others during the lectures, and it is presumably to him that the *Exposition* owes its elegance and power. An important supplement to it are the five lectures on the Saint-Simonian religion which Abel Transon delivered about the same time to the students of the *Ecole Polytechnique* [221] and which are appended to some of the editions of the *Exposition*.

It is difficult without tiresome repetition to give an adequate idea of this most comprehensive expression of Saint-Simonian thought, since much of it is of course a more or less faithful reproduction of views we have already met. It is, however, not merely, as it claims to be, the sole publication in which the whole of the contribution of Saint-Simon (and, we should add, the young Comte) has been brought into a comprehensive system; but it also develops it further, and it is these developments by Enfantin and his friends which we must mainly consider.

A large part of the more important first volume of the *Exposition* is given to a broad philosophic survey of history and of the "law of development of humanity revealed to the genius of Saint-Simon," [222] which, based on the study of mankind as a "collective being," [223] shows us with certainty what its future will be.[224] This law asserts in the first instance the alternation of *organic* and *critical* states, in the former of which "all aspects of human activity are ordered, foreseen and co-ordinated by a general theory," while in the critical states society is an agglomeration of isolated individuals struggling against each other.[225] The final destiny towards which we are tending is a state where all antagonism between men will have entirely disappeared and the exploitation of men by men is replaced by their joint and harmonic action upon nature.[226] But this definite state, where the "systematisation of effort," [227] the "organisation of labor" [228] for a common purpose [229] is perfected, is reached only in stages. The basic fact of the ever decreasing antagonism between men, which will lead in the end to the "universal association," [230] implies a "steady diminution of the exploitation of men by men"—a phrase which forms the leitmotif of the whole *Exposition*.[231] While the positive advance towards the universal association is marked by the stages of the family, town, nation, and the federation of nations having a common creed and church,[232] the decrease of exploitation is shown by the changing relations between the classes. From the stage when cannibalism was practiced on the captive, through slavery and serfdom to the present relations between proletarians and proprietors, there has been a constant decrease of the degree of exploitation.[233] But men are still divided into two classes, the exploiters and the exploited.[234] There is still a class of disinherited proletarians.[235] As the eloquent Abel Transon put it to the young polytechnicians in a passage of his lectures which better than anything in the *Exposition* sums up the main argument:

"The peasant or craftsman is no longer attached to the man or to the soil, he is not subjected to the whip like the slave; he owns *a greater part* of his labor than the serf, but still, the law is cruel at his expense. All the fruit of his labor does not belong to him. He has to share it with other people who are not useful to him either by their knowledge or by their power. In short, there are no *masters* for him nor *lords,* but there are BOURGEOIS, and so that's what a BOURGEOIS is.

"As the owner of land and capital the bourgeois disposes of these at his will and does not place them in the hands of the workers except on condition that he receive a premium from the price of their work, a premium that will support him and his family. Whether a direct heir of the man of conquest or else an emancipated son of the peasant class, this difference of origin merges into the common character which I have just described; only in the first case is the title of his possession based on a fact which is now condemned, on the action of the sword; in the second case the origin is more honorable, it is the work of industry. But *in the eyes of the future* this title is in either case illegitimate and without value because it hands over to the mercy of a privileged class all those whose fathers have not left them any instruments of production." [236]

The cause of this still existing state of affairs is the "constitution of property, the transmission of wealth by inheritance within the family." [237] But the institution of "property is a social fact, subject, as all other social facts, to the law of progress." [238] According to the *Exposition* the new order will be created by

"the transfer to the State, which will become an *association of workers,* of the right of inheritance which to-day is confined to the members of the family. The privileges of birth which have already received such heavy blows in so many respects must entirely disappear." [239]

"If, as we proclaim, humanity moves toward a state where all the individuals will be classed according to their capacities and remunerated according to their work, its is evident that the right of property, as it exists, must be abolished, because, by giving to a certain class of men the possibility to live on the work of others and in complete idleness, it preserves the exploitation of one part of the population, the most useful one, that which works and produces, in favor of those who only destroy." [240]

They explain that to them land and labor are merely "instruments of work; and the proprietors and capitalists . . . are the depositaries of these instruments; their function [241] is to distribute them among the workers." [242] But they perform this function very inefficiently. The Saint-Simonians had studied Sismondi's *Nouveaux principes d'économie politique* which in 1826 had appeared in a new edition, in which the author for the first time describes how the ravages of economic crises were caused by "chaotic competition." But while Sismondi had no real remedy to propose and later seems even to have deplored the effects of his teaching,[243] the Saint-Simonians had one. Their description of the defects of competition is almost entirely taken from Sismondi:

"In the present state of affairs, where the distribution [of the instruments of production] is effected by the capitalists and proprietors, none of these functions is performed except after much groping, experimenting, and many unfortunate experiences; and even so the result obtained is always imperfect, always temporary. Each person is left to act on his own individual knowledge; no general conspectus guides production; it takes place without judgment, without foresight; it is deficient at one point and excessive at another." [244]

The economic crises are thus due to the fact that the distribution of the instruments of production is effected by isolated individuals, ignorant of the requirements and needs of industry and of the people, and of the means that can satisfy them.[245] The solution which the Saint-Simonians propose was at the time completely new and original. In the new world which they invite us to contemplate

"there will be no longer any proprietors, no isolated capitalists, who by their habits are strangers to industrial activity, yet who decide the character of the work and the fate of the workers. A *social* institution is charged with these functions which to-day are so badly performed; it is the *depository* of all the instruments of production; it presides over the exploitation of all the material resources; from its point of vantage it has a comprehensive view of the whole which enables it to perceive at one and the same time all the parts of the industrial *workshop;* through its ramifications it is in touch with all the different places, with all kinds of industries, and with all the workers; it can thus take account of all the general and individual wants, bring men and instruments to where the need for them makes itself felt; in a word, it can direct the production and put it in harmony with consumption and entrust the tools to the most deserving industrialists, because it incessantly endeavours to discover their capacity and is in the best position to develop them . . . In this new world . . . the disturbances which follow from the lack of general accord and from the blind distribution of the agents and instruments of production would disappear and with them also the misfortunes, the reverses and failures of firms against which to-day no peaceful worker is protected. In a word, industrial activity is *organised,* everything is connected, everything foreseen; the division of labor is perfected and the combination of efforts becomes every day more powerful." [246]

The "social institution" which is to perform all these functions is not left vague and undetermined as it was by most later socialists. It is the banking system, properly reconstructed and centralized and crowned by a single *banque unitaire, directrice,* which is to serve as the planning body:

"The social institution of the future will direct all industries in the interest of the whole society and specially of the peaceful workers. We call this institution provisionally the general system of banks, making all reservations against the too narrow interpretations which one might give to this term.

"The system will comprise in the first instance a central bank which constitutes the government in the material sphere; this bank will become the depository of all wealth, of the whole productive fund, of all the instruments of production, in short of everything that to-day makes up the whole mass of private property." [247]

We need not follow the *Exposition* further into the detail of the proposed organization.[248] The main points given will suffice to show that in their description of the organization of a planned society they went much further than later socialists until quite recent times, and also how heavily later socialists have drawn on their ideas. Till the modern discussion of the problem of calculation in a socialist community this description of its working has not been further advanced. There was very little justification for dubbing this very realistic picture of a planned society "utopian." Marx, characteristically, added to it the one part of classical English economics which was out of tune with its general analysis of competition, the "objective" or labor theory of value. The general results of the fusion of Saint-Simonian and Hegelian ideas, of which Marx is of course the best-known exponent, will occupy us later.[249]

But in so far as that general socialism which today is common property is concerned, little had to be added to Saint-Simonian thought. As a further indication of how profoundly the Saint-Simonians have influenced modern thought, it need only be mentioned to what a great extent all European languages have drawn from their vocabulary. "Individualism," [250] "industrialist," [251] "positivism," [252] and the "organization of labor" [253] all occur first in the *Exposition*. The concept of the "class struggle" and the contrast between the "bourgeoisie" and the "prolétariat" in the special technical sense of the terms are Saint-Simonian creations. The word "socialism" itself, although it does not yet appear in the *Exposition* (which uses "association" in very much the same sense), appears in its modern meaning for the first time [254] a little later in the Saint-Simonian *Globe*.[255]

§ 5.   With the appearance of the *Exposition,* and of a number of articles by Enfantin [256] and others in the new Saint-Simonian journals *Organisateur* and *Globe* which we need not further consider, the development of their ideas which is of interest to us came more or less suddenly to an end. If we cast a quick glance over the further history of the School, or rather the Saint-Simonian Church, as it presently became, it will show why its immediate influence was not greater, or rather, why that influence was not more clearly recognized. The reason is that under Enfantin's influence the doctrine was turned into a religion; [257] the sentimental and mystic elements gained the upper hand over the ostensibly scientific and rational, just as they did in the last phases of Saint-Simon's and later of Comte's life. Already the second year of the *Exposition* shows an increasing tendency in that direction. But in its further career the literary activities are of less importance and it is to the organization of the Church and to the practical application of its doctrines that we must look for the picturesque qualities and sensational doings of the new church which have attracted more attention than the earlier and more important phase of its activity.[258]

The new religion consisted at first merely of a vague pantheism and a fervent belief in human solidarity. But the dogma was much less important than the cult and the hierarchy. The School became a Family over which Enfantin and Bazard presided as the two Supreme Fathers—new popes with a college of apostles and various other grades of members below them. Services were organized at which not only the doctrine was taught, but at which the members soon began publicly to confess their sins. Itinerant preachers spread the doctrine all over the country and founded local centers.

For a time the success was considerable, not only in Paris but throughout France and even in Belgium. Among their group they counted then P. Leroux, Adolphe Blanqui, Pecqueur and Cabet. Le Play was also a member [259] and in Brussels they gained a new enthusiast for social physics in the astronomer and statistician, A. Quetelet, who had already been profoundly influenced by the circle of the *Ecole Polytechnique*. [260]

The July revolution of 1830 found them altogether unprepared but naïvely assuming that it would place them into power. It is said that Bazard and Enfantin even requested Louis Philippe to hand over to them the Tuileries since they were the only legitimate power on earth. One effect of the revolution on their doctrines appears to have been that they felt compelled to make some concessions to the democratic tendencies of the age. The originally authoritarian socialism thus began its temporary partnership with liberal democracy. The reasons for this step were explained by the Saint-Simonians with an amazing frankness, rarely equaled by later socialists: "We demand at this moment liberty of religious practice in order that a single religion can be more easily erected on the ruins of the religious past of humanity; . . . the liberty of the press, because this is the indispensable condition for the subsequent creation of a legitimate direction of thought; the liberty of teaching, in order that our doctrine can be more easily propagated and become one day the only one loved and followed by all; the destruction of the monopolies as a means of arriving at the definite organisation of the industrial body." [261] Their real views, however, are better shown by their early discovery of, and enthusiasm for, the organising genius of Prussia [262]—a sympathy which, as we shall presently see, was reciprocated by the "Young Germans," one of whom, with some justification, remarked that the Prussians had long been Saint-Simonians.[263] The only other doctrinal development during this period which we need mention is their increasing interest in railways, canals and banks, to which so many of them were to give their lifework after the dispersal of the School.

Already Enfantin's early attempt to turn the School into a Religion had created a certain tension among the leaders and caused some desertions. The main crisis came when he began to develop new theories about the position of women and the relation between the sexes. There was practically nothing in the teaching of Saint-Simon himself to justify this new departure, and the first elements of this doctrine were probably an importation from Fourierism, with its theory of the couple, man and woman, constituting the true social individual. For Enfantin there was only a short step from the principle of the emancipation of women to the doctrine of the "rehabilitation of the flesh" and the distinction between the "constant" and "inconstant" types among both sexes, which both should be able to have it their own way. These doctrines and the rumors which got around about their practical application (for which, it must be admitted, the Saint-Simonians gave ample cause in their writings [264]) created a considerable scandal. A break between Enfantin and Bazard followed, and the latter left the movement and died nine months later. His chair was left vacant for the *Mère suprême,* an honor which George Sand had declined. With Bazard some of the most eminent members, Carnot, Leroux, Lechevalier and Transon seceded, the last two becoming Fourierists; and a few months later even Rodrigues, the living link with Saint-Simon, broke with Enfantin.

Faced with a serious setback, since financial difficulties made it necessary to discontinue the *Globe,* and as they had begun to attract the attention of the police, Enfantin with forty faithful apostles withdrew to a house at Ménilmontant, at the outskirts of Paris, to begin a new life in accordance with the precepts of the doctrine. The forty men started there a community life without servants, dividing the menial tasks between them and observing, to silence the ugly rumors, strict celibacy. But if their life was half modeled on that of a monastery, in other respects it was more like that of a Nazi *Führerschule*. Athletic exercises and courses in the doctrine were to prepare them for a more active life in the future.

Although they voluntarily confined themselves to their estate, they did not cease in their attempts to attract notoriety. The forty apostles who in their fantastic costumes cultivated their garden and tended their home became for a while the sensation of the Parisians, who flocked there in thousands to watch the spectacle. In consequence the "retreat" by no means reassured the police. Proceedings were instituted against Enfantin, Chevalier and Duveyrier for outraging public morality and ended with their being condemned to imprisonment for one year. The march of the whole group to the law courts in their peculiar costumes and with their spades and other implements on their shoulders, and the sensational defense of the accused, was almost the last public appearance of the group. When Enfantin entered the St. Pelagier prison to serve his sentence the movement began rapidly to decline and the establishment in Ménilmontant soon broke up. A group of disciples still gave the people much to talk about by their journey to Constantinople and the East *pour chercher la femme libre*.[265] But when Enfantin left the prison, although he organized another journey to the East, it was for a more sensible purpose. He and a group of Saint-Simonians spent some years in Egypt, trying to organize the piercing of the Isthmus of Suez. And although they at first failed to obtain support, it is largely due to their efforts that later the Suez Canal Company was founded.[266] As we shall have occasion to mention again, most of them continued to devote their lives to similar useful efforts—Enfantin to founding the Paris-Lyon-Méditerranée railway system and many of his disciples to organizing railway and canal constructions in other parts of France and elsewhere.[267]

V

SAINT-SIMONIAN INFLUENCE

§ 1. It is not easy today to appreciate the immense stir which the Saint-Simonian movement caused for a couple of years, not only in France, but throughout Europe, or to gauge the extent of the influence which the doctrine has exercised. But there can be little doubt that this influence was far greater than is commonly realized. If one were to judge that influence by the frequency with which the Saint-Simonians were mentioned in the literature of the time, it would seem that their celebrity was as short-lived as it was great. We must not forget, however, that in its later years the school had covered itself with ridicule by its pseudo-religious harlequinades and its various escapades and follies, and that in consequence many men who had absorbed most of its social and philosophical teaching might well have been ashamed to admit their association with the cranks of Ménilmontant and the men who went to the East in search of the *femme libre.* It was only natural that people should come to treat their Saint-Simonian period as a youthful folly of which they did not wish to boast. But that did not mean that the ideas they had then absorbed did not continue to operate in and through them, and a careful investigation, which has yet to be undertaken, would probably show how surprisingly wide that influence has extended.

Here we are not primarily interested in tracing the influence of persons or groups. From our point of view it would be even more significant if it could be shown that a similar situation has produced similar ideas elsewhere without any direct influence from the Saint-Simonians. Yet any study of similar contemporaneous movements elsewhere soon reveals a close connection with the French prototypes. Even if it is doubtful whether in all these cases we are really entitled

156

to speak of influence, and whether we should not rather say that all those who happened to have similar ideas soon found their way to Saint-Simonism, it will be worth while to cast a rapid glance over the variety of channels through which this influence acted, since the extent of it is yet so little understood, and particularly because the spreading of Saint-Simonism also meant a spreading of Comtian positivism in its early form.

The first point which it is important to realize is that this influence was by no means confined to people mainly interested in social and political speculation, but that it was even stronger in literary and artistic circles, which often became almost unconsciously the medium of spreading Saint-Simonian conceptions on other matters. In France the Saint-Simonian ideas about the social function of art made a deep impression on some of the greatest writers of the time, and are held responsible for the profound change in the literary atmosphere which then took place.[268] The demand that all art should be tendentious, that it should serve social criticism and for this purpose represent life as it is in all its ugliness led to a veritable revolution in letters.[269] Not only authors who like George Sand or Béranger had been closely associated with the Saint-Simonians, but some of the greatest writers of the period such as H. de Balzac,[270] V. Hugo, and Eugène Sue absorbed and practiced much of the Saint-Simonian teaching. Among composers Franz Liszt had been a frequent visitor to their meetings and Berlioz with a *Chant d'Inauguration des Chemins de Fer* applied Saint-Simonian precepts to music.

§ 2.   The influence of Saint-Simonism in England was also partly in the literary field. The main expositor of their ideas here became for a time Thomas Carlyle, whose indebtedness to Saint-Simonian doctrine is well known and who even translated and attempted to publish with an anonymous introduction Saint-Simon's *Nouveau Christianisme*.[271] He is the first of the many instances we shall meet where Saint-Simonism or Comtian and German influences so readily blended. Carlyle's views on the philosophy of history, his exposition of the Law of Progress in *Sartor Resartus,* his division of history into positive and negative periods, are all mainly of Saint-Simonian origin, and his interpretation of the French Revolution is penetrated with Saint-Simonian thought. The influence which he in turn exercised need not be stressed here, but it is worth pointing out that the later English Positivists recognized that his teaching had largely prepared the way for them.[272]

Better known is the influence which the Saint-Simonians exercised on J. S. Mill. In his *Autobiography* [273] he describes them as "the writers by whom, more than by any others, a new mode of thinking was brought home" to him and recounts how particularly one of their publications, which seemed to him far superior to the rest, Comte's early *System of Positive Policy,*

"harmonized well with my existing notions to which it seemed to give a scientific shape. I already regarded the methods of physical science as the proper models for political. But the chief benefit which I derived at this time from the trains of thought suggested by the Saint-Simonians and by Comte, was, that I obtained a clearer conception than ever before of the peculiarities of an era of transition in opinion, and ceased to mistake the moral and intellectual characteristics of such an era, for the normal attributes of humanity."

Mill goes on to explain how, although he lost sight for a time of Comte, he was kept *au courant* of the Saint-Simonian's progress by G. d'Eichthal (who had also introduced Carlyle to Saint-Simonism),[274] how he read nearly everything they wrote and how it was "partly by their writings that [his] eyes were opened to the very limited and temporary value of the old political economy, which assumes private property and inheritance as indefeasible facts and freedom of production and exchange as the *dernier mot* of social improvement." From a letter to d'Eichthal [275] it appears that he became so far convinced as to be "inclined to think that [their] social organization, under some modification or other . . . is likely to be the final and permanent condition of our race," although he differed from them in believing that it would take many or at least several stages till mankind would be capable of realizing it. We have here undoubtedly the first roots of J. S. Mill's socialist leanings. But in Mill's case, too, this was largely a preparation for the still more profound influence which Comte was later to exercise on him.

§ 3.   In no country outside France, however, did the Saint-Simonian doctrine arouse greater interest than in Germany.[276] This interest began to show itself surprisingly early. Already the first *Organisateur* seems to have reached a considerable number of readers in that country.[277] Some years later it seems to have been Comte's pupil Gustave d'Eichthal who, even before his similar efforts in England, on a visit to Berlin in 1824, succeeded in interesting several people in Comte's *Système de Politique Positive,* with the result that a fairly detailed review, the only one the book ever received in any language, appeared in the *Leipziger Literatur-Zeitung.*[278] And in Friedrich Buchholz, then a well-known political writer, d'Eichthal gained Comte a warm admirer, who not only in a flattering letter to Comte expressed complete agreement,[279] but who also in 1826 and 1827 published in his *Neue Monatsschrift für Deutschland* four anonymous articles on Saint-Simon's work, followed by a translation of the concluding part of the *Système Industriel.*[280]

It was, however, only in the autumn of 1830 that general interest in the Saint-Simonian movement awoke in Germany; and during the next two or three years it went like wildfire through the German literary world. The July Revolution had made Paris once more the center of attraction for all progressives, and the Saint-Simonians, then at the height of their reputation, were the outstanding intellectual movement in that Mecca of all liberals. A veritable flood of books, pamphlets and articles of the Saint-Simonians [281] and translations of some of their writings [282] appeared in German and there was little that could not be learned about them from German sources. The wave of excitement even reached the old Goethe, who subscribed to the *Globe* (probably since its liberal days) and who, after he had warned Carlyle as early as October, 1830, "to keep away from the Société St. Simonienne," [283] and after several recorded conversations on the subject, in May, 1831, still felt impelled to spend a day reading to get at the bottom of the Saint-Simonian doctrine.[284]

The whole German literary world seems to have been agog for news about the novel French ideas and to some, as Rahel von Varnhagen describes it, the Saint-Simonian *Globe* became the indispensable intellectual daily bread.[285] The news about the Saint-Simonian movements appears to have been the decisive factor which in 1831 drew Heinrich Heine to Paris,[286] and, as he later said, he had not been twenty-four hours in Paris before he sat in the midst of the

Saint-Simonians.[287] From Paris he and L. Boerne did much to spread information about the Saint-Simonians in Germany literary circles. Another important source of information for those who had stayed behind, particularly the Varnhagens, was the American Albert Brisbane, then not yet a Fourierist, but already spreading socialist ideas on his travels.[288] How profoundly these ideas were affecting the Young German poets Laube, Gutzkow, Mundt and Wiebarg has been well described by Miss E. M. Butler in her book on the *Saint-Simonian Religion in Germany,* where with much justification she describes the whole Young German school as a Saint-Simonian movement.[289] In their short but spectacular existence as a group between 1832 and 1835 they persistently, if more crudely than their French contemporaries, applied the Saint-Simonian principle that art must be tendentious, and in particular popularized their feminist doctrines and their demands for the "rehabilitation of the flesh." [290]

§ 4.   Much more important for our purpose, but unfortunately much less explored,[291] is the relation of the Saint-Simonians to another connected German group, the Young Hegelians. The curious affinity which existed between the Hegelian and the Saint-Simonian ideas and which was strongly felt by the contemporaries will occupy us later. Here we are concerned only with the actual extent to which the younger Hegelian philosophers were directly affected by Saint-Simonian ideas, and how much therefore the decisive change which led to the separation of the Young Hegelians from the orthodox followers of the philosopher may have been partly due to that influence. Our actual knowledge on this point is small, yet, as there existed close personal contacts between the Young Germans and the members of what later became the Young Hegelian group, and as some of the former as well as some of the authors of the German works on Saint-Simon were Hegelians,[292] there can be little doubt that in the group as a whole the interest in Saint-Simonism cannot have been much smaller than among the Young Germans.

The period of German thought which is still so little explored and yet so crucial for the understanding of the later developments is the eighteen-thirties, during which it seems the seeds were sown which bore fruit only in the next decade.[293] We meet here with the difficulty that after the Saint-Simonians had discredited themselves, people became most reluctant to acknowledge any indebtedness, especially as the Prussian censorship was likely to object to any reference to that dangerous group. As early as 1834, G. Kuehne, a Hegelian philosopher closely connected with the Young Germans, said of Saint-Simonism, "the French counterpart of Hegelianism," that "it will scarcely any longer be permissible to mention the name, yet the basic feature of this view of life, which in this particular form has become a caricature, will prove to have been completely embedded in social relations." [294] And when we remember that the men who were to play the decisive rôle in the revolt against orthodox Hegelianism and in the birth of German socialism, A. Ruge, L. Feuerbach, D. F. Strauss, Moses Hess and K. Rodbertus, were all in their twenties when the rage for Saint-Simonism swept through Germany,[295] it seems almost certain that they all imbibed Saint-Simonian doctrine at the time. Only of one of them, although the one from whom socialist doctrines are known to have spread more than from anybody else in the Germany of the time, Moses Hess, is it definitely known that he visited Paris in the early 'thirties,[296] and the traces of Saint-Simonian and Fourierist doctrines can easily be seen in his first book of 1837.[297] In the case of some of the others, as particularly in that of the most influential of the Young Hegelians, Ludwig Feuerbach, in whom Positivism and Hegelianism were so completely combined and who exercised great influence on Marx and Engels, we have no direct evidence of his having known the Saint-Simonian writings. It would be even more significant, if this Hegelian, who in providing a positivist *Weltanschauung* for the next generations of German scientists was to play a rôle similar to that of Comte in France, had arrived at his view independently of the contemporary movements in that country. But it seems practically certain that he must have come to know them in the formative period of his thought. It is hard to believe that the young university lecturer in philosophy, who, in the summer of 1832, when Germany was reverberating with discussions of Saint-Simonism, spent months in Frankfurt reading to prepare himself for an intended visit to Paris,[298] should, almost alone among men of his kind, have escaped their influence. It seems much more likely that, as in the case of others, it was precisely the fame of this school which attracted him to Paris. And although the intended visit did not take place, Feuerbach probably absorbed much of Saint-Simonian thought at that time and thus prepared himself to replace the Saint-Simonian influence among his younger contemporaries. If one reads his work with this probability in mind, it becomes difficult to believe that the obvious resemblances between his work and that of Comte are accidental.[299]

An important rôle in spreading French socialist thought in Germany during this period was also played by various members of the large colony of German journeymen in Paris, whose organizations became so important for the growth of the socialist movement and among whom for a time W. Weitling was the outstanding figure.[300] He and numerous other travelers must have provided a continuous stream of information about the development of French doctrine, even before, in the beginning of the 'forties, Lorenz von Stein and Karl Grün went to Paris for a systematic study of French socialism. With the appearance of the two books [301] which were the results of these visits, particularly with Lorenz von Stein's most detailed and sympathetic account in his widely read *Socialism and Communism in Present-Day France* (1842), the whole of Saint-Simonian doctrine became common property in Germany. That Stein—incidentally another Hegelian who was most ready to absorb and spread Saint-Simonian ideas—was, with Feuerbach, one of the strongest influences that were brought to bear on Karl Marx's early development is well known.[302] Yet the belief that it was only through Stein and Grün (and later, perhaps, Thierry and Mignet) that Marx made his acquaintance with Saint-Simonian ideas and that he studied them at first hand only later in Paris, is probably mistaken. It seemed certain that he was directly affected by the early wave of Saint-Simonian enthusiasm when he was a boy of thirteen or fourteen. He himself told his friend, the Russian historian M. Kowalewski, how his paternal friend and later father-in-law, Baron Ludwig von Westphalen, had been infected by the general enthusiasm and had talked to the boy about the new ideas.[303] The fact, often noted by German scholars,[304] that many parts of Marx's doctrine, particularly the theory of the class struggle and certain aspects of his interpretation of history, bear a much closer resemblance to those of Saint-Simon than to those of

Hegel, becomes even more interesting when we realize that the influence of Saint-Simon on Marx seems to have preceded that of Hegel.

Friedrich Engels, in whose separate writings Saint-Simonian elements are perhaps even more conspicuous than in those of Marx, was at one time closely associated with some of the members of the Young German movement, particularly Gutzkow, and later received his first introduction to socialist theory from M. Hess.[305] The other leaders of German socialist thought are similarly indebted. How closely most of Rodbertus' doctrines resemble those of the Saint-Simonians has often been noticed and, in view of the whole situation, there can be little doubt about the direct derivation.[306] Among the leading members of the active socialist movement in Germany, we know at least of W. Liebknecht that he steeped himself in Saint-Simonian doctrine when still very young,[307] while Lassalle received most of it from his masters Lorenz von Stein and Louis Blanc.[308, 309]

§ 5.   We have not yet said anything about the relations of Saint-Simonism to later French socialist schools. But this part of their influence is on the whole so well known that we can be brief. The only one of the early French socialists who was independent of Saint-Simon was of course his contemporary Charles Fourier [310]—who, with Robert Owen and Saint-Simon, is usually regarded as one of the three founders of socialism. But although the Saint-Simonians borrowed from him some elements of their doctrines—particularly with respect to the relations between the sexes—neither he nor, for that matter, Robert Owen, contributed much to that aspect of socialism which is relevant here: the deliberate organisation and direction of economic activity. His contribution there is more of a negative character. A fanatic for economy, he could see nothing but waste in the competitive institutions and surpassed even the Saint-Simonians in his belief in the unbounded possibilities of technological progress. There was indeed much of the engineer mentality in him and, like Saint-Simon, he recruited his pupils largely among the polytechnicians. He is probably the earliest representative of the myth of "scarcity in the midst of plenty," which to the engineering mind seemed as obvious 120 years ago as it does now.

Victor Considérant, the leader of the Fourierist school which gave their doctrines more coherence than did their master, was a poly-technician, and most of the influential members, like Transon and Lechevalier, were old Saint-Simonians.[311] Of the rival socialist sects nearly all the leaders were former Saint-Simonians who had developed particular aspects of that doctrine: Leroux, Cabet, Buchez and Pecqueur, or, like Louis Blanc, whose *Organisation du Travail* is pure Saint-Simonism, had borrowed extensively from it. Even the most original of the later French socialists, Proudhon, however much he may have contributed to political doctrine, was in his properly social-ist doctrines largely Saint-Simonian.[312] It can be said that by about 1840 Saint-Simonian ideas had ceased to be the property of a par-ticular school and had come to form the basis of all the socialist movements. And the socialism of 1848—apart from the strong democratic and anarchistic elements which by then had been carried into it as new and alien elements—was in doctrine and personnel still largely Saint-Simonian.

§ 6.   Although there is already some danger that we may appear unduly to exaggerate the importance of that little group of men, we have by no means yet surveyed the full extent of their influence. To be inspirers of practically all socialist movements [313] during the past hundred years would be enough to secure them an important place in history. The influence which Saint-Simon exercised on the study of social problems through Comte and Thierry, and the Saint-Simonians through Quetelet and Le Play is hardly less important and will oc-cupy us again. A full account of the spreading of their ideas through Europe would have to give considerable attention to the profound influence they exercised on G. Mazzini,[314] the whole Young Italian Movement, Silvio Pellico, Gioberti, Garibaldi, and others [315] in Italy, and to trace their effects on such divers figures as A. Strindberg in Sweden,[316] A. Herzen in Russia,[317] and others in Spain and South America.[318] Nor can we stop here to consider the frequent occur-rence of similar types who sometime rallied to the Saint-Simonian flag as did the Belgian industrialist, sociologist and benefactor Ernest Solvay,[319] or the *Néo-Saint-Simoniens* who in post-war France pub-lished a new *Producteur*.[320] Such conscious or unconscious re-births we meet throughout the last hundred years.[321]

There is, however, one direct effect of Saint-Simonian teaching which deserves more consideration: the founders of modern socialism also did much to give Continental capitalism its peculiar form; "monopoly capitalism," or "finance capitalism," growing up through the intimate connection between banking and industry (the banks organizing industrial concerns as the largest shareholders of the component firms), the rapid development of joint-stock enterprises and the large railway combines are largely Saint-Simonian creations.

The history of this is mainly one of the *Crédit Mobilier* type of bank, the kind of combined deposit and investment institution which was first created by the brothers Pereire in France and then imitated under their personal influence or by other Saint-Simonians almost all over the European Continent. One might almost say that after the Saint-Simonians had failed to bring about the reforms they desired through a political movement, or after they had grown older and more worldly, they undertook to transform the capitalist system from within and thus to apply as much of their doctrines as they could by individual effort. And it cannot be denied that they succeeded in changing the economic structure of the Continental countries into something quite different from the English type of competitive capitalism. Even if the *Crédit Mobilier* of the Pereires ultimately failed, it and its industrial concerns became the model on which the banking and capital structure in most of the industrial countries of Europe were developed, partly by other Saint-Simonians. For the Pereires the aim of their *Crédit Mobilier* was most definitely to create a center of administration and control which was to direct according to a coherent program the railway systems, the town planning activities and the various public utilities and other industries which by a systematic policy of mergers they attempted to consolidate into a few large undertakings.[322] In Germany G. Mevissen and A. Oppenheim, who had early come under Saint-Simonian influence, went similar ways with the foundation of the Darmstaedter Bank and other banking ventures.[323] In Holland other Saint-Simonians worked in the same direction,[324] and in Austria,[325] Italy, Switzerland and Spain [326] the Pereires or their subsidiaries or connections created similar institutions. What is known as the "German" type of bank with its close connection with industry and the whole system of *Effektenkapitalis-*

mus as it has been called is essentially the realization of Saint-Simonian plans.[327] This development was closely connected with the other favorite activity of the Saint-Simonians in later years, railway construction,[328] and their interest in public works of all kinds,[329] which, as years went by, became more and more their chief interest. As Enfantin organized the Paris-Lyon-Méditerranée railway system, the Pereires built railways in Austria, Switzerland, Spain and Russia and P. Talabot in Italy, employing as engineers on the spot other Saint-Simonians to carry out their directions. Enfantin, looking back at the works of the Saint-Simonians in late life, was well entitled to say that they had "covered the earth with a net-work of railways, gold, silver, and electricity." [330]

If with their far-flung plans for industrial organization they did not succeed in creating large combines, as was later done with the assistance of the Governments in the process of cartelization, this was largely due to the policy of Free Trade on which France had embarked and of which some of the old Saint-Simonians, particularly M. Chevalier, but also the Pereires, were still among the chief advocates. But already others from the same circle, notably Pecqueur,[331] were agitating in the same direction as their friend Friedrich List in Germany. Yet they could not succeed till another branch from the same stem, positivism and "historicism," had succeeded in effectively discrediting "orthodox" political economy. The arguments, however, which were later to justify a policy of supporting the growth of cartels were already created by the Saint-Simonians.

However far their practical influence extended, it was greatest in France during the second Empire. During this period they had not only the support of the Press because some of the leading journalists were old Saint-Simonians; [332] but the most important fact was that Napoleon III himself was so profoundly influenced by Saint-Simonian ideas that Saint-Beuve could call him "Saint-Simon on horseback." [333] He remained on friendly terms with some of its members and even committed himself to part of their ideas in his programmatic *Idées Napoléoniennes* and some other pamphlets.[334] It is thus not surprising that the years of the second Empire became the great period of the Saint-Simonian *réalisations*. So closely indeed did they become associated with the regime that its end meant more or less also the end of their direct influence in France.[335]

When to this influence of the French Empire we add the facts that Bismarck's social policy and ideas were largely derived from Lassalle and thus via Louis Blanc, Lorenz von Stein and Rodbertus from Saint-Simon,[336] and that the theory of the *soziale Königtum* and state socialism, which guided the execution of that policy, can be traced, through L. von Stein and Rodbertus and others, to the same source,[337] we begin to get the measure of this influence in the nineteenth century. Even if this influence was tempered by others which in any case would have worked in the same direction, the statement of the German K. Grün, which may conclude this survey, appears certainly in no way to exaggerate their importance. "Saint-Simonism," he wrote in 1845, "is like a seed-pod that has been opened and whose husk has been lost, while the individual seeds have found soil everywhere and have come up, one after the other." And in his enumeration of all the different movements which have been thus fertilized, we find for the first time the term "scientific socialism," [338] applied to the work of Saint-Simon who "had throughout his life been searching for the new science."

VI

SOCIOLOGY: COMTE, AND HIS SUCCESSORS

§ 1. Eight years after the first *Système de politique positive* [339] there began to appear that work of Comte to which his fame is mainly due. The *Cours de philosophie positive,* the literary version of the series of lectures which he had first started in 1826, and then, after recovery from his mental illness, delivered in 1829, extended to six volumes which appeared between 1830 and 1842.[340] In devoting the best years of his manhood to this theoretical task, Comte remained faithful to the conviction which had led to his break with Saint-Simon: that the political reorganization of society could be achieved only after the spiritual foundation had been laid by a reorganization of all knowledge.[341] But he never lost sight of the political task. The main philosophical work was duly followed by the definite *Système de politique positive* (4 vols., 1851–1854) which, in spite of all its bizarre excrescences, is a consistent execution of the plans of his youth. And if his death in 1857 had not prevented it, this would have been followed by the third part of the original plan, a similarly elaborate treatise on technology or "the action of man upon nature."

No attempt can be made here to give an adequate summary of the whole of Comte's philosophy or of its evolution. We are concerned only with the birth of the new discipline, of which Saint-Simon and the younger Comte had only dreamt but which the latter's mature works brought into existence. Yet, as the whole of Comte's work is directed towards this end, this is not a sufficient restriction of our task. We shall have to confine ourselves to a consideration of those aspects of his immense work which, either because of their influence on other leading thinkers of the period, or because they are particularly representative of the intellectual tendencies of the age, are of

168

special significance. They concern mainly the methods appropriate to the study of social phenomena, a subject which is extensively treated in the *Cours*. But it should perhaps be pointed out that it is because the subjects which mainly concern us are treated in that work that we shall confine ourselves to its contents, and that we cannot accept the belief, at one time widely held, that there is a fundamental break between it and Comte's later work, brought about by the increasingly pathological state of his mind.[342]

A few further facts of Comte's life may be recalled here which will help to understand his views and the extent and limits of his influence. The most important feature of his career is, perhaps, that trained as a mathematician he remained one by profession. Through the greater part of his life he derived his income from coaching and examining in mathematics for the *Ecole polytechnique*—but the professorship at the institution which he coveted remained denied to him. The repeated disappointments and the quarrels caused by his recriminations, which in the end lost him even the modest positions which he held, explain to some extent his increasing isolation, his outspoken contempt for most of his scientific contemporaries, and the almost complete neglect of his work in his own country during his life-time. Although in the end he found a few enthusiastic disciples, it is on the whole not difficult to see why to most people he seems to have appeared a singularly unattractive figure, whose whole intellectual style has often repelled those who have most in common with him.[343] The man who prided himself that in a few years of his youth he had absorbed all the knowledge from which he could construct a grandiose systematization of all human science and who, through a great part of his life, practiced a "cerebral hygiene" consisting in not reading any new publications, was not likely to be readily accepted as that *preceptor mundi et universae scientiae* he claimed to be. The excessive length and prolixity and the clumsy style of his mature works were a further bar to its popularity. Yet if this restricted the number of people who became directly acquainted with his work, it was made up for by the profound effect it had on some of the most influential thinkers of the age. Although largely indirect, his influence is among the most potent in the nineteenth century, certainly where the study of social phenomena is concerned.

§ 2. The whole of Comte's philosophy hinges, of course, upon the celebrated law of the three stages which we have already met in his early essays. His very task is determined for him by that law: all the simpler sciences like physics, chemistry, and biology having reached the positive stage, it was reserved for Comte to do the same for the crowning science of the human race and thus to complete the main development of the human mind. The stress which Comte himself and still more his interpreters have put on the *three* separate stages is, however, rather misleading. The great contrast is between, on the one hand, the theological and the metaphysical stage (the latter being a mere "modification" [344] of the first), and, on the other, the positive stage. What he is concerned with is the continuous and gradual emancipation from the anthropomorphic interpretation of all phenomena [345] which each science completely achieves only as it reaches the positive stage. The metaphysical stage is no more than the phase of dissolution of the theological stage, the critical phase in which man has already abandoned the cruder personalistic view which seeks spirits and deities in all phenomena, but has merely replaced them with abstract entities or essences which have as little place in the truly positivist view of science. In the positive phase every attempt to explain phenomena by causes or a statement of the "mode of production" is abandoned; [346] it aims at directly connecting the observed phenomena by rules about the coexistence or sequence or, to use a modern phrase not yet used by Comte, at merely "describing" their interrelations by general and invariable laws. In other words, since the habits of thought which man had acquired in interpreting the actions of his own kind had long held up the study of external nature, and the latter had only made real progress in proportion as it got rid of this human habit, the way to progress in the study of man must be the same: we must cease to consider man anthropomorphically and must treat him as if we knew about him as little as we know about external nature. Although Comte does not say so in so many words, he comes very near doing so, and therefore one cannot help wondering how he could have failed to see the paradoxical nature of this conclusion. [347]

But that in the positive treatment of social phenomena man must not be treated differently from the way in which we approach the phenomena of inanimate nature is only a negative characteristic of the character which the new "natural science" [348] of society will assume. We have yet to see what the positive characteristics of the "positive" method are. This is a far more difficult task, as Comte's statements on most of the epistemological problems involved are distressingly naïve and unsatisfactory. The basis of Comte's views is the apparently simple contention that "the fundamental character of all positive philosophy is to regard all phenomena as subject to invariable natural *laws,* whose precise discovery and reduction to the smallest number possible is the aim of all our effort." [349] All science deals with observed facts,[350] and, as he states in a sentence which he quotes with pride from his essay of 1825, "any proposition which does not admit of being reduced to a simple enunciation of fact, special or general, can have no real or intelligible sense." [351] But the question to which it is exceedingly difficult to find an answer in Comte's work is what precisely is meant by the "phenomena" which are all subject to invariable laws, or what he regards as "facts." The statement that all phenomena are subject to invariable natural laws clearly makes sense only if we are given some guidance on what individual events are to be regarded as the same phenomena. It evidently cannot mean that everything which appears the same to our senses must behave in the same manner. The task of science is precisely to reclassify the sense impressions on the basis of their coexistence with or succession to others so as to make it possible to establish regularities for the behavior of the newly constructed units of reference. But this is exactly what Comte objects to. The construction of such new entities as the "ether" is definitely a metaphysical procedure and any attempt to explain the "mode of production" of the phenomena as distinct from the study of the laws which connect the directly observed facts is to be proscribed. The emphasis lies on the establishment of direct relationship among the immediately given facts. But what these facts (which may be "particular" or "general"!) are seems to constitute no problem for Comte, who approaches the question with an entirely naïve and uncritical realism. As in the whole of 19th century positivism,[352] this concept is left exceedingly obscure.

§ 3. The only indication of what is meant by the term "fact" as used by Comte we obtain from its regular conjunction with the adjective "observed," together with his discussion of what he means by observation. This is of great importance for its meaning in the field with which we are concerned, the study of human and social phenomena. "True observation," we are told, "must necessarily be external to the observer" and the "famous internal observation is no more than a vain parody of it," which presupposes the "ridiculously contradictory situation of our intelligence contemplating itself during the habitual performance of its own activity." [353] Comte accordingly consistently denies the possibility of all psychology, that "last transformation of theology," [354] or at least of all introspective knowledge of the human mind. There are only two ways in which the phenomena of the individual mind can properly become the object of positive study: either through the study of the organs which produce them, that is through "phrenological psychology"; [355] or, since "affective and intellectual functions" have the peculiar characteristic of "not being subject to direct observation during their performance," through the study of "their more or less immediate and more or less durable results" [356]—which would seem to mean what is now called the behaviorist approach. To these only two legitimate ways of studying the phenomena of the individual mind is later added, as the result of the creation of sociology, the study of the "collective mind," the only form of psychology proper which is admitted into the positive system.

As regards the first of these aspects we need here say no more than that it is remarkable that even Comte should have fallen so completely under the influence of the founder of "phrenology," the "illustrious Gall" whose "immortal works are irrevocably impressed upon the human mind," [357] as to believe that his attempt at localizing particular mental "faculties" in particular parts of the brain should provide an adequate substitute for all other forms of psychology.

The "behaviorist" approach in Comte deserves rather more attention, because in this primitive form it shows particularly clearly its weakness. Only a few pages after Comte has confined the study of the individual mind to the observation of its "more or less immediate and more or less durable results" this becomes the direct observation of "the series of intellectual and moral acts, which belongs more to natural history proper" and which he seems to regard as in some sense objectively given and known without any use of introspection or any other means different from "external observation." Thus Comte not only tacitly admits intellectual phenomena among his "facts" which are to be treated like any objectively observed facts of nature; he even admits, to all intents and purposes, that our knowledge of man, which we possess only because we are men ourselves and think like other men, is an indispensable condition of our interpretation of social phenomena. It can only mean this when he emphasizes that wherever we have to deal with "animal" life (as distinguished from merely vegetative life, *i.e.,* those phenomena which appear only in the higher part of the zoological scale),[358] investigation cannot succeed unless we begin with "the consideration of man, the sole being where this order of phenomena can ever be directly intelligible." [359]

§ 4.   Comte's theory of the three stages is closely connected with the second main characteristic of his system, his classification, or the theory of the "positive hierarchy," of the sciences. In the beginning of the *Cours* he still plays with the Saint-Simonian idea of the unification of all sciences by reducing all phenomena to one single law, the law of gravitation.[360] But gradually he abandons this belief and in the end it becomes even the subject of violent denunciation as an "absurd utopia." [361] Instead, the "fundamental" or theoretical sciences (as distinguished from their concrete applications) are arranged in a single linear order of decreasing generality and increasing complexity, beginning with mathematics (including theoretical mechanics) and leading through astronomy, physics, chemistry, and biology (which includes all study of man as an individual) to the new and final science of social physics or sociology. As each of these fundamental sciences is "based" on those preceding it in the hierarchical order, in the sense that it makes use of all the results of the preceding sciences *plus* some new elements peculiar to itself, it is an "indispensable complement of the law of the three stages" that the different sciences can reach the positive stage only successively in this "invariable and necessary order." But as the last of these sciences has for its object the growth of the human mind and therefore particularly the development of science itself, it becomes, once established, the universal science which will progressively tend to absorb all knowledge in its system, although this ideal may never be fully realized.

Here we are interested only in the meaning of the assertion that sociology "rests" on the results of all other sciences and therefore could only be created after all the other sciences had reached the positive stage. This has nothing to do with the undeniable contention that the biological study of man as one of the most complicated organisms will have to make use of the results of all the other natural sciences. Comte's sociology, as we shall see presently, does not deal with man as a physical unit but with the evolution of the human mind as a manifestation of the "collective organism" which mankind as a whole constitutes. It is the study of the organization of society and the laws of the evolution of the human mind which are supposed to require the use of the results of all the other sciences. Now this would be justified if Comte really contended that the aim of sociology (and that part of biology which in his system replaces individual psychology) was to explain mental phenomena in physical terms, that is, if he wanted seriously to carry out his early dreams of unification of all sciences on the basis of some single universal law.[362] But this he has explicitly abandoned. His schematism leads him indeed to assert that none of the phenomena belonging to any of the sciences higher up in his hierarchy can ever fully be reduced to, or explained in terms of, the preceding sciences. It is just as impossible to explain sociological phenomena purely in biological terms as, in his opinion, it will remain forever impossible to reduce chemical phenomena altogether to physical. While there will always be sociological laws which cannot be reduced to mechanical or biological laws, this break between sociology and biology is no different from the presumed difference between chemistry and physics.

When, however, Comte tries to prove his contention that sociology depends on a sufficient development of the other sciences, he fails completely, and the examples he gives as illustrations are almost childish. That in order to understand any social phenomena we have to know the *explanation* of the change of day and night and of the

changes of the seasons "by the circumstances of the earth's daily ro-
tation and annual movements," or that "the very conception of the
stability in human association could not be positively established till
the discovery of gravitation," [363] is simply not true. The results of the
natural sciences may be essential data for sociology to the extent to
which they actually affect the actions of the men who use them. But
that is true, whatever the state of natural knowledge is, and there is
no reason why the sociologist need know more of natural science
than those whose actions he tries to explain, and therefore no reason
why the development of the study of society should have to wait on
the natural sciences having reached a certain stage of development.

Comte claims that with the application of the positive method to
social phenomena the unity of method of all sciences is established.
But beyond the general characteristic of the positive method, "to
abandon, as necessarily vain, all search for causes, be it primary or
final, and to confine itself to the study of the invariable relations
which constitute the effective laws of all observable events," [364] it is
difficult to say in what precisely this positive method consists. It certainly is not, as one might expect, the universal application of mathematical methods. Although mathematics is to Comte the source of
the positive method, the field where it appeared first and in its purest
form,[365] he does not believe that it can be usefully applied in the
more complicated subjects, even chemistry,[366] and he is scornful
about the attempts to apply statistics to biology [367] or the calculus of
probability to social phenomena.[368] Even observation, the one common element of all sciences, does not appear in the same form in all
of them. As the sciences become more complicated, new methods of
observation become available while others appropriate to the less
complicated phenomena cease to be useful. Thus, while in astronomy
the mathematical method and pure observation rule, in physics and
chemistry the experiment comes in as a new help. And as we proceed further, biology brings the comparative method and sociology,
finally, the "historical method," while mathematics and the experiment become in turn inapplicable.[369]

There is one more aspect of the hierarchy of the sciences which
must be briefly mentioned, as it is relevant to points which we shall
presently have to consider. As we ascend the hierarchical scale of the

sciences, and the phenomena with which they deal become more complex, they also become more subject to modification by human action and at the same time less "perfect" and therefore more in need of improvement by human control. Comte has nothing but contempt for people who admire the "wisdom of nature," and he is quite certain that a few competent engineers in creating an organism for a particular task would do infinitely better.[370] And the same applies necessarily to the most complicated and therefore most imperfect of all natural phenomena, human society. The paradox that the instrument of the human mind, which according to this theory should be the most imperfect of all phenomena, should yet at the same time have the unique power to control and improve itself, does not trouble Comte in the least.

§ 5.   There is one respect in which Comte not only admits but even stresses a difference in the method, not only of sociology, but of all organic sciences from that of inorganic sciences. Yet, although this break occurs between chemistry and biology, the importance of this "inversion" of procedure, as Comte calls it himself, is of even greater importance with respect to sociology and we shall quote in full the passage in which he himself explains it with direct reference to the study of social phenomena. "There exists necessarily," he explains, "a fundamental difference between the whole of inorganic philosophy and the whole of organic philosophy. In the first, where solidarity between the phenomena, as we have shown, is little pronounced, and can only little affect the study of the subject, we have to explore a system where the elements are better known than the whole, and are usually even alone directly observable. But in the second, on the contrary, where man and society constitute the principal object, the opposite procedure becomes most often the only rational one, as another consequence of the same logical principle, because the whole of the object is here certainly much better known and more immediately accessible." [371]

This astounding assertion that where we have to deal with social phenomena the whole is better known than the parts is put forward as an indisputable axiom without much explanation. It is of crucial importance for the understanding of the new science of sociology as

created by Comte and accepted by his direct successors. Its significance is further enhanced by the fact that this collectivist approach
is characteristic of most of the students who approach such phenomena from what we have called a "scientistic" point of view.[372]
But it must be admitted that it is not easy to see why this should be
so, and Comte gives us little help in this respect.

One possible justification of this view which would occur first to
the modern mind, played at best a very minor rôle in Comte's
thought: the idea that mass phenomena may show statistical regularities while the composing elements seem to follow no recognizable
law.[373] This idea, made familiar by Comte's contemporary Quetelet,[374] is certainly not the foundation of Comte's own argument. It is
indeed more than doubtful whether Comte ever took notice of Quetelet's work beyond showing indignation about the latter's using, in the
subtitle of a work dealing with "mere statistics," [375] the term "social
physics," which Comte regarded as his intellectual property. But
though Quetelet seems thus to have been indirectly responsible
for the substitution of the new word "sociology," [376] for what Comte
till well on in the fourth volume of the *Cours* still describes as "social physics," [377] his main idea, which should have fitted so well into
Comte's general approach and was to play so important a rôle in
later scientistic sociology, found no place in Comte's system.

We shall probably have to see the explanation in Comte's general
attitude of treating whatever phenomena a science had to deal with
as immediately given "things" and in his desire to establish a similarity between biology, the science immediately beneath sociology in
the positive hierarchy, and the science of the "collective organism."
And since in biology it was unquestionably true that the organisms
were better known to us than their parts, the same had to be asserted
of sociology.

§ 6. The exposition of Comte's sociology, which was to constitute
the fourth volume of the *Cours*, extended in fact to three volumes
each considerably longer than any of the first three dealing with all
the other sciences. The fourth volume, published in 1839, contains
mainly the general considerations on the new science and its static
part. The two remaining ones contain a very full and detailed ex-

position of sociological dynamics, that general theory of the history of the human mind, which was the main aim of Comte's labors.

The division of the subject into statics and dynamics,[378] which Comte believes to be appropriate to all sciences, he takes over, not directly from mechanics, but from biology to which it had been applied by the physiologist De Blainville, whose work had influenced Comte to an extent equaled only by Lagrange, Fourier, and Gall.[379] The distinction, which according to De Blainville in biology corresponds to that between anatomy and physiology, or organization and life, is made to correspond in sociology with the two great watchwords of positivism, order and progress. Static sociology deals with the laws of co-existence of social phenomena, while dynamic sociology is concerned with the laws of succession in the necessary evolution of society.

When it comes to the execution of this scheme it proves, however, that Comte has extraordinarily little to say on the static part of his subject. His disquisitions about the necessary *consensus* between all the parts of any social system, the *idée mère* of solidarity as he often calls it, which in social phenomena is even more marked than in biological, remain pretty empty generalizations, as Comte has no way (or intention) of establishing why particular institutions, or which kinds of institutions, should necessarily go together, or others be incompatible. The comments on the relations between the individual, the family, and society, in the single chapter devoted to social statics, rise little above the commonplace.[380] In the discussion of the division of labor, although a distant echo of Adam Smith,[381] there is no trace of a comprehension of the factors which regulate it; and how little he understands them becomes evident when he expressly denies that a division of intellectual labor similar to that applying to material labor is possible.[382]

The whole of his statics is, however, no more than a brief sketch and of minor importance compared with the dynamic part of sociology, the fulfillment of his main ambition. It is the attempt to prove the basic contention, which Comte, as a young man of twenty-six, had expressed in a letter to a friend when he promised to show that "there were laws governing the development of the human race as definite as those determining the fall of a stone." [383] History was to be made a science, and the essence of all science is that it should be capable of prediction.[384] The dynamic part of sociology was therefore to become a philosophy of history, as it is commonly but somewhat misleadingly called, or a theory of history as it would be more correctly described. The idea which was to inspire so much of the thought of the second half of the nineteenth century, was to write "abstract history," "history without the names of men or even people." [385] The new science was to provide a theoretical scheme, an abstract order in which the major changes of human civilization must necessarily follow each other.

The basis of this scheme is of course the law of the three stages and the main content of dynamic sociology is a detailed elaboration of the law. It is thus a curious feature of the Comtian system that this same law which is supposed to prove the necessity of the new science is at the same time its main and almost sole result. We need not trouble here with its elaboration in detail, beyond saying that in Comte's hands human history becomes largely identified with the growth of the natural sciences.[386] What is relevant to us are only the general implications of the idea of a natural science which deals with the laws of intellectual development of the human race, and the practical conclusions drawn from it with regard to the future organization of society. The idea of recognizable laws, not only of the growth of individual minds, but of the development of the knowledge of the human race as a whole, presupposes that the human mind could, so to speak, look down on itself from a higher plane and be able not merely to understand its operation from the inside, but observe it, as it were, from the outside. The curious thing about this proposition, particularly in its Comtian form, is that although it explicitly recognizes that the interactions of individual minds may produce something in a sense superior to what an individual mind can ever achieve, it yet claims for the same individual mind not only the power to grasp this development as a whole and to recognize the principle on which it works and even the course it must follow, but also the power to control and direct it and thereby to improve upon its uncontrolled working.

What this belief really amounts to is that the products of the process of mind can be comprehended as a whole by a simpler process than the laborious one of understanding them, and that the individual mind, looking at these results from the outside, can then directly connect these wholes by laws applying to them as entities, and finally, by extrapolating the observed development, achieve a kind of shortcut to the future development. This empirical theory of the development of the collective mind is at the same time the most naïve and the most influential result of the application of the procedure of the natural sciences to social phenomena, and of course based on the illusion that the phenomena of the mind are in the same sense given as objective things, and subject to external observation and control as physical phenomena. It follows from this approach that our knowledge is to be regarded as "relative" and conditioned by assignable factors—not merely from the point of view of some hypothetical more highly organized mind, but from our own point of view. It is from this point of view that the belief springs that we ourselves can recognize the "mutability" [387] of our mind and of its laws and the belief that the human race can undertake to control its own development. This idea that the human mind can, as it were, lift itself up by its own bootstraps, has remained a dominant characteristic of most sociology to the present day,[388] and we have here the root (or rather one of the roots, the other being Hegel) of that modern hubris which has found its most perfect expression in the so-called "sociology of knowledge." And the fact that this idea of the human mind controlling its own development has from its beginning been one of the leading ideas of sociology also provides the link which has always connected it with socialist ideals so that in the popular mind sociological and socialist often mean the same thing.[389]

It is this search for the "general laws of the continuous variations of human opinions" [390] which Comte calls the "historical method," the "indispensable complement of the positive logic." [391] But although, partly under Comte's influence, this is what the term historical method increasingly came to mean in the second half of the nineteenth century, we cannot leave this subject without pointing out that it is, of course, nearly the opposite of what historical approach really means or did mean to the great historians who in the beginning of the century tried by the application of the historical method to understand the genesis of social institutions.[392]

§ 7. It is hardly surprising that, with this ambitious conception of the task of the single theoretical science of society which he admits into his system, Comte should have nothing but contempt for the already existing social disciplines. It would hardly be worth while to dwell on this attitude if it were not so characteristic of the view taken at all times of the social sciences by men blinded by the scientistic prejudice, and if his own efforts had not, at least in part, to be explained by his almost complete ignorance of the achievements of the then existing social sciences. Some, as particularly the study of language, he regards as hardly worth mentioning.[393] But he takes the trouble to denounce political economy at some length, and here his severity stands in a strange contrast to his exceedingly slender knowledge of the object of his abuse. Indeed, as even one of his admirers, who has devoted a whole book to Comte's relation to economics,[394] could not help emphasizing, his knowledge of economics was practically non-existent. He knew and even admired Adam Smith, partly for his descriptive work in economics, but mainly for his *History of Astronomy*. In his early years he had made the acquaintance of J. B. Say and some other members of the same circle, particularly Destutt de Tracy. But the latter's treatment of economics in his great treatise on "ideology" between logic and morals appeared to Comte merely a frank admission of the "metaphysical" character of economics.[395] For the rest, the economists did not seem to Comte to be worth bothering about. He knew *a priori* that they had merely performed their necessary destructive rôle, typical representatives of the negative or revolutionary spirit which was characteristic of the metaphysical phase. That no positive contribution to the reorganization of society could be expected from them was evident from the fact that they had not been trained as scientists: "being almost invariably lawyers or literary men, they had no opportunity of discipline in that spirit of positive rationality which they suppose they have introduced into their researches. Precluded by their education from any idea of scientific observation of even the smallest phenomena, from any notions of natural laws, from all perception of what demonstration is, they must obviously be incapable of applying a method in which they had no practice to the most difficult of all analyses." [396] Comte indeed would admit to the study of sociology only men who had successively

and successfully mastered all the other sciences and thus properly prepared themselves for the most difficult task of the study of the most complex of all phenomena.[397] Although the further development of the new science could not again present difficulties as great as those he had himself surmounted in first creating it,[398] only the very best minds could hope successfuly to grapple with them. The special difficulty of this task arises from the absolute necessity of dealing with all aspects of society at the same time, a necessity dictated by the particularly close "consensus" of all social phenomena. To have sinned against this principle and to have attempted to deal with economic phenomena in isolation, "apart from the analysis of the intellectual, moral, and political state of society," [399] is one of his main reproaches against the economists. Their "pretended science" presents to "all competent and experienced judges most decidedly the character of purely metaphysical concepts." [400] "If one considers impartially the sterile disputes which divide them concerning the most elementary concepts of value, utility, production, etc., one may fancy oneself attending the strangest debates of medieval scholastics on the fundamental attributes of their metaphysical entities." [401] But the main defect of political economy is its conclusion, "the sterile aphorism of absolute industrial liberty," [402] the belief that there is no need of some "special institution immediately charged with the task of regularizing the spontaneous co-ordination" which should be regarded as merely offering the opportunity for imposing real organization.[403] And he particularly condemns the tendency of political economy to "answer to all complaints that in the long run all classes, and especially the one most injured on the existing occasion, will enjoy a real and permanent satisfaction; a reply which will be regarded as derisive, as long as man's life is incapable of being indefinitely lengthened." [404]

§ 8.   It cannot be too much emphasized in any discussion of Comte's philosophy that he had no use for any knowledge of which he did not see the practical use.[405] And "the purpose of the establishment of social philosophy is to re-establish order in society." [406] Nothing seems to him "more repugnant to the real scientific spirit, not even the theological spirit," [407] than disorder of any kind, and nothing is perhaps more characteristic of the whole of Comte's work than "the inordinate demand for 'unity' and 'systematization'" which J. S. Mill described as the *fons errorum* of all Comte's later speculations.[408] But even if the "frenzy for regulation" [409] is not quite as preponderant in the *Cours* as it became in the *Système de philosophie positive,* the practical conclusions to which the *Cours* leads, just because they are still free from the fantastic exaggeration of the later work, show this feature already in a marked degree. With the establishment of the "definitive" [410] philosophy, positivism, the critical doctrine which has characterized the preceding period of transition has completed its historic mission and the accompanying dogma of the unbounded liberty of conscience will disappear.[411] To make the writing of the *Cours* possible was, as it were, the last necessary function of "the revolutionary dogma of free enquiry," [412] but now that this is achieved, the dogma has lost its justification. All knowledge being once again unified, as it has not been since the theological stage began to decay, the next task is to set up a new intellectual government where only the competent scientists will be allowed to decide the difficult social questions.[413] Since their action will in all respects be determined by the dictates of science, this will not mean arbitrary government, and "true liberty," which is nothing else than "a rational submission to the preponderance of the laws of nature," [414] will even be increased.

The detail of the social organization which positive science will impose need not concern us here. So far as economic life is concerned, it still resembles in many respects the earlier Saint-Simonian plans, particularly in so far as the leading rôle of the bankers in guiding industrial activity is concerned.[415] But he dissents from the later outright socialism of the Saint-Simonians. Private property is not to be abolished, but the rich become the "necessary depositaries of the public capitals" [416] and the owning of property a social function.[417] This is not the only point in which Comte's system resembles the later authoritarian socialism which we associate with Prussia rather than socialism as we used to know it. In fact in some passages this resemblance with Prussian socialism, even down to the very words used, is really amazing. Thus when he argues that in the future society the "immoral" concept of individual rights will disappear and there will be only duties,[418] or that in the new society there will be no private persons but only state functionaries of various units and grades,[419] and that in consequence the most humble occupation will be ennobled by its incorporation into the official hierarchy just as the most obscure soldier has his dignity as a result of the solidarity of the military organism,[420] or finally when, in the concluding section of the first sketch of the future order, he discovers a "special disposition towards command in some and towards obedience in others" and assures us that in our innermost heart we all know "how sweet it is to obey,"[421] we might match almost every sentence with identical statements of recent German theoreticians who laid the intellectual foundations of the doctrines of the Third Reich.[422] Having been led by his philosophy to take over from the reactionary Bonald the view that the individual is "a pure abstraction" [423] and society as a whole a single collective being, he is of necessity led to most of the characteristic features of a totalitarian view of society.

The later development of all this into a new Religion of Humanity with a fully developed cult is outside our subject. Needless to say that Comte, who was so completely a stranger to the one real cult of humanity, tolerance (which he would admit only in indifferent and doubtful matters),[424] was not the man to make much of that idea, which in itself does not lack a certain greatness. For the rest we cannot better summarize this last phase of Comte's thought than by the well-known epigram of Thomas Huxley, who described it as "Catholicism *minus* Christianity."

§ 9.   Before we cast a glance on the direct influence of Comte's main work we must briefly consider certain simultaneous and in a sense parallel efforts which, from the same intellectual background, but by a different route, produced an impression which tended to strengthen the tendencies of which Comte's work is the main representative. The Belgian astronomer and statistician Quetelet, who must be mentioned here in the first place, differs from Comte not only by being a great scientist in his own field but also by the great contributions which he has made to the methods of social study. He did this precisely by that application of mathematics to social study which Comte condemned. Through his application of the "Gaussian" normal curve of error to the analysis of statistical data he became, more than any other single person, the founder of modern statistics and particularly of its application to social phenomena. The value of this achievement is undisputed and indisputable. But in the general atmosphere in which Quetelet's work became known the belief was bound to arise that the statistical methods, which he had so successfully applied to some problems of social life, were destined to become the sole method of study. And Quetelet himself contributed not a little to create that belief.

The intellectual environment out of which Quetelet rose [425] is exactly the same as that of Comte: it was the French mathematicians of the circle of the *Ecole polytechnique*,[426] above all Laplace and Fourier, from whom he drew the inspiration for the application of the theory of probability to the problem of social statistics, and in most respects he, much more than Comte, must be regarded as the true continuer of their work and of that of Condorcet. His statistical work proper is not our concern. It was the general effect of his demonstration that something like the methods of the natural sciences could be applied to certain mass phenomena of society and of his implied and even explicit demand that all problems of social science should be treated in a similar fashion, which operated in a direction parallel to Comte's teaching. Nothing fascinated the ensuing generation so much as Quetelet's "average man" and his celebrated conclusion of his studies of moral statistics that "we pass from one year to another with the sad perspective of seeing the same crimes reproduced in the same order and calling down the same punishments in the same proportions. Sad condition of humanity! . . . We might enumerate in advance how many individuals will stain their hands in the blood of their fellows, how many will be forgers, how many will be poisoners, almost we can enumerate in advance how many births and deaths there should occur. There is a budget which we pay with a frightful regularity; it is that of prisons, chains and the scaffold." [427] His views on the application of the mathematical methods have become more characteristic of later positivist method than anything deriving directly from Comte: "The more advanced the sciences have become, the more they have tended to enter the domain of mathematics, which is a sort of center towards which they converge. We can judge of the perfection to which a science has come by the facility, more or less great, with which it may be approached by calculation." [428]

Although Comte had condemned this view and particularly all attempts to find social laws by means of statistics, his and Quetelet's general endeavors to find natural laws of the development of the human race as a whole, to extend the Laplacean conception of universal determinism to cultural phenomena, and to make mass phenomena the sole object of the science of society were sufficiently akin to lead to a gradual fusion of their doctrines.

In the same category of contemporary efforts with similar methodological tendencies we must at least briefly mention the work of F. Le Play, polytechnician and ex-Saint-Simonian, whose descriptive social surveys became the model of much later sociological work. Though differing from Comte as well as Quetelet in more respects than they have in common, he contributed like them to the reaction against theoretical individualism, classical economics, and political liberalism, thus strengthening the particular effects of the scientistic influences with which we are here concerned.[429]

§ 10. The tracing of influences is the most treacherous ground in the history of thought and we have in the last chapter already so much sinned against the canons of caution in this field that we shall now be brief. Yet the curious course which Comte's influence took is so important for the understanding of the intellectual history of the nineteenth century, and the cause of so many still prevailing misconceptions about his rôle, that a few more words about it are indispensable. In France, as already observed, Comte's immediate influence on thinkers of importance was small. But, as J. S. Mill points out, "the great treatise of M. Comte was scarcely mentioned in French literature or criticism, when it was already working powerfully on the minds of many British students and thinkers." [430] It was this influence on Mill himself and a few other leading English thinkers which became decisive for Comte's effect on European thought.[431] Mill himself, in the sixth book of his *Logic,* which deals with the methods of the moral sciences, became little more than an expounder of Comtian doctrine. The philosopher George Lewes and

George Eliot are some of the better known names of Comte's English adherents. And nothing could be more characteristic of the tremendous impact of Comte on England than that the same Miss Martineau who in her younger years had been the faithful and most successful popularizer of Ricardo's economics, should become, not only the translator and most skilful condenser of Comte's work, but also one of his most enthusiastic disciples. As important almost as Mill himself for the spreading of positivist views among students of social phenomena was their adoption by the historian H. T. Buckle, although in this case the influence of Comte was reinforced and perhaps outweighed by that of Quetelet.

It was largely through the medium of these English writers that Comtian positivism made its entry into Germany.[432] Mill's *Logic,* Buckle's and Lecky's historical works, and later Herbert Spencer, made Comte's ideas familiar to many who were often completely unaware of their source. And although it is perhaps doubtful whether many of the German scholars who in the second half of the nineteenth century professed views closely similar to Comte's had derived them directly from him, there were probably in no other country a greater number of influential men who tried to reform the social sciences on essentially Comtean lines. No other country seems at that time to have been more receptive of new ideas, and positivist thought together with Quetelet's new statistical methods was definitely the fashion of the period and was accepted in Germany with corresponding enthusiasm.[433] The curious phenomenon that there (and elsewhere) positivist influences should have so readily combined with that of Hegel will require separate investigation.

We have no space here more than briefly to mention the successors which in France at last took up the Comtian tradition. Before we mention the sociologists proper we must at least mention the names of Taine and Renan, both, incidentally, representatives of that curious combination of Comtian and Hegelian thought to which we have just referred. Of the sociologists almost all the best-known ones (with the exception of Tarde), Espinas, Lévy-Bruhl, Durkheim, Simiand, stand directly in the Comtian tradition, although in their case, too, this has in part come back to France *via* Germany and with the modifications which it there experienced.[434] To attempt to trace this later influence of Comte on French thought during the Third Republic would mean to write a history of sociology in the country where for a time it gained the greatest influence. Many of the best minds who devoted themselves to social studies were here attracted by the new science and it is perhaps not too much to suggest that the peculiar stagnation of French economics during that period is at least partly due to the predominance of the sociological approach to social phenomena.[435]

That Comte's direct influence remained confined to comparatively few, but that through these very few it extended exceedingly far, is even more true of the present generation than it was of earlier ones. There will be few students of the social sciences now who have ever read Comte or know much about him. But the number of those who have absorbed most of the important elements of his system through the intermediation of a few very influential representatives of his tradition, such as Henry Carey and T. Veblen [436] in America, J. K. Ingram, W. Ashley and L. T. Hobhouse [437] in England, or K. Lamprecht [438] and K. Breysig in Germany, is very large indeed. Why this influence of Comte should so frequently have been much more effective in an indirect manner, those who have attempted to study his work will have no difficulty in understanding.

Part Three

COMTE AND HEGEL

COMTE AND HEGEL

§ 1

THE DISCUSSIONS of every age are filled with the issues on which its leading schools of thought differ. But the general intellectual atmosphere of the time is always determined by the views on which the opposing schools agree. They become the unspoken presuppositions of all thought, the common and unquestioningly accepted foundations on which all discussion proceeds.

When we no longer share these implicit assumptions of ages long past, it is comparatively easy to recognize them. But it is different with regard to the ideas underlying the thought of more recent times. Here we are frequently not yet aware of the common features which the opposing systems of thought shared, ideas which for that very reason often have crept in almost unnoticed and have achieved their dominance without serious examination. This can be very important because, as Bernard Bosanquet once pointed out, "extremes of thought may meet in error as well as in truth." [1] Such errors sometimes become dogmas merely because they were accepted by the different groups who quarreled on all the live issues, and may even continue to provide the tacit foundations of thought when most of the theories are forgotten which divided the thinkers to whom we owe that legacy.

When this is the case, the history of ideas becomes a subject of eminently practical importance. It can help us to become aware of much that governs our own thought without our explicitly knowing it. It may serve the purposes of a psychoanalytical operation by bringing to the surface unconscious elements which determine our reasoning, and perhaps assist us to purge our minds from influences which seriously mislead us on questions of our own day.

191

My purpose is to suggest that we are in such a position. My thesis will be that in the field of social thought not only the second half of the nineteenth century but also our own age owes much of its characteristic approach to the agreement between two thinkers who are commonly regarded as complete intellectual antipodes: the German "idealist" Georg Wilhelm Friedrich Hegel and the French "positivist" Auguste Comte. In some respects these two men do indeed represent such complete extremes of philosophical thought that they seem to belong to different ages and scarcely even to talk about the same problems. But my concern here will be only incidentally with their philosophical systems as a whole. It will be chiefly with their influence on social theory. It is in this field that the influence of philosophical ideas can be most profound and most lasting. And there is, perhaps, no better illustration of the far-reaching effects of the most abstract ideas than the one I intend to discuss.

§ 2.   The suggestion that in these manners we have to deal with a common influence of Hegel and Comte has still so much the air of a paradox that I had better say at once that I am by no means the first to notice similarities between them. I could give you a long list, and shall presently mention a few outstanding examples, of students of the history of ideas who have pointed out such resemblances. The curious fact is that these observations have again and again been made with the air of surprise and discovery, and that their authors always seem a little uneasy about their own temerity and afraid of going beyond pointing out a few isolated points of agreement. If I am not mistaken, these coincidences go much further, however, and, in their effects on the social sciences, were much more important than has yet been realized.

Before I mention some instances of such earlier notice I must, however, correct a common mistake which is largely responsible for the neglect of the whole issue. It is the belief that the similarities are due to an influence which Hegel exercised on Comte.[2] This belief is due mainly to the fact that the publication of Comte's ideas is commonly dated from the appearance of the six volumes of his *Cours de Philosophie Positive* from 1830 to 1842, while Hegel died in 1831. All the essential ideas of Comte were, however, expounded by him as early as 1822 in his youthful *System of Positive Polity;* [3] and this *opuscule fondamentale,* as he later called it, appeared also as one of the works of the Saint-Simonian group and as such probably reached a wider audience and exercised a greater influence than the *Cours* immediately did. It seems to me to be one of the most pregnant tracts of the nineteenth century, infinitely more brilliant than the now better known ponderous volumes of the *Cours.* But even the *Cours,* which is little more than an elaboration of the ideas sketched in that small tract, was planned as early as 1826 and delivered as a series of lectures before a distinguished audience in 1828.[4] Comte's main ideas were thus published within a year of Hegel's *Philosophy of Law,* within a couple of years of the *Encyklopaedie,* and of course before the posthumous appearance of the *Philosophy of History,* to mention only Hegel's main works which are relevant here. In other words, although Comte was Hegel's junior by twenty-eight years, we must regard them to all intents and purposes as contemporaries, and there would be about as much justification for thinking that Hegel might have been influenced by Comte, as that Comte was influenced by Hegel.

You will now appreciate the significance of the first, and in many ways the most remarkable, instance in which the similarity between the two thinkers was noticed. In 1824 Comte's young pupil Gustave d'Eichthal went to study in Germany. In his letters to Comte he soon reported excitedly from Berlin about his discovery of Hegel.[5] "There is," he wrote with regard to Hegel's lectures on the philosophy of history, "a marvelous agreement between your results, even though the principles are different, at least in appearance." He went on to say that "the identity of results exists even in the practical principles, as Hegel is a defender of the governments, that is to say, an enemy of the liberals." A few weeks later d'Eichthal was able to report that he had presented a copy of Comte's tract to Hegel, who had expressed satisfaction and greatly praised the first part, although he had doubts about the meaning of the method of observation recommended in the second part. And Comte not much later even expressed the naïve hope that "Hegel seemed to him in Germany the man most capable to push the positive philosophy." [6]

The later instances in which the similarity has been noticed are numerous, as I have already said. But although such widely used books as R. Flint's *Philosophy of History* [7] and J. T. Merz's *History of European Thought* [8] comment upon it, and such distinguished and diverse scholars as Alfred Fouillée [9] Émile Meyerson,[10] Thomas Wittaker,[11] Ernst Troeltsch,[12] and Eduard Spranger [13] have discussed it—I will keep for a note a score of other names I could mention [14] —little attempt has yet been made at a systematic examination of these similarities, though I must not omit mention of Friedrich Dittmann's comparative study of the philosophies of history of Comte and Hegel,[15] on which I shall draw in some measure.

§ 3.   More significant, perhaps, than any list of the names of those who have noticed the similarities is the long series of social thinkers of the last hundred years who testify to this kinship in a different and more effective manner. Indeed, still more surprising than the neglect of the similarities in the two original doctrines is the similar failure to notice the surprising number of leading figures who succeeded in combining in their own thought ideas derived from Hegel and Comte. Again, I can quote only a few of the names which belong here.[16] But if I tell you that the list includes Karl Marx, Friedrich Engels, and probably Ludwig Feuerbach in Germany, Ernest Renan, Hippolyte Taine, and Emile Durkheim in France, Giuseppe Mazzini in Italy— and I should probably add Benedetto Croce and John Dewey from the living—you will begin to see how far this influence reaches. When later I shall have occasion to show how we can trace to the same source such widespread intellectual movements as that peculiarly unhistorical approach to history which paradoxically is called historicism, much of what has been known as sociology during the last hundred years, and especially its most fashionable and most ambitious branch, the sociology of knowledge, you will perhaps understand the importance which I attach to this combined influence.

Before addressing myself to my main task, I must go through one more preliminary: I ought, in fairness, to acquaint you with a serious deficiency with which I approach it. So far as Comte is concerned, it is true that I strongly disagree with most of his views. But this disagreement is still of a kind which leaves room for profitable discussion because there exists at least some common basis. If it is true that criticism is worth-while only when one approaches one's object with at least this degree of sympathy, I am afraid I cannot claim this qualification with regard to Hegel. Concerning him I have always felt, not only what his greatest British admirer said, that his philosophy was "a scrutiny of thought so profound that it was for the most part unintelligible," [17] but also what John Stuart Mill experienced who "found by actual experience . . . that conversancy with him tends to deprave one's intellect." [18] I ought to warn you, therefore, that I do not pretend to understand Hegel. But, fortunately for my task, a comprehension of his system as a whole is not necessary. I think I know well enough those parts of his doctrines which have, or are supposed to have, influenced the development of the social sciences. Indeed, they are so well known that my task will consist largely in showing that many of the developments commonly ascribed to Hegel's influence might well in fact be due to Comte's. It seems to me that it is largely the support which the Hegelian tradition received from this quarter that accounts for the otherwise inexplicable fact that in the social sciences Hegelian thought and language continued to rule for so long after, in the other fields of science, the rule of his philosophy had long been superseded by that of exact science.

§ 4.   There is one feature, however, which their general theories of knowledge have in common, and which I must mention—for its own sake as well as because it will give me an opportunity to refer to an interesting question which I shall not have time to consider elsewhere in this paper: the original source of their common ideas.

The point of their doctrines to which I refer is one on which at first they may appear to hold diametrically opposed views: their attitude to empirical research. For Comte this constitutes the whole of science; for Hegel it is entirely outside what he calls science, although he by no means underrates the importance of factual knowledge within its sphere. What brings them together is their belief that empirical science must be purely descriptive, confined to establishing regularities of the observed phenomena. They are both strict phenomenalists in this sense, denying that empirical science can proceed from description to explanation. That the positivist Comte regards all explanation, all discussion of the manner in which the phenomena are produced, as futile metaphysics, while Hegel reserves it to his idealistic philosophy of nature, is a different matter. In their views on the functions of empirical research they agree almost completely, as Émile Meyerson has beautifully shown.[19] When Hegel argues, for example, that "empirical science has no business to assert the existence of anything that is not given to sense perception," [20] he is as much a positivist as Comte.

Now this phenomenalist approach to the problems of empirical science derives in modern times without question from Descartes, to whom both philosophers are directly indebted. And the same is, I believe, true of the second basic feature which they have in common and which will show up strongly in the more detailed points on which they agree: their common rationalism, or better, intellectualism. It was Descartes who first combined these apparently incompatible ideas of a phenomenalist or sensualist approach to physical science and a rationalist view of man's task and functions.[21] With respect to the points in which we are chiefly interested, it was mainly through Montesquieu,[22] d'Alembert,[23] Turgot, and Condorcet in France, Herder,[24] Kant, and Fichte in Germany, that the Cartesian heritage was passed on to Hegel and Comte. But what in those men had been merely bold and stimulating suggestions became with our two philosophers the bases of the two ruling systems of thought of their time. In thus stressing the common Cartesian origin of what I believe to be the common errors of Hegel and Comte, I wish, of course, not in the least to deprecate the great services which Descartes has rendered to modern thought. But as has been true with so many fertile ideas, a stage is often reached when their very success brings about their application to fields in which they are no longer appropriate. And this, I believe, is what Comte and Hegel have done.

§ 5.   When we turn to the field of social theory we find that the central ideas which Hegel and Comte have in common are so closely related that we can almost express them all in one sentence, if we give due weight to every single word. Such a statement would have to run somewhat like this: the central aim of all study of society must be to construct a universal history of all mankind, understood as a scheme of the necessary development of humanity according to recognizable laws. It is characteristic of the extent to which their ideas have entered into the whole intellectual make-up of our time, that, thus baldly stated, they now sound almost commonplace. Only when we analyze in greater detail the meaning and the implications of this statement do we become aware of the extraordinary nature of the undertaking which it proposes.

The laws which both seek—and it makes little difference that Comte presents them as "natural laws" [25] while for Hegel they are metaphysical principles—are in the first instances laws of the development of the human mind. They both claim, in other words, that our individual minds, which contribute to this process of development, are at the same time capable of comprehending it as a whole. It is the necessary succession of stages of the human mind determined by these dynamic laws which accounts for a corresponding succession of different civilizations, cultures, *Volksgeister,* or social systems.

Their common stress on the predominance of the intellectual development in this process, incidentally, in no way conflicts with the fact that the most influential tradition which they both inspired came misleadingly to be called the "materialist" interpretation of history. Comte, in this as in many other points nearer to Marx than Hegel, laid the foundation for this development with his stress on the predominant importance of our knowledge of nature; and the basic contention of the so-called materialist (or better, technological) interpretation of history is, after all, merely that it is our knowledge of nature and of technological possibilities which governs the development in other fields. The essential point, the belief that one's own mind should be capable of explaining itself, and the laws of its past and future development—I cannot explain here why to me this seems to involve a contradiction [26]—is the same with both, and it is derived by Marx, and through him by his disciples, from Hegel and Comte.

The conception of laws of succession of distinct stages in the development of the human mind in general, and in all its particular manifestations and concretizations, of course implies that these wholes or collectives can be directly apprehended as individuals of a species: that we can directly perceive civilizations or social systems as objectively given facts. Such a claim is not surprising in a system of idealism like Hegel's, that is, as a product of a conceptual realism or of "essentialism." [27] But it seems at first out of place in a naturalist system like Comte's. The fact is, however, that his phenomenalism which eschews all mental constructions and allows him to admit only of what can be directly observed, forces him into a position very similar to Hegel's. Since he cannot deny the existence of social structures, he must claim that they are immediately given to experience. In fact, he goes so far as to claim that the social wholes are undoubtedly better known and more directly observable than the elements of which they consist,[28] and that therefore social theory must start from our knowledge of the directly apprehended wholes.[29] Thus he, no less than Hegel, starts from intuitively apprehended abstract concepts of society or civilization, and then deductively derives from it his knowledge of the structure of the object. He even goes so far, surprisingly enough in a positivist, as to claim explicitly that from this conception of the total we can derive a priori knowledge about the necessary relations of the parts.[30] It is this which justifies it if Comte's positivism has sometimes been described as a system of idealism.[31] Like Hegel he treats as "concrete universals" [32] those social structures which in fact we come to know only by composing them, or building them up, from the familiar elements; and he even surpasses Hegel in claiming that only society as a whole is real and that the individual is only an abstraction.[33]

§ 6. The similarity of the treatment of social evolution by Hegel and Comte goes far beyond these methodological aspects. For both, society appears as an organism in a fairly literal sense. Both compare the stages through which social evolution must pass with the different ages through which individual man passes in his natural growth. And for both, the growth of the conscious control of his destiny by man is the main content of history.

Neither Comte nor Hegel was of course a historian, properly speaking—although it is not so very long since it was the fashion to describe them, in contrast to their predecessors, as "true historians" [34] because they were "scientific," which, presumably, meant that they aimed at the discovery of laws. But what they presented as the "historical method" soon began to displace the approach of the great historical school of a Niebuhr or a Ranke. It is customary to trace to

Hegel the rise of the later historicism [35] with its belief in the necessary succession of "stages" which manifest themselves in all fields of social life; but Comte's influence had probably more to do with it than Hegel's.

In the confused state of terminology on these matters,[36] it is perhaps necessary to say explicitly that I draw a sharp distinction between the "historical school" of the early nineteenth century and the majority of the later professional historians, and the historicism of a Marx, a Schmoller, or a Sombart. It was the latter who believed that with the discovery of laws of development they had the only key to true historical understanding, and who in an altogether unjustified arrogance claimed that the earlier writers, and particularly those of the eighteenth century, had been "unhistorical." It seems to me that in many respects David Hume, for example, had much more justification when he believed his "to be the historical age and [his] to be the historical nation" [37] than the historicists who tried to turn history into a theoretical science. The abuses to which this historicism ultimately led is best seen by the fact that even a thinker so close to it as Max Weber was once driven to describe the whole *Entwicklungsgedanke* as a "romantic swindle." [38] I have little to add to the masterly analysis of this historicism by my friend Karl Popper, hidden away in a wartime volume of *Economica*,[39] except that the responsibility for it seems to me to rest at least as much with Comte and positivism as with Plato and Hegel.

This historicism, let me repeat, was much less an affair of the historians proper than of the representatives of the other social sciences who applied what they believed to be the "historical method." Gustav Schmoller, the founder of the younger historical school in economics, is perhaps the best example of one who was clearly guided by the philosophy of Comte rather than that of Hegel.[40] But if the influence of this kind of historicism was perhaps most marked in economics, it was a fashion which, first in Germany and then elsewhere, affected all the social sciences. It could be shown to have influenced the history of art [41] no less than anthropology or philology. And the great popularity which "philosophies of history" have enjoyed during the last hundred years, theories which ascribed to the historical process an intelligible "meaning" and which pretended to show us a recognizable destiny of mankind, is essentially the result of this joint influence of Hegel and Comte.

§ 7.   I will not dwell here on another and perhaps only superficial resemblance between their theories: the fact that with Comte the necessary development proceeds according to the famous law of the three stages, while with Hegel a similar threefold rhythm is the result of the growth of mind as a dialectical process which proceeds from thesis to antithesis and synthesis. More important is the fact that for both men history leads to a predetermined end, that it can be interpreted teleologically as a succession of achieved purposes.

Their historical determinism—by which is meant, not merely that historical events are somehow determined, but that *we* are able to recognize why they were bound to take a particular course—necessarily implies a thorough fatalism: man cannot change the course of history. Even the outstanding individuals are, with Comte, merely "instruments" [42] or "organs of a predestined movement," [43] or with Hegel *Geschäftsführer des Weltgeistes,* managers of the World Spirit whom Reason cunningly uses for its own purposes.

There is no room for freedom in such a system: for Comte freedom is "the rational submission to the domination of natural laws," [44] that is, of course, his natural laws of inevitable development; for Hegel it is the recognition of necessity.[45] And since both are in possession of the secret of the "definitive and permanent intellectual unity" [46] to which evolution is tending according to Comte, or of the "absolute truth" in Hegel's sense, they both claim for themselves the right to impose a new orthodoxy. But I have to admit that in this as in many other respects the much abused Hegel is still infinitely more liberal than the "scientific" Comte. There are in Hegel no such fulminations against the unlimited liberty of conscience as we find throughout the work of Comte, and Hegel's attempt to use the machinery of the Prussian state to impose an official doctrine [47] appears very tame compared with Comte's plan for a new "religion of humanity" and all his other thoroughly anti-liberal schemes for regimentation which even his old admirer John Stuart Mill ultimately branded as "liberticide." [48]

I have not the time to show in any detail how these similar political attitudes are reflected in equally similar evaluations of different historical periods or of different institutions. I will merely mention, as particularly characteristic, that the two thinkers show the same dislike of Periclean Greece and of the Renaissance, and the same admiration for Frederick the Great.[49]

§ 8. The last major point of agreement between Hegel and Comte which I will mention is no more than a consequence of their historicism. But it has exercised so much independent influence that I must discuss it separately. It is their thorough moral relativism, their conviction either that all moral rules can be recognized as justified by the circumstances of the time, or that only those are valid which can be thus explicitly justified—it is not always clear which they mean. This idea is, of course, merely an application of historical determinism, of the belief that we can adequately explain why people at different times believed what they actually did believe. This pretended insight into the manner in which people's thought is determined implies the claim that we can know what they ought to believe in given circumstances, and the dismissal as irrational or inappropriate of all moral rules which cannot be thus justified.

In this connection historicism shows most clearly its rationalist or intellectualist character: [50] Since the determination of all historical development is to be intelligible, only such forces as can be fully understood by us can have been at work. Comte's attitude on this is really not very different from Hegel's statement that all that is real is rational and all that is rational is also real [51]—only that instead of rational Comte would have said historically necessary and therefore justified. Everything appears to him as in this sense justified in its time, slavery and cruelty, superstition and intolerance, because—this he does not say but it is implied in his reasoning—there are no moral rules which we must accept as transcending our individual reason, nothing which is a given and unconscious presupposition of all our thought, and by which we must judge moral issues. Indeed, he significantly could not conceive of, any other possibility except either a system of morals designed and revealed by a higher being, or one demonstrated by our own reason.[52] And between these two the necessary superiority of the "demonstrated morals" seemed to him unquestionable. Comte was both more consistent and more extreme than Hegel. He had indeed already stated the main conception in his very first publication when, at the age of nineteen, he wrote: "There is nothing good and nothing bad, absolutely speaking; everything is relative, this is the only absolute statement." [53]

It is possible, however, that with regard to this particular point I am attributing too much importance to the influence of our two philosophers, and that they were merely following a general fashion of their time which fitted in with their systems of thought. How rapidly moral relativism was then spreading we can see clearly in an interesting exchange of letters between Thomas Carlyle and John Stuart Mill. As early as January 1833 we find Carlyle writing to Mill with reference to a recently published *History of the French Revolution*: [54] "Has not this man Thiers a wonderful system of Ethics *in petto*? He will prove to you that the power to have done a thing almost (if not altogether) gave you the right to do it: every hero of his turns out to be perfectly justified—he has succeeded in doing." [55] To which Mill replied: "You have characterized Thiers' system of ethics most accurately. I am afraid it is too just a specimen of the young French *Litterateurs,* and that this is *all* they have made, ethically speaking, of their attempts to imitate the Germans in identifying themselves with the *past.* By dint of shifting their point of view to make it accord with that of whomever they are affecting to judge, coupled with their historical fatalism, they have arrived at the annihilation of all moral distinctions except *success* and *not success.*" [56] It is interesting that Mill, who knew very well how these ideas had been spread in France by the Saint-Simonians, yet explicitly ascribes their appearance in a young French historian to German influence.

That these views lead both Comte and Hegel to a complete moral and legal positivism [57]—and at times desperately close to the doctrine that Might is Right—I can mention only in passing. I believe that quite a good case could be made out that they are among the main sources of the modern tradition of legal positivism. It is, after all, only another manifestation of the same general attitude that refuses to admit anything as relevant which cannot be recognized as the expression of conscious reason.

§ 9. This brings me back to the common central idea which under-lies all these particular similarities of the doctrines of Comte and Hegel: the idea that we can improve upon the results of the earlier individualist approaches with their modest endeavor to understand how individual minds interact, by studying Human Reason, with a capital R, from the outside as it were, as something objectively given and observable as a whole, as it might appear to some supermind. From the belief that they had achieved the old ambition of *se ipsam cognoscere mentem,* and that they had reached a position where they were able to predict the future course of the growth of Reason, it was only one step more to the still more presumptuous idea that Reason should now be able to pull itself up by its own bootstraps to its definitive or absolute state. It is in the last analysis this intellectual *hubris,* the seeds of which were sown by Descartes, and perhaps already by Plato, which is the common trait in Hegel and Comte. The concern with the movement of Reason as a whole not only prevented them from understanding the process through which the interaction of individuals produced structures of relationships which performed actions no individual reason could fully comprehend, but it also made them blind to the fact that the attempt of conscious reason to control its own development could only have the effect of limiting this very growth to what the individual directing mind could foresee.[58] Although this aspiration is a direct product of a certain brand of rationalism, it seems to me to be the result of a misunder-stood rationalism, better called intellectualism—a rationalism which fails in its most important task, namely, in recognizing the limits of what individual conscious reason can accomplish.

Hegel and Comte both singularly fail to make intelligible how the interaction of the efforts of individuals can create something greater than they know. While Adam Smith and the other great Scottish individualists of the eighteenth century—even though they spoke of the "invisible hand"—provided such an explanation,[59] all that Hegel and Comte give us is a mysterious teleological force. And while eighteenth-century individualism, essentially humble in its aspira-tions, aimed at understanding as well as possible the principles by which the individual efforts combined to produce a civilization in order to learn what were the conditions most favorable to its further growth, Hegel and Comte became the main source of that hubris of collectivism which aims at "conscious direction" of all forces of society.

§ 10. I must now attempt to illustrate briefly, by a few more examples, the hints I have already given about the course which the common influence of Hegel and Comte took. One of the most interesting to study in detail would be that once very famous but now largely forgotten German philosopher, Ludwig Feuerbach. It would be even more significant if that old Hegelian who became the founder of German positivism had arrived at that position without any knowledge of Comte; but circumstances make it very probable that he too had at an early stage become acquainted with Comte's first *Système*.[60] How enormous his influence was, not only on the other radical Young Hegelians but on the whole rising generation, is best seen in the account given by Friedrich Engels, who describes how they "all became at once Feuerbachians." [61]

The blend of Hegelianism and positivism which Feuerbach provided [62] became characteristic of the thought of the whole group of German social theorists who appeared in the 1840's. Only one year after Feuerbach had broken away from Hegel because, as he later said, he had recognized that the absolute truth meant merely the absolute professor,[63] the same year in which the last volume of Comte's *Cours* appeared and when, incidentally, the young Karl Marx sent his first work to the printers, namely, in 1842, another author, who was very influential and representative of the time, Lorenz von Stein, published his *Socialism and Communism in France,* which admittedly attempted a fusion of Hegelian and Saint-Simonian and therefore Comtian thought.[64] It has often been noticed that in this work Stein anticipated much of the historical theories of Karl Marx.[65] This fact becomes even more suggestive when we find that another man who was later discovered as a precursor of Karl Marx, the Frenchman Jules Lechevalier, was an old Saint-Simonian who had actually studied under Hegel in Berlin.[66] He preceded Stein by ten years, but remained for some time an isolated figure in France. But in Germany Hegelian positivism, if I may so call it, became the dominant trend of thought. It was in this atmosphere that both Karl

Marx and Friedrich Engels formed their now famous theories of history, largely Hegelian in language but, I believe, much more indebted to Saint-Simon and Comte than is commonly realized.[67] And it was those similarities which I have discussed which made it so easy for them to retain Hegelian language for the exposition of a theory which, as Marx himself said, in some respects turned Hegel upside down.

It is probably also more than an accident that it was almost at the same time, in 1841 and in 1843, that two men who were much nearer to a natural science approach to social study than they were to Hegel, Friedrich List [68] and Wilhelm Roscher,[69] began the tradition of historicism in economics which became the model that the other social sciences soon eagerly followed. It was in those fifteen or twenty years following 1842 [70] that the ideas developed and spread which gave Germany for the first time a leading position in the social sciences; and it was to some extent by way of re-export from Germany (though partly also from England through Mill and Buckle), that French historians and sociologists such as Taine [71] and Durkheim[72] became familiar with the positivist tradition at the same time as with Hegelianism.

It was under the banner of this historicism made in Germany that in the second half of the ninteenth century the great attack on individualist social theory was conducted, that the very foundations of individualist and liberal society came to be questioned, and that both historical fatalism and ethical relativism became dominant traditions. And it was particularly under its influence that, from Marx to Sombart and Spengler, "philosophies of history" became the most influential expression of the attitude of the age to social problems.[73] Its most characteristic expression, however, is probably the so-called sociology of knowledge which to the present day in its two distinct yet closely similar branches still shows how the two strands of thought originating from Comte and Hegel operate sometimes side by side and sometimes in combination.[74] And, last but not least, most of modern socialism derives its theoretical foundation from that *Alliance intellectuelle franco-allemande,* as Celestin Bouglé has called it,[75] which was in the main an alliance of German Hegelianism and French positivism.

Let me conclude this historical sketch by one more remark. After 1859, as far as the social sciences are concerned, the influence of Darwin could do little more than confirm an already existing tendency. Darwinism may have assisted the introduction into the Anglo-Saxon world of ready-fashioned evolutionary theories. But if we examine such scientific "revolutions" as were attempted in the social sciences under the influence of Darwin, for example by Thorstein Veblen and his disciples, they appear in fact as little more than a revival of the ideas which German historicism had developed under the influence of Hegel and Comte. I suspect, though I have no proof, that on closer investigation even this American branch of historicism would prove to have more direct connections with the original source of these ideas.[76]

§ *11.* It is impossible in this brief paper to do full justice to so big a subject. Least of all can I hope, with the few remarks I have been able to make on the filiation of ideas, to have convinced you that they are correct in every detail. But I trust I have at least provided sufficient evidence to persuade you of the burden of my argument: that we are still, largely without knowing it, under the influence of ideas which have almost imperceptibly crept into modern thought because they were shared by the founders of what seemed to be radically opposed traditions. In these matters we are to a great extent still guided by ideas which are at least a century old, just as the nineteenth century was mainly guided by the ideas of the eighteenth. But while the ideas of Hume and Voltaire, of Adam Smith and Kant, produced the liberalism of the nineteenth century, those of Hegel and Comte, of Feuerbach and Marx, have produced the totalitarianism of the twentieth.

It may well be true that we as scholars tend to overestimate the influence which we can exercise on contemporary affairs. But I doubt whether it is possible to overestimate the influence which ideas have in the long run. And there can be no question that it is our special duty to recognize the currents of thought which still operate in public opinion, to examine their significance, and, if necessary, to refute them. It was an attempt to fulfill at least the first part of this duty which I have tried to outline in this paper.

NOTES

Part One

1. This is not universally true. The attempts to treat social phenomena "scientistically," which became so influential in the 19th century, were not completely absent in the 18th. There is at least a strong element of it in the work of Montesquieu, and of the Physiocrats. But the great achievements of the century in the theory of the social sciences, the works of Cantillon and Hume, of Turgot and Adam Smith, were on the whole free from it.

2. The earliest example of the modern narrow use of the term "science" given in Murray's *New English Dictionary* dates from as late as 1867. But T. Merz (*History of European Thought in the Nineteenth Century*, vol. I, 1896, p. 89) is probably right when he suggests that "science" has acquired its present meaning about the time of the formation of the British Association for the Advancement of Science (1831).

3. E.g. J. Dalton's *New System of Chemical Philosophy*, 1808; Lamarck's *Philosophie Zoologique*, 1809, or Fourcroy's *Philosophie chimique*, 1806.

4. We shall use the term Science with a capital letter when we wish to emphasize that we use it in the modern narrow meaning.

5. See M. R. Cohen, "The Myth about Bacon and the Inductive Method," *Scientific Monthly*, vol. XXIII, 1926, p. 505.

6. Murray's *New English Dictionary* knows both "scientism" and "scientis-tic," the former as the "habit and mode of expression of a man of science," the latter as "characteristic of, or having the attributes of, a scientist (used depreciatively)." The terms "naturalistic" and "mechanistic," which have often been used in a similar sense, are less appropriate because they tend to suggest the wrong kind of contrast.

7. See e.g. J. Fiolle, *Scientisme et Science*, Paris, 1936, and A. Lalande, *Vocabulaire technique et critique de la philosophie*, 4th ed., vol. II, p. 740.

8. Perhaps the following passage by a distinguished physicist may help to show how much the scientists themselves suffer from the same attitude which has given their influence on other disciplines such a baneful character: "It is difficult to conceive of anything more scientifically bigoted than to postulate that all possible experience conforms to the same type as that with which we are already familiar, and therefore to demand that explanation use only elements familiar in everyday experience. Such an attitude bespeaks an unimaginativeness, a mental obtuseness and obstinacy, which might be expected to have exhausted their pragmatic justification at a lower plane of mental activity." (P. W. Bridgman, *The Logic of Modern Physics*, 1928, p. 46.)

9. On the significance of this "law of inertia" in the scientific sphere and its effects on the social disciplines see H.

207

Münsterberg, *Grundzüge der Psychologie*, 1909, vol. I, p. 137; E. Bernheim, *Lehrbuch der historischen Methode und Geschichts-philosophie*, 5th ed., 1908, p. 144, and L. v. Mises, *Nationalökonomie*, 1940, p. 24. The phenomenon that we tend to overstrain a new principle of explanation is, perhaps, more familiar with respect to particular scientific doctrines than with respect to Science as such. Gravitation and evolution, relativity and psycho-analysis, all have for certain periods been strained far beyond their capacity. That for Science as a whole the phenomenon has lasted even longer and had still more far-reaching effects is not surprising in the light of this experience.

10. This view was, I believe, first explicitly formulated by the German physicist G. Kirchhoff in his *Vorlesungen über die mathematische Physik; Mechanik*, 1874, p. 1, and later made widely known through the philosophy of Ernst Mach.

11. The word "explain" is only one of many important instances where the natural sciences were forced to use concepts originally formed to describe human phenomena. "Law" and "cause," "function" and "order," "organism" and "organization" are others of similar importance where Science has more or less succeeded in freeing them from their anthropomorphic connotations, while in other instances, particularly, as we shall see, in the case of "purpose," though it cannot entirely dispense with them, it has not yet succeeded in doing so and is therefore with some justification afraid of using these terms.

12. Cf. T. Percy Nunn, *Anthropomorphism and Physics* (*Proceedings of the British Academy*, vol. XIII), 1926.

13. L. S. Stebbing, *Thinking to Some Purpose* ("Pelican" Books), 1939, p. 107. Cf. also B. Russell, *The Scientific Outlook*, 1931, p. 85.

14. The comparison becomes more adequate if we conceive that only small groups of characters, say words, appear to us simultaneously, while the groups as such appear to us only in a definite time sequence, as the words (or phrases) actually do when we read.

15. The old puzzle over the miracle that qualities which are supposed to attach to the things are transmitted to the brain in the form of indistinguishable nervous processes differing only in the organ which they affect, and then in the brain re-translated into the original qualities, ceases to exist. We have no evidence for the assumption that the things in the external world in their relations to each other differ or are similar in the way our senses suggest to us. In fact we have in many instances evidence to the contrary.

16. It may just be mentioned that this classification is probably based on a pre-conscious learning of those relationships in the external world which are of special relevance for the existence of the human organism in the kind of environment in which it developed, and that it is closely connected with the infinite number of "conditioned reflexes" which the human species had to acquire in the course of its evolution. The classification of the stimuli in our central nervous system is probably highly "pragmatic" in the sense that it is not based on all observable relations between the external things, but stresses those relations between the external world (in the narrower sense) and our body which in the course of evolution have proved significant for the survival of the species. The human brain will e.g. classify external stimuli largely by their association with stimuli emanating from the reflex action of parts of the human body caused by the same external stimulus without the intervention of the brain.

17. That different people classify external stimuli in the "same" way does not mean that individual sense qualities are the same for different people (which would be a meaningless statement) but that the systems of sense qualities of different people have a common structure (are homeomorphic systems of relations).

18. Most of the problems of this latter group will, however, raise problems of the kind characteristic of the social sciences proper when we attempt to explain them.

19. Sometimes the German term *Geisteswissenschaften* is now used in English to describe the social sciences in the specific narrow sense with which we are here concerned. But considering that this German term was introduced by the translator of J. S. Mill's *Logic* to render the latter's "moral sciences," there seems to be little case for using this translation instead of the original English term.

20. It has often been suggested that for this reason economics and the other theoretical sciences of society should be described as "teleological" sciences. This term is, however, misleading as it is apt to suggest that not only the actions of individual men but also the social structures which they produce are deliberately designed by somebody for a purpose. It leads thus either to an "explanation" of social phenomena in terms of ends fixed by some superior power or to the opposite and no less fatal mistake of regarding all social phenomena as the product of conscious human design, to a "pragmatic" interpretation which is a bar to all real understanding of these phenomena. Some authors, particularly O. Spann, have used the term "teleological" to justify the most abstruse metaphysical speculations. Others, like K. Englis, have used it in an unobjectionable manner and sharply distinguished between "teleological" and "normative" sciences. (See particularly the illuminating discussions of the problem in K. Englis, *Teleologische Theorie der Wirtschaft*, Brünn, 1930.) But the term remains nevertheless misleading. If a name is needed the term "praxeological" sciences, deriving from A. Espinas, adopted by T. Kotarbinsky and E. Slutsky, and now clearly defined and extensively used by L. v. Mises (*Nationalökonomie*, Geneva, 1940) would appear to be the most appropriate.

21. While the great majority of the objects or events which determine human action, and which from that angle have to be defined not by their physical characteristics but by the human attitudes towards them, are means for an end, this does not mean that the purposive or "teleological" nature of their definition is the essential point. The human purposes for which different things serve are the most important but still only one kind of human attitudes which will form the basis of such classification. A ghost or a bad or good omen belong no less to the class of events determining human action which have no physical counterpart, although they cannot possibly be regarded as instruments of human action.

22. I believe also in the discussions on psychological methods.

23. It is sheer illusion when some sociologists believe that they can make "crime" an objective fact by defining it as those acts for which a person is punished. This only pushes the subjective element a step further back, but does not eliminate it. "Punishment" is still a subjective thing which cannot be defined in objective terms. If, e.g., we see that every time a person commits a certain act he is made to wear a chain round his neck, this does not tell us whether it is a reward or a punishment.

24. This is a development which has

probably been carried out most consistently by L. v. Mises and I believe that most peculiarities of his views which at first strike many readers as strange and unacceptable are due to the fact that in the consistent development of the subjectivist approach he has for a long time moved ahead of his contemporaries. Probably all the characteristic features of his theories, from his theory of money (so much ahead of the time in 1912!) to what he calls his *a priorism*, his views about mathematical economics in general and the measurement of economic phenomena in particular, and his criticism of planning all follow directly (although, perhaps, not all with the same necessity) from this central position. See particularly his *Grundprobleme der Nationalökonomie* (Jena, 1933) and *Human Action*, 1949.

25. This was seen very clearly by some of the early economists, but later obscured by the attempts to make economics "objective" in the sense of the natural sciences. Ferdinando Galiani, e.g., in his *Della Moneta* (1751) emphasized that "those things are equal which afford equal satisfaction to the one with respect to whom they are said to be equivalent. Anyone who seeks equality elsewhere, following other principles, and expects to find it in weight, or similarity of appearance, will show little understanding of the facts of human life. A sheet of paper is often the equivalent of money, from which it differs both in weight and appearance; on the other hand, two moneys of equal weight and quality, and similar appearance, are often not equal." (Translation from A. E. Monroe, *Early Economic Thought*, 1930, p. 303)

26. Except probably linguistics, for which it may indeed be claimed with some justification that it "is of strategic importance for the methodology of the social sciences" (E. Sapir, *Selected Writings*, University of California Press 1949, p. 166). Edward Sapir, whose writings were unknown to me when I wrote this essay, stresses many of the points here emphasized. See, for instance, *ibid.* p. 46: "no entity in human experience can be adequately defined as the mechanical sum or product of its physical properties," and "all significant entities in experience are thus revised from the physically given by passing through the filter of the functionally or relatedly meaningful."

27. In the extreme Ricardian form the statement is, of course, that a change in the value of the product will affect *only* the value of the land and leave the value of the co-operating labor altogether unaffected. In this form (connected with Ricardo's "objective" theory of value) the proposition can be regarded as a limiting case of the more general proposition stated in the text.

28. For some further discussion of these problems see the author's article "Economics and Knowledge," *Economica*, February, 1937, and reprinted in *Individualism and Economic Order*, Chicago, 1948.

29. Cf. C. V. Langlois and C. Seignobos, *Introduction to the Study of History*, trans. by G. G. Berry, London 1898, p. 218: "Actions and words all have this characteristic, that each was the action or word of an individual; the imagination can only represent to itself *individual* acts, copies from those which are brought before us by direct observation. As these are the actions of men living in society, most of them are performed simultaneously by several individuals, or are directed to some common end. These are collective acts; but in the imagination as in direct observation, they always reduce to a sum of individual actions. The "social fact," as recognized by certain sociologists, is

a philosophical construction, not a historical fact."

30. Cf. the excellent discussions of the effects of conceptual realism (*Begriffsrealismus*) on economics in W. Eucken, *The Foundations of Economics*, London, 1950, pp. 51 *et seq.*

31. In some contexts concepts which by another social science are treated as mere theories to be revised and improved upon may have to be treated as data. One could, e.g., conceive of a "science of politics" showing what kind of political action follows from the people holding certain views on the nature of society and for which these views would have to be treated as data. But while in man's actions towards social phenomena, i.e., in explaining his political actions, we have to take his views about the constitution of society as given, we can on a different level of analysis investigate their truth or untruth. The fact that a particular society may believe that its institutions have been created by divine intervention we would have to accept as a fact in explaining the politics of that society; but it need not prevent us from showing that this view is probably false.

32. Cf. Robbins, *An Essay on the Nature and Significance of Economic Science*, 2nd ed., 1935, p. 105: "In Economics . . . the ultimate constituents of our fundamental generalizations are known to us by immediate acquaintance. In the natural sciences they are known only inferentially." Perhaps the following quotation from an earlier essay of my own (*Collectivist Economic Planning*, 1935, p. 11) may help further to explain the statement in the text: "The position of man, midway between natural and social phenomena—of the one of which he is an effect and of the other a cause—brings it about that the essential basic facts which we need for the explanation are part of common experience, part of the stuff of our thinking. In the social sciences it is the elements of the complex phenomena which are known to us beyond the possibility of dispute. In the natural sciences they can be at best surmised." Cf. also C. Menger, *Untersuchungen über die Methoden der Socialwissenschaften*, 1883, p. 157, note: "Die letzten Elemente, auf welche die exacte theoretische Interpretation der Naturphänomene zurückgehen muss, sind 'Atome' und 'Kräfte'. Beide sind unempirischer Natur. Wir vermögen uns 'Atome' überhaupt nicht, und die Naturkräfte nur unter einem Bilde vorzustellen, und verstehen wir in Wahrheit unter den letzteren lediglich die uns unbekannten Ursachen realer Bewegungen. Hieraus ergeben sich für die exacte Interpretation der Naturphänomene in letzter Linie ganz ausserordentliche Schwierigkeiten. Anders in den exacten Socialwissenschaften. Hier sind die menschlichen *Individuen und ihre Bestrebungen*, die letzten Elemente unserer Analyse, empirischer Natur und die exacten theoretischen Socialwissenschaften somit in grossem Vortheil gegenüber den exacten Naturwissenschaften, Die 'Grenzen des Naturerkennens' und die hieraus für das theoretische Verständnis der Naturphänomene sich ergebenden Schwierigkeiten bestehen in Wahrheit nicht für die exacte Forschung auf dem Gebiete der Socialerscheinungen. Wenn A. Comte die 'Gesellschaften' als reale Organismen, und zwar als Organismen komplicirterer Art, denn die natürlichen, auffasst und ihre theoretische Interpretation als das unvergleichlich kompliciertere und schwierigere wissenschaftliche Problem bezeichnet, so findet er sich somit in einem schweren Irrthume. Seine Theorie wäre nur gegenüber Socialforschern richtig, welche den, mit Rücksicht auf den heutigen Zustand der theoretischen Naturwissenschaften, geradezu wahn-

witzigen Gedanken fassen würden, die Gesellschaftsphänomene nicht in specifisch socialwissenschaftlich, sondern in naturwissenschaftlich-atomistischer Weise interpretiren zu wollen."

33. I have borrowed the term *compositive* from a manuscript note of Carl Menger who in his personal annotated copy of Schmoller's review of his *Methoden der Socialwissenschaften* (*Jahrbuch für Gesetzgebung, etc.,* N.F., 7, 1883, p. 42) wrote it above the word *deductive* used by Schmoller. Since writing this I have noticed that Ernst Cassierer in his *Philosophie der Aufklärung* (1932, pp. 12, 25, 341) uses the term "compositive" in order to point out rightly that the procedure of the natural sciences presupposes the successive use of the "resolutive" and the "compositive" technique. This is useful and links up with the point that, since the elements are directly known to us in the social sciences, we can start here with the compositive procedure.

34. As Robbins (l.c., p. 86) rightly says, economists in particular regard "the things which psychology studies as the data of their own deductions."

35. That this task absorbs a great part of the economist's energies should not deceive us about the fact that by itself this "pure logic of choice" (or "economic calculus") does not explain any facts, or at least does no more so by itself than does mathematics. For the precise relationship between the pure theory of the economic calculus and its use in the explanation of social phenomena I must once more refer to my article "Economics and Knowledge" (*Economica,* February, 1937). It should perhaps be added that while economic theory might be very useful to the director of a completely planned system in helping him to see what he ought to do to achieve his ends, it would not help us to explain his actions —except in so far as he was actually guided by it.

36. Cf. M. R. Cohen, *Reason and Nature,* p. 356: "If, then, social phenomena depend upon more factors than we can readily manipulate, even the doctrine of universal determinism will not guarantee an attainable expression of laws governing the specific phenomena of social life. Social phenomena, though determined, might not to a finite mind in limited time display any laws at all."

37. Pareto himself has clearly seen this. After stating the nature of the factors determining the prices in his system of equations, he adds (*Manuel d'économie politique,* 2nd ed., 1927, pp. 233-4): "It may be mentioned here that this determination has by no means the purpose of arriving at a numerical calculation of prices. Let us make the most favorable assumptions for such a calculation; let us assume that we have triumphed over all the difficulties of finding the data of the problem and that we know the *ophélimités* of all the different commodities for each individual, and all the conditions of production of all the commodities, etc. This is already an absurd hypothesis to make. Yet it is not sufficient to make the solution of the problem possible. We have seen that in the case of 100 persons and 700 commodities there will be 70,699 conditions (actually a great number of circumstances which we have so far neglected will still increase that number); we shall, therefore, have to solve a system of 70,699 equations. This exceeds practically the power of algebraic analysis, and this is even more true if one contemplates the fabulous number of equations which one obtains for a population of forty millions and several thousand commodities. In this case the roles would be changed: it would not be mathematics which would assist political economy, but political econ-

omy which would assist mathematics. In other words, if one really could know all these equations, the only means to solve them which is available to human powers is to observe the practical solution given by the market." Compare also A. Cournot, *Researches into the Mathematical Principles of the Theory of Wealth* (1838), trans. by N. T. Bacon, New York, 1927, p. 127, where he says that if in our equations we took the entire economic system into consideration "this would surpass the powers of mathematical analysis and of our practical methods of calculation, even if the values of all the constants could be assigned to them numerically."

38. Cf. above pp. 20 *et seq.*

39. The attempts often made to evade this difficulty by an *illustrative* enumeration of some of the physical attributes by which we recognize the object as belonging to one of these mental categories are just begging the question. To say that when we speak about a man being angry we mean that he shows certain physical symptoms helps us very little unless we can exhaustively enumerate all the symptoms by which we ever recognize, and which always when they are present mean, that the man who shows them is angry. Only if we could do this would it be legitimate to say that in using this term we mean no more than *certain* physical phenomena.

40. This must also serve as a justification for what may have seemed the very loose way in which we have throughout, in illustrative enumerations of mental entities, indiscriminately lumped together such concepts as "sensation," "perceptions," "concepts," or "ideas." These different types of mental entities all have in common that they are classifications of possible external stimuli (or complexes of such stimuli). This contention will perhaps

appear less strange now than would have been the case fifty years ago, since in the configurations or *Gestalt* qualities we have become familiar with something which is intermediate between the old "elementary" sense qualities and concepts. It may be added that on this view there would, however, seem to be no justification for the unwarranted ontological conclusions which many members of the *Gestalt* school draw from their interesting observations; there is no reason to assume that the "wholes" which we perceive are properties of the external world and not merely ways in which our mind classifies complexes of stimuli; like other abstractions, the relations between the parts thus singled out may be significant or not.

Perhaps it should also be mentioned here that there is no reason to regard values as the only purely mental categories which do therefore not appear in our picture of the physical world. Although values must necessarily occupy a central place wherever we are concerned with purposive action, they are certainly not the only kind of purely mental categories which we shall have to employ in interpreting human activities: the distinction between true and false provides at least one other instance of such purely mental categories which is of great importance in this connection. On the connected point that it is not necessarily value considerations which will guide us in selecting the aspects of social life which we study, see note 62 below.

41. Which, as we have already seen, does, of course, not mean that it will always treat only elements which have common properties as members of the same class.

42. Cf. p. 42 above.

43. Cf. the comment on this by Carl Menger in the passage quoted in note 32 above.

44. Cf. above p. 23.

45. It should, perhaps, be emphasized that there is no necessary connection between the use of mathematics in the social sciences and the attempts to measure social phenomena—as particularly people who are acquainted only with elementary mathematics are apt to believe. Mathematics may—and in economics probably is—absolutely indispensable to describe certain types of complex structural relationships, though there may be no chance of ever knowing the numerical values of the concrete magnitudes (misleadingly called "constants") which appear in the formulae describing these structures.

46. M. R. Cohen, *Reason and Nature*, p. 305.

47. Cf. L. Hogben (in *Lancelot Hogben's Dangerous Thoughts*, 1939, p. 99): "Plenty is the excess of free energy over the collective calory debt of human effort applied to securing the needs which all human beings share."

48. The description of this contrast as one between the view from the inside and the view from the outside, though, of course, metaphorical, is less misleading than such metaphors usually are and perhaps the best short way to indicate the nature of the contrast. It brings out that what of social complexes is directly known to us are only the parts and that the whole is never directly perceived but always reconstructed by an effort of our imagination.

49. It would, of course, be false to believe that the first instinct of the student of social phenomena is any less to "go and see." It is not ignorance of the obvious but long experience which has taught him that directly to look for the wholes which popular language suggests to exist leads nowhere. It has, indeed, rightly become one of the first maxims which the student of social phenomena learns (or ought to learn) never to speak of "society" or a "country" acting or behaving in a certain manner, but always and exclusively to think of individuals as acting.

50. Cf. above p. 38.

51. Cf. F. Kaufmann, "Soziale Kollektiva," *Zeitschrift für Nationalökonomie*, Vol. I, 1930.

52. It should be noted that, though observation may assist us to understand what people mean by the terms they use, it can never tell us what a "market" or "capital," etc., really are, i.e., which are the significant relations that it is useful to single out and combine into a model.

53. On this whole problem, see M. Ginsberg, *The Psychology of Society*, 1921, chapter IV.—What is said in the text does of course not preclude the possibility that our study of the way in which individual minds interact may reveal to us a structure which operates in some respects similarly to the individual mind. And it might be possible that the term collective mind would prove the best term available to describe such structures—though it is most unlikely that the advantages of the use of this term would ever outweigh its disadvantages. But even if this were the case the employment of this term should not mislead us into thinking that it describes any observable object that can be directly studied.

54. *Cours de philosophie positive*, Vol. IV (2nd-4th ed.), p. 258.

55. Cf. Ernst Mach, *Erkenntnis und Irrtum*, 3rd ed., 1917, p. 28, where, however, he points out correctly that "Könnten wir die Menschen aus grösserer Entfernung, aus der Vogelperspektive, vom Monde aus beobachten, so würden die feineren Einzelheiten mit den von individuellen Erlebnissen herrührenden Einflüssen für uns verschwinden, und wir würden nichts wahrnehmen, als Menschen, die mit grosser Regelmässigkeit wachsen, sich nähren, sich fortpflanzen."

56. G. Meinecke, *Die Entstehung des Historismus,* 1936. The term historicism applied to the older historical school discussed by Meinecke is inappropriate and misleading since it was introduced by Carl Menger (see *Untersuchungen über die Methoden der Sozialwissenschaften,* 1883 pp. 216-220 —with reference to Gervinus and Roscher—and *Die Irrthümer des Historismus,* 1884) to describe the distinguishing features of the younger historical school in economics represented by Schmoller and his associates. Nothing shows more clearly the difference between this younger historical school and the earlier movement from which it inherited the name than that it was Schmoller who accused Menger of being an adherent of the "Burke-Savigny school" and not the other way round. (Cf. G. Schmoller, "Zur Methodologie der Staats-und Socialwissenschaften," *Jahrbuch für Gesetzgebung,* etc., N.F., Vol. VII, 1886, p. 250).

57. Although in its German origins the connection of historicism with positivism is perhaps less conspicuous than is the case with its English followers such as Ingram or Ashley, it was no less present and is overlooked only because historicism is erroneously connected with the historical method of the older historians, instead of with the views of Roscher, Hildebrandt and particularly Schmoller and his circle.

58. It will be noted that this, still restricted, use of the term "science" (in the sense in which the Germans speak of *Gesetzeswissenschaft*) is wider than the even narrower sense in which its meaning is confined to the theoretical sciences of nature.

59. Cf. e.g., E. F. M. Durbin, "Methods of Research—A Plea for Co-operation in the Social Sciences," *Economic Journal,* June, 1938, p. 191, where the writer argues that in the social sciences "unlike the natural sciences, our sub-divisions are largely (though not entirely) *abstractions from* reality rather than *sections* of reality" and asserts of the natural sciences that "in all these cases the object of study are real independent objects and groups. They are not aspects of something complex. They are real things." How this can be really asserted, e.g., of Crystallography (one of Mr. Durbin's examples) is difficult to comprehend.—This argument has been extremely popular with the members of the German historical school in economics, though, it should be added, Mr. Durbin is probably entirely unaware how closely his whole attitude resembles that of the *Kathedersozialisten* of that school.

60. For a good survey of the modern theories of historical relativism see M. Mandelbaum, *The Problem of Historical Knowledge,* New York, 1938.

61. Cf. note 64 below.

62. It is not possible to pursue further here the interesting question of the reasons which make the historian ask particular questions and which make him ask at different times different questions about the same period. We ought, however, perhaps briefly to refer to one view which has exercised wide influence, since it claims application not only to history but to all *Kulturwissenschaften.* It is Rickert's contention that the social sciences, to which, according to him, the historical method is alone appropriate, select their object exclusively with reference to certain values with respect to which they are important. Unless by "value consideration" (*Wertbezogenheit*) any kind of practical interest in a problem is meant so that this concept would include the reasons which make us, say, study the geology of Cumberland, this is certainly not necessarily the case. If, merely to indulge my taste in detective work, I try to find out why in the year x Mr. N. has been elected mayor

of Cambridge, this is no less historical work though no known value may have been affected by the fact that Mr. N. rather than somebody else has been elected. It is not the reason why we are interested in a problem but the character of the problem which makes it a historical problem.

63. It does not alter the essential fact that the theorizing will usually already have been done for the historian by his source which in reporting the "facts" will use such terms as "state" or "town" which cannot be defined by physical characteristics but which refer to a complex of relationships which, made explicit, is a "theory" of the subject.

64. The confusion which reigns in this field has evidently been assisted by a purely verbal confusion apt to arise in German in which most of the discussions of this problem have been conducted. In German the singular or unique is called the *Individuelle*, which almost inevitably calls forth a misleading association with the term for the individual (*Individuum*). Now, individual is the term which we employ to describe those natural units which in the physical world our senses enable us to single out from the environment as connected wholes. Individuals in this sense, whether human individuals or animals or plants, or stones, mountains or stars, are constant collections of sense attributes which, either because the whole complex can move together in space relatively to its environment, or for cognate reasons, our senses spontaneously single out as connected wholes. But this is precisely what the objects of history are *not*. Though singular (*individuell*), as the individual is, they are not definite individuals in the sense in which this term is applied to natural objects. They are not given to us as wholes but only found to be wholes.

65. There is, of course, also a legitimate sense in which we may speak of "historical theories," where "theory" is used as a synonym for "factual hypothesis." In this sense the unconfirmed explanation of a particular event is often called a historical theory, but such a theory is of course something altogether different from the theories which pretend to state laws which historical developments obey.

66. L. Brunschvicg, in *Philosophy and History, Essays presented to E. Cassirer,* ed. by R. Klibansky and H. J. Paxton, Oxford, 1936, p. 30.

67. Cf. C. V. Langlois and C. Seignobos, *Introduction to the Study of History,* trans. by G. G. Berry, London, 1898, p. 222: "If former humanity did not resemble humanity of to-day, documents would be unintelligible."

68. Cf. W. Eucken, *Grundlagen der Nationalökonomie,* 1940, pp. 203-205.

69. "Man is what is known to all." Cf. H. Diehls, *Die Fragmente der Vorsokratiker,* 4th ed., Berlin, 1922; Democritus, Fragment No. 165, Vol. II, p. 94. I owe the reference to Democritus in this connection to Professor Alexander Rüstow.

70. On this concept of the "pragmatic" interpretation of social institutions as for the whole of this section compare Carl Menger, *Untersuchungen über die Methode der Sozialwissenschaften,* 1883 (L. S. E. reprint 1933), book II, chapter 2, which is still the most comprehensive and most careful survey known to me of the problems here discussed.

71. See above note 11.

72. Cf. M. Schlick, *Fragen der Ethik,* Vienna, 1930, p. 72.

73. On the use of teleological concepts in biology compare the careful discussion in J. H. Woodger, *Biological Principles,* 1929, particularly the section on "Teleology and Causation," pp. 429-451; also the earlier discussion in the same work (p. 291) on the so-

called "scientific habit of thought" causing the "scandal" of biologists not taking organization seriously and "in their haste to become physicists, neglecting their business."

74. *Untersuchungen, etc.,* p. 163: "Hier ist es wo uns das merkwürdige, vielleicht das merkwürdigste Problem der Sozialwissenschaften entgegentritt: Wieso vermögen dem Gemeinwohl dienende und für dessen Entwicklung höchst bedeutsame Institutionen ohne einen auf ihre Begründung gerichteten Gemeinwillen zu entstehen?" If for the ambiguous and somewhat question-begging term "social welfare" we substitute in this statement "institutions which are necessary conditions for the achievement of man's conscious purposes" it is hardly saying too much that the way in which such "purposive wholes" are formed and preserved is *the* specific problem of social theory, just as the existence and persistence of organisms is the problem of biology.

75. How much intellectual progress has been obstructed here by political passions is readily seen when we compare the discussion of the problem in the economic and political sciences with, say, the study of language where, what in the former is still disputed, is a commonplace which nobody dreams of questioning.

76. Menger speaks in this connection rightly of "a pragmatism which, against the wishes of its representatives, leads inevitably to socialism." (*Untersuchungen, etc.,* p. 208.) Today this view is most frequently found in the writings of the American "Institutionalists" of which the following (taken from Professor W. H. Hamilton's article on "Institution" in the *Encyclopaedia of the Social Sciences,* Vol. VIII, pp. 87-89) is a good example: "The tangled thing called capitalism was never created by design or cut to a blueprint; but now that it is here,

contemporary schoolmen have intellectualized it into a purposive and self-regulating instrument of general welfare." From this it is of course only a few steps to the demand "that order and direction should be imposed upon an unruly society."

77. A typical example of the treatment of social institutions as if they were true artifacts, in a characteristic scientistic setting, is provided by J. Mayer, *Social Science Principles in the Light of Scientific Method,* Durham, N. C., 1941, p. 20, where society is explicitly "designated as an 'artificial creation,' much as an automobile or steel mill is, that is to say, made by the artifice of man."

78. The best illustration, perhaps, of how we constantly make use of the experience or knowledge acquired by others, is the way in which, by learning to speak, we learn to classify things in a certain manner without acquiring the actual experiences which have led successive generations to evolve this system of classification. There is a great deal of knowledge which we never consciously know implicit in the knowledge of which we are aware, knowledge which yet constantly serves us in our actions, though we can hardly be said to "possess" it.

79. See above pp. 64-79.

80. *Ibid.,* pp. 54-58. Cf. also Part I, p. 289, and Menger, *Untersuchungen, etc.,* pp. 165 *et seq.*

81. A. N. Whitehead, *An Introduction to Mathematics* (Home University Library), 1911, p. 61.

82. It cannot be objected to this that what is meant by conscious control is not control by a single mind but by a concerted and "co-ordinated" effort of all, or all the best minds, instead of by their fortuitous interplay. This phrase about the deliberate co-ordination merely shifts the task of the individual mind to another stage but leaves the

ultimate responsibility still with the co-ordinating mind. Committees and other devices for facilitating communications are excellent means to assist the individual in learning as much as possible; but they do not extend the capacity of the individual mind. The knowledge that can be consciously co-ordinated in this manner is still limited to what the individual mind can effectively absorb and digest. As every person with experience of committee work knows, its fertility is limited to what the best mind among the members can master; if the results of the discussion are not ultimately turned into a coherent whole by an individual mind, they are likely to be inferior to what would have been produced unaided by a single mind.

83. L. T. Hobhouse, *Democracy and Reaction*, 1904, p. 108.

84. J. Needham, *Integrative Levels. A Revaluation of the Idea of Progress* (Herbert Spencer Lecture), Oxford, 1937, p. 47.

85. K. Mannheim, *Man and Society in an Age of Reconstruction*, 1940, p. 213.

86. See above pp. 76-80.

87. Interesting illustrations of the length to which these absurdities have been carried will be found in E. Gruenwald, *Das Problem der Soziologie des Wissens*, Vienna, 1934, a posthumously published sketch of a very young scholar which still constitutes the most comprehensive survey of the literature of the subject.

88. Cf. above p. 78.

89. It is, perhaps, not so obvious as to make it unnecessary to mention it, that the fashionable disparagement of any activity which, in science or the arts, is carried on "for its own sake," and the demand for a "conscious social purpose" in everything, is an expression of the same general tendency and based on the same illusion of complete knowledge as those discussed in the text.

90. Some further aspects of the big problems here just touched upon are discussed in my *Road to Serfdom*, 1944, particularly chapters VI and XIV.

91. It is characteristic of the spirit of the time, and of positivism in particular, when A. Comte speaks (*Système de Politique Positive*, Vol. I, p. 356) of "La supériorité necessaire de la morale démontrée sur la morale révélée," characteristic especially in its implied assumption that a rationally constructed moral system is the only alternative to one revealed by a higher being.

92. For those who wish to pursue further the matters discussed in the last section a few references to several relevant works may be added which have appeared since this was first published. In addition to the *Selected Writings of Edward Sapir* (ed. by D. G. Mandelbaum, University of California Press, 1949, especially pp. 46 f, 104, 162, 166, 546 ff and 553) already mentioned earlier, the reader will with advantage consult G. Ryle, "Knowing How and Knowing That," *Proceedings of the Aristotelian Society*, N. S. XLVI, 1945, and the corresponding passages in the same author's *The Concept of Mind*, London, 1949, K. R. Popper, *The Open Society and its Enemies*, London, 1946, and M. Polany, *The Logic of Liberty*, London, 1951.

93. Once again one of the best illustrations of this tendency is provided by K. Mannheim, *Man and Society in an Age of Reconstruction*, 1940, particularly pp. 240-244, where he explains that "functionalism made its first appearance in the field of the natural sciences, and could be described as the technical point of view. It has only recently been transferred to the social sphere . . . Once this technical approach

was transferred from natural sciences to human affairs, it was bound to bring about a profound change in man himself . . . The functional approach no longer regards ideas and moral standards as absolute values, but as products of the social process which can, if necessary, be changed by scientific guidance combined with political practice . . . The extension of the doctrine of technical supremacy which I have advocated in this book is in my opinion inevitable . . . Progress in the technique of organization is nothing but the application of technical conceptions to the forms of co-operation. A human being, regarded as part of the social machine, is to a certain extent stabilized in his reactions by training and education, and all his recently acquired activities are co-ordinated according to a definite principle of efficiency within an organized framework."

94. The best description of this feature of the engineering approach by an engineer which I have been able to find occurs in a speech of the great German optical engineer Ernst Abbe: "Wie der Architekt ein Bauwerk, bevor eine Hand zur Ausführung sich rührt, schon im Geist vollendet hat, nur unter Beihilfe von Zeichenstift und Feder zur Fixierung seiner Idee, so muss auch das komplizierte Gebilde von Glas und Metall sich aufbauen lassen rein verstandesmässig, in allen Elementen bis ins letzte vorausbestimmt, in rein geistiger Arbeit, durch theoretische Ermittlung der Wirkung aller Teile, bevor diese Teile noch körperlich ausgeführt sind. Der arbeitenden Hand darf dabei keine andere Funktion mehr verbleiben als die genaue Verwirklichung der durch die Rechnungen bestimmten Formen und Abmessungen aller Konstruktionselemente, und der praktischen Erfahrung keine andere Aufgabe als die Beherrschung der Methoden und Hilfsmittel, die für letzteres, die

körperliche Verwirklichung, geeignet sind" (quoted by Franz Schnabel, *Deutsche Geschichte im neunzehnten Jahrbundert*, vol. III, 1934, p. 222—a work which is a mine of information on this as on all other matters of the intellectual history of Germany in the nineteenth century).

95. It would take too long here to explain in any detail why, whatever delegation or division of labor is possible in preparing an engineering 'blueprint,' it is very limited and differs in essential respects from the division of knowledge on which the impersonal social processes rest. It must suffice to point out that not only must the precise nature of the result be fixed which anyone who has to draw up part of an engineering plan must achieve, but also that, in order to make such delegation possible, it must be known that the result can be achieved at no more than a certain maximum cost.

96. The most persistent advocate of such *in natura* calculation is, significantly, Dr. Otto Neurath, the protagonist of modern "physicalism" and "objectivism."

97. Cf. the characteristic passage in B. Bavinck, *The Anatomy of Modern Science* (trans. from the 4th German edition by H. S. Hatfield), 1932, p. 564: "When our technology is still at work on the problem of transforming heat into work in a manner better than that possible with our present-day steam and other heat engines . . . , this is not directly done to cheapen production of energy, but first of all because it is an end in itself to increase the thermal efficiency of a heat engine as much as possible. If the problem set is to transform heat into work, then this must be done in such a way that the greatest possible fraction of the heat is so transformed . . . The ideal of the designer of such machines is therefore the efficiency of the Carnot

cycle, the ideal process which delivers the greatest theoretical efficiency."

It is easy to see why this approach, together with the desire to achieve a calculation *in natura,* leads engineers so frequently to the construction of systems of "energetics" that it has been said, with much justice, that "das Charakteristikum der Weltanschauung des Ingenieurs ist die energetische Weltanschauung" (L. Brinkmann, *Der Ingenieur,* Frankfurt, 1908, p. 16). We have already referred (above p. 41) to this characteristic manifestation of scientistic "objectivism," and there is no space here to return to it in greater detail. But it deserves to be recorded how widespread and typical this view is and how great the influence it has exercised. E. Solvay, G. Ratzenhofer, W. Ostwaldt, P. Geddes, F. Soddy, H. G. Wells, the "Technocrats" and L. Hogben are only a few of the influential authors in whose works "energetics" play a more or less prominent rôle. There are several studies of this movement in French and German (Nyssens, *L'énergetique,* Brussels, 1908; G. Barnich, *Principes de politique positive basée sur l'énergetique sociale de Solvay,* Brussels, 1918; Schnehen, *Energetische Weltanschauung,* 1907; A. Dochmann, *F. W. Ostwald's Energetik,* Bern, 1908; and the best, Max Weber, "Energetische Kulturtheorien," 1909, reprinted in *Gesammelte Aufsätze zur Wissenschaftslehre,* 1922), but none of them adequate and none, to my knowledge, in English.

The section from the work of Bavinck from which a passage has been quoted above condenses the gist of the enormous literature, mostly German, on the "philosophy of technology" which has had a wide circulation and of which the best known is E. Zschimmer, *Philosophie der Technik,* 3rd ed., Stuttgart, 1933. (Similar ideas pervade the well-known American works of Lewis Mumford.) This German literature is very instructive as a psychological study, though otherwise about the dreariest mixture of pretentious platitudes and revolting nonsense which it has ever been the ill fortune of the present author to peruse. Its common feature is the enmity towards all economic considerations, the attempted vindication of purely technological ideals, and the glorification of the organization of the whole of society on the principle on which a single factory is run. (On the last point see particularly F. Dessauer, *Philosophie der Technik,* Bonn, 1927, p. 129.)

98. That this is fully recognized by its advocates is shown by the popularity among all socialists from Saint-Simon to Marx and Lenin, of the phrase that the whole of society should be run in precisely the same manner as a single factory is now being run. Cf. V. I. Lenin, *The State and Revolution* (1917), "Little Lenin Library," 1933, p. 78. "The whole of society will have become a single office and a single factory with equality of work and equality of pay"; and for Saint-Simon and Marx, p. 121 above and note 72 to Part II.

99. Cf. now on these problems my essay on "The Use of Knowledge in Society," *American Economic Review,* XXXV, No. 4 (September, 1945), reprinted in *Individualism and Economic Order,* Chicago, 1948, pp. 77-91.

100. It is important to remember in this connection that the statistical aggregates which it is often suggested the central authority could rely upon in its decisions, are always arrived at by a deliberate disregard of the peculiar circumstances of time and place.

101. Cf. in this connection the suggestive discussion of the problem in K. F. Mayer, *Goldwanderungen,* Jena, 1935, pp. 66-68, and also the present author's article "Economics and

Knowledge" in *Economica*, February, 1937, reprinted in *Individualism and Economic Order*, Chicago, 1948, pp. 33-56.

102. *The Scientific Outlook*, 1931, p. 211.

103. *Ibid.*, p. 211. The passage quoted could be interpreted in an unobjectionable sense if "certain purposes" is taken to mean not particular predetermined results but as capacity to provide what the individuals at any time wish—i.e., if what is planned is a machinery which can serve many ends and need not in turn be "consciously" directed towards a particular end.

104. A. Bebel, *Die Frau und der Sozialismus*, 13th ed., 1892, p. 376.

"Der Sozialismus ist die mit klarem Bewusstsein and mit voller Erkenntnis auf alle Gebiete menschlicher Taetigkeit angewandte Wissenschaft." Cf. also E. Ferri, *Socialism and Positive Science* (trans. from the Italian edition of 1894). The first clearly to see this connection seems to have been M. Ferraz, *Socialisme, Naturalisme et Positivisme*, Paris, 1877.

105. M. R. Cohen, *Reason and Nature*, 1931, p. 449. It is significant that one of the leading members of the movement with which we are concerned, the German philosopher Ludwig Feuerbach, explicitly chose the opposite principle, *homo homini Deus*, as his guiding maxim.

Part Two

1. D'Alembert was fully aware of the significance of the tendency he was supporting and anticipated later positivism to the extent of expressly condemning everything that did not aim at the development of *positive* truths and even suggesting that "all occupations with purely speculative subjects should be excluded from a healthy state as profitless pursuits." Yet he did not include in this the moral sciences and even, with his master Locke, regarded them as *a priori* sciences comparable with mathematics and of equal certainty with it. See on all this G. Misch, "Zur Entstehung des französischen Positivismus," *Archiv für Philosophie, Abt. I, Archiv für Geschichte der Philosophie*, vol. 14 (1901), especially pp. 7, 31 and 158; M. Schinz, *Geschichte der französischen Philosophie seit der Revolution, I. Bd. Die Anfänge des französischen Positivismus*, Strassburg, 1914, pp. 58, 67-69,

71, 96, 149; and H. Gouhier, *La jeunesse d'Auguste Comte et la formation du positivisme*, Vol. II, Paris, 1936, Introduction.

2. Cf. E. Mach, *Die Mechanik in ihrer Entwicklung*, 3rd ed., 1897, p. 449.

3. In his famous work *Du culte des dieux fétishes* (1760).

4. *Œuvres de Turgot*, ed. Daire, Paris, 1844, Vol. II, p. 656. Compare also *ibid.*, p. 601.

5. See particularly the detailed analysis by Misch and the books by Schinz and Gouhier quoted in note 1 above, and also M. Uta, *La théorie du savoir dans la philosophie d'Auguste Comte*, Paris (Alcan), 1928.

6. To avoid giving a wrong impression it should perhaps also be stressed at this point that the Liberalism of the French Revolution was of course not yet based on the understanding of the market mechanism provided by Adam

Smith and the Utilitarians but rather on the Law of Nature and the rationalistic-pragmatic interpretation of social phenomena which is essentially pre-Smithian and of which Rousseau's social contract is the prototype. One might indeed trace much of the contrast, which with Saint-Simon and Comte became an open opposition to classical economics, back to the differences which existed, say, between Montesquieu and Hume, Quesnay and Smith, or Condorcet and Bentham. Those French economists who like Condillac or J. B. Say followed essentially the same trend as Smith never had an influence on French political thought comparable to that of Smith in England. The result of this was that the transition from the older rationalist views of society, which regarded it as a conscious creation of man, to the newer view which wanted to re-create it on scientific principles, took place in France without passing through a stage in which the working of the spontaneous forces of society was generally understood. The revolutionary cult of Reason was symptomatic of the general acceptance of the pragmatic conception of social institutions—the very opposite of the view of Smith. And in a sense it would be as true to say that it was the same veneration of Reason as the universal creator which led to the triumphs of science that led to the new attitude to social problems as it is to say that it was the influence of the new habits of thought created by the triumphs of science and technology. If socialism is not a direct child of the French Revolution, it springs at least from that rationalism which distinguished most of the French political thinkers of the period from the contemporary English liberalism of Hume and Smith and (to a lesser degree) Bentham and the philosophical Radicals. On all this see now the first essay in my volume on *Individualism*

and Economic Order, University of Chicago Press, 1948.

7. See his *Esquisse d'un tableau historique des progrès de l'esprit humain* (1793), ed. O. H. Prior, Paris, 1933, p. 11.

8. Cf. his *Tableau général de la science qui a pour objet l'application du calcul aux sciences politiques et morales, Œuvres,* ed. Arago, Paris, 1847–49, Vol. I, pp. 539-573.

9. *Œuvres,* ed. Arago, Vol. I, p. 392.

10. Condorcet, *Rapport et projet de décret sur l'organization générale de l'instruction publique* (1792), ed. G. Compayre, Paris, 1883, p. 120.

11. *Esquisse,* ed. Prior, p. 11.

12. *Ibid.,* p. 200.

13. *Ibid.,* p. 203. The famous passage in which this sentence occurs figures, characteristically, as motto of book VI, "On the Logic of the Moral Sciences" of J. S. Mill's *Logic.*

14. It is worthy of mention that the man who was so largely responsible for the creation of what in the late 19th century came to be regarded as "historical sense," i.e., of the *Entwicklungsgedanke* with all its metaphysical associations, was the same man who was capable of celebrating in a discourse the deliberate destruction of papers relating to the history of the noble families of France. "To-day Reason burns the innumerable volumes which attest the vanity of a caste. Other vestiges remain in public and private libraries. They must be involved in a common destruction."

15. Quoted by Gouhier, *La jeunesse d'Auguste Comte,* Vol. II, p. 31, from the *Décade philosophique,* Vol. I, 1794.

16. See E. Allain, *L'œuvre scolaire de la Révolution, 1789–1802,* Paris, 1891; C. Hippeau, *L'instruction publique en France pendant la Révolution,* Paris, 1883 and F. Picavet. *Les Idéologues,* Paris, 1891, pp. 56-61.

17. See E. Allain, *op. cit.* pp. 117-120.

18. After 1803 the ancient languages were at least partly restored in Napoleon's *lycées.*

19. H. de Saint-Simon, *Mémoire sur la science de l'homme* (1813) in *Œuvres de Saint-Simon and d'Enfantin,* Paris, 1877-78, Vol. XL, p. 16.

20. Particularly of saltpetre for the production of gunpowder.

21. See Pressard, *Histoire de l'association philotechnique,* Paris 1889, and Gouhier, *La jeunesse d'Auguste Comte,* Vol. II, p. 54.

22. On the foundation and history of the Ecole Polytechnique see A. Fourcy, *Histoire de l'Ecole Polytechnique,* Paris, 1828; G. Pinet, *Histoire de l'Ecole Polytechnique,* Paris, 1887; G.-G. J. Jacobi, Ueber die Pariser polytechnische Schule (Vortrag gehalten am 22. Mai 1835 in der physikalisch-ökonomischen Gesellschaft zu Königsberg) in *Gesammelte Werke,* Berlin, 1891, Vol. VI, p. 355; F. Schnabel, *Die Anfänge des technischen Hochschulwesens,* Stuttgart, 1925; and F. Klein, *Vorlesungen über die Entwicklung der Mathematik,* Berlin 1926, Vol. I, pp. 63-89.

23. Carnot had published in 1783 an *Essay on Machines in General* (in the second edition of 1803 called *Principes fondamentaux de l'équilibre du mouvement*) in which he not only expounded Lagrange's new view of mechanics but developed the idea of the "ideal machine" which takes nothing away from the force which puts it into motion. His work did much to prepare the way for that of his son, Sadi Carnot, "the founder of the Science of Energy." His younger son, Hippolyte, was the leading member of the Saint-Simonian group and actual writer of the *Doctrine de Saint-Simon* which we shall meet later. Lazare Carnot, the father, had been a life-long admirer and protector of Saint-Simon himself. As Arago reports of Lazare Carnot, he "always discoursed with [Arago] on the political organisation of society precisely as he speaks in his work of a machine." See F. Arago, *Biographies of Distinguished Men,* transl. by W. H. Smith, etc., London, 1857, pp. 300-304, and E. Dühring, *Kritische Geschichte der allgemeinen Principien der Mechanik,* 3rd ed., Leipzig, 1887, pp. 258-261.

24. L. de Launay, *Un grand français, Monge, Fondateur de l'Ecole Polytechnique,* Paris, 1933, p. 130.

25. Cf. A. Comte, "Philosophical considerations on the Sciences and Men of Science" (1825, in *Early Essays on Social Philosophy,* London, "New Universal Library," p. 272), where he says that he knows "but one conception capable of giving a precise idea of [the characteristic doctrines fitted to constitute the special existence of the class of Engineers], that of the illustrious Monge, in his *Géometrie descriptive,* where he gives a general theory of the arts of construction."

26. G.-G. J. Jacobi, *l.c.,* p. 370.

27. Fourcroy, Vauquelin, Chaptal.

28. In March 1808, shortly after he had arrived in Paris (nominally on a diplomatic mission), Alexander von Humboldt wrote to a friend: "Je passe ma vie à l'Ecole Polytechnique et aux Tuileries. Je travaille à l'Ecole, j'y couche; j'y mis tous les nuit, tous les matins. J'habite la même chambre avec Gay-Lussac." (K. Bruhns, *Alexander von Humboldt,* 1872, Vol. II, p. 6.

29. Laplace, *Essai philosophique sur les probabilités* (1814), edition *Les Maîtres de la Pensée Scientifique,* Paris, 1921, p. 3.

30. Cf. for instance the reference to it in Abel Transon, *De la religion Saint-Simonienne. Aux Elèves de l'Ecole Polytechnique,* Paris, 1830, p. 27. See also note 69 below.

31. See O. Neurath, *Empirische Soziologie*, Vienna, 1931, p. 129. On the postulate of universal determinism which is really involved, see particularly K. Popper, *Logik der Forschung*, 1935, p. 183, Ph. Frank, *Das Kausalgesetz*, and R. von Mises, *Probability, Statistics and Truth*, 1939, pp. 284-294. —Equally characteristic of the positivist spirit and no less influential in spreading it is the famous anecdote about Laplace's answer to Napoleon when asked why in his *Mécanique Céleste* the name of God did not appear: "Je n'ai pas besoin de cette hypothèse."

32. E. Dühring, *Kritische Geshichte*, etc., 3rd ed., p. 569, *et seq.*

33. H. de Balzac after remarking in one of his novels (*Autre étude de femme*) how different periods had enriched the French language by certain characteristic words, takes *organiser* as an example and adds that it is "un mot de l'empire qui contient Napoléon tout entier."

34. É. Keller, *Le général de la Moricière*, quoted by Pinet, *Histoire de l'Ecole Polytechnique*, Paris, 1887, p. 136.

35. A. Thibaudet, quoted by Gouhier, *La jeunesse d'Auguste Comte*, Vol. I, p. 146.

36. See Arago, *Œuvres*, Vol. III, p. 109, and F. Bastiat, *Baccalauréat et Socialisme*, Paris, 1850.

37. See G. Pinet, *Ecrivains et Penseurs Polytechniciens*, Paris, 1898.

38. See, however, the essays of Lavoisier and Lagrange in Daire, *Mélanges d'économie politique*, 2 vols., Paris, 1847-8, Vol. I, pp. 575-607.

39. See Arago, *Œuvres*, Vol. II, p. 34, where he points out that Ampère (a physiologist by training) was one of the few connecting links between the two groups.

40. On Cuvier's influence see the account in J. T. Merz, *A History of European Thought in the Nineteenth Century*, Vol. I, 1906, pp. 136 *et seq.*, where the following characteristic passage is quoted (p. 154) from Cuvier's *Rapport historique sur le progrès des sciences naturelles depuis 1789*, Paris, 1810, p. 389: "Experiments alone, experiments that are precise, made with weights, measures and calculation, by comparison of all substances employed and all substances obtained; this to-day is the only legitimate way of reasoning and demonstration. Thus, though the natural sciences escape the application of the calculus, they glory in being subject to the mathematical spirit, and by the wise course they have invariably adopted, they do not expose themselves to the risk of taking a backward step." Cf. also Lord Acton, *Lectures on Modern History*, pp. 22 and 338, note 82.

41. A. C. Thibaudeau (*Bonaparte and the Consulate*, 1834, English translation by G. K. Fortescue, 1908, p. 153) points out that, although the terms 'idéologues' and 'idéologie,' commonly ascribed to Napoleon, were introduced as technical terms by Destutt de Tracy with the first volume of his *Eléments d'Idéologie*, published in 1801, at least the word 'idéologie' was known in French as early as 1684.

42. On the whole ideological school see the comprehensive exposition in F. Picavet, *Les Idéologues, Essai sur l'histoire des idées et des théories scientifiques, philosophiques, religieuses, en France depuis 1789*, Paris, 1891, and, published since this essay first appeared, E. Cailliet, *La Tradition littéraire des idéologues*, Philadelphia, 1943.

43. The expression was indeed used in very much the same wide sense as their German contemporaries used the term anthropology. On the German parallel to the *idéologues* see F. Günther, *Die Wissenschaft vom Menschen*,

ein Beitrag zum deutschen Geistesleben im Zeitalter des Rationalismus (in *Geschichtliche Untersuchungen*, herausgegeben von K. Lamprecht, Bd. 5, Heft 1) 1907.

44. Picavet, *l.c.*, p. 337.

45. *Ibid.*, p. 314.

46. *Ibid.*, p. 250. Also see pp. 131-5, where Cabanis' predecessor in these efforts, Volney, is discussed. In 1793, Volney had published a *Catéchisme du Citoyen Français*, later to become *La loi naturelle ou les principes physiques de la morale* in which he unsuccessfully attempted to create morals as a physical science.

47. *Ibid.*, p. 226.

48. On Destutt de Tracy see H. Michel, *L'Idée d'état*, Paris, 1895, pp. 282-286; on Louis Say see A. Schatz, *L'Individualisme économique et social*, Paris, 1907, pp. 153 *et seq.*

49. See Picavet, *l.c.*, p. 82.

50. See the passage from Napoleon's reply to the Council of State at its session of December 20th, 1812, quoted by Pareto (*Mind and Society*, Vol. III, p. 1244) from the *Moniteur universel*, Paris, December 21st, 1812: "All the misfortunes that our beautiful France has been experiencing have to be ascribed to 'ideology,' to that cloudy metaphysics which goes ingeniously seeking first causes and would ground legislation of the peoples upon them instead of adapting laws to what we know of the human heart and the lessons of history. Such errors could only lead to a régime of men of blood and have in fact done so. Who cajoled the people by thrusting upon it a sovereignty it was unable to exercise? Who destroyed the sacredness of the laws and respect for the laws by basing them not on the sacred principles of justice, on the nature of things and the nature of civil justice, but simply on the will of an assembly made up of individuals who are strangers to any knowledge of law, whether civil, administrative, political or military? When a man is called upon to reorganize a state, he must follow principles that are forever in conflict. The advantages and disadvantages of the different systems of legislation have to be sought in history." See also H. Taine, *Les origines de la France contemporaine*, 1876, Vol. II, pp. 214-233. Not because of its historical correctness which may be questioned, but in order to show how all this appeared to the next generation, the following characteristic statement by a leading Saint-Simonian may be quoted: "Après 1793, *l'Académie des Sciences* prend le sceptre; les *mathématiciens* et *physiciens* remplacent les littérateurs: Monge, Fourcroy, Laplace . . . règnent dans le royaume de l'intelligence. En même temps, Napoléon, membre de l'Institut, classe de *mécanique*, étouffe au berceau les enfants légitimes de la philosophie du XVIIIᵉ siècle." (P. Enfantin, *Colonisation de l'Algérie*, 1843, pp. 521-2.)

51. See A. C. Thibaudeau, *Le Consulat et l'Empire*, Paris, 1835-37, Vol. III, p. 396.

52. See J. B. Say, *Traité d'économie politique*, 2nd ed. 1814, Avertissement.

53. See G. Chinard, *Jefferson et les idéologues*, Baltimore, 1925.

54. Cf. Merz, *l.c.*, Vol. I, p. 149.

55. The date, and therefore the age, is not quite certain.

56. See H. Gouhier, *La jeunesse d'Auguste Comte et la formation du positivisme*, Vol. II, *Saint Simon jusqu'à la restauration*, Paris, 1936, which for the first forty-five years of Saint-Simon's life supersedes all earlier biographies, including the best of them, G. Weill, *Un précurseur du socialisme, Saint-Simon et son œuvre*, Paris, 1894, and M. Leroy, *La vie véritable du comte de Saint-Simon, 1760–1825*, Paris, 1925, and G. Dumas, *Psycho-*

logie de deux messies positivistes, Saint-Simon et Auguste Comte, Paris, 1905.

57. "J'ai employé mon argent à acquérir de la science; grande chère, bon vin, beaucoup d'empressements vis-à-vis des professeurs auxquels ma bourse était ouverte, me procuraient toutes les facilités que je pouvais désirer." Quoted by M. Leroy, *l.c.*, p. 210.

58. Léon Halévy, "Souvenirs de Saint-Simon," *La France littéraire*, March, 1832, partially reproduced by G. Brunet in *Revue d'histoire économique et sociale*, 1925, p. 168.

59. See Madame de Staël, *De la littérature considérée dans ses rapports avec les institutions sociales* (1800). The passages quoted occur in the "Discours préliminaire," Vol. I, p. 58, and in Vol. II, 2nd part, Ch. VI, p. 215 of the 3rd ed. of 1818.

60. See *Œuvres de Saint-Simon et d'Enfantin*, Paris, 1865–1878 (henceforth quoted as *O.S.S.E.*), Vol. XV, pp. 7-60, and the new edition reprinted from the original with an Introduction by A. Pereire, Paris, 1925. Nearly all the important passages from Saint-Simon's works are conveniently brought together in *L'œuvre d'Henri de Saint-Simon*, Textes choisies avec une Introduction par C. Bouglé, Notice bibliographique de A. Pereire, Paris, 1925. In the references given below, the first refers to the *Œuvres*, the second (in brackets) to the separate edition of the *Lettres* of 1925. For the complicated history of the various editions and manuscripts of this work see Gouhier, *La jeunesse d'Auguste Comte*, Vol. II, pp. 224 *et seq.*

61. *O.S.S.E.*, XV, p. 11 (3).

62. *Ibid.*, p. 51 (55).

63. *Ibid.*, p. 49 (53).

64. *Ibid.*, p. 48 (52).

65. *Ibid.*, pp. 50-3 (54-8).

66. In *Lettres*, ed. A. Pereire, pp. xv, 93.

67. *O.S.S.E.*, XV, p. 39 (39).

68. *Ibid.*, p. 40 (40).

69. *O.S.S.E.*, XV, pp. 39-40, 55 (39, 61). The passage in which Saint-Simon praises the significance of that universal law is a curious anticipation of Laplace's famous world formula (*ibid.*, p. 59 [67]): "Faites la supposition que vous avez acquis connoissance de la manière dont la matière s'est trouvée repartie à une époque quelconque, et que vous avez fait le plan de l'Univers, en désignant par des nombres la quantité de matière qui se trouvoit contenue dans chacune des ces parties, il sera clair à vos yeux qu'en faisant sur ce plan d'application de la loi de la pesanteur universelle, vous pourriez prédire (aussi exactment que l'état des connoissances mathématiques vous le permettroit) tousles changements successifs qui arriveraient dans l'Univers." But although Laplace published his formula only in 1814, we must, no doubt, assume that the idea would have been familiar from his lectures delivered in 1796 to which he later added the introduction containing the famous phrase.

70. *O.S.S.E.*, XV, p. 26 (23).

71. *Ibid.*, p. 28 (25).

72. *Ibid.*, p. 55 (61). Cf. also p. 57 (65): "L'obligation est imposée à chacun de donner constamment à ses forces personelles une direction utîle à l'humanité; les bras du pauvre continueront à nourir le riche, mais le riche reçoit le commandement de faire travailler sa cervelle, et si sa cervelle n'est pas propre au travail, il sera bien obligé de faire travailler ses bras; car Newton ne laissera sûrement pas sur cette planète (une des plus voisines du soleil) des ouvriers volontairement inutiles dans l'atelier." The idea of the organization of society on the example of the workshop, which appears here for the first time in literature, has, of course, since played an important rôle in all socialist literature. See particu-

larly G. Sorel, "Le syndicalisme révolutionaire" in *Mouvement Socialiste*, November 1st and 15th, 1905. Compare also the passage in K. Marx, *Das Kapital*, Vol. I, Ch. 12, section 4, 10th ed., pp. 319-324.

73. *Lettres*, ed. A. Pereire, p. 54. The passage has been discreetly suppressed by his pupils who edited the *Œuvres*.

74. *O.S.S.E.*, XV, p. 54 (59).

75. 2 Vols. 1807–8. The *Introduction* has not been included in the *Œuvres de Saint-Simon et d'Enfantin* and must be consulted in *Œuvres choisies de C.-H. de Saint-Simon*, Bruxelles, 1859, Vol. I, pp. 43-264.

76. *Œuvres choisies*, I ("Mon Portefeuille") : "Trouver une synthèse scientifique qui codifie les dogmes du nouveau pouvoir et serve de base à une réorganisation de l'Europe."

77. *Œuvres choisies*, I, p. 219. See also pp. 195, 214-5, and 223-4.

78. *Ibid.*, p. 214: "Je crois à la nécessité d'une religion pour le maintien de l'ordre social; je crois que le déisme est usé, je crois que le physicisme n'est point assez solidement établi pour pouvoir servir de base à une religion. Je crois que la force des choses veut qu'il y ait deux doctrines distinctes: le Physicisme pour les gens instruits, et le Déisme pour la classe ignorante."

79. Saint-Simon uses "Deism" and "Theism" indiscriminately for Monotheism.

80. *Ibid.*, p. 195.

81. *Ibid.*, p. 146.

82. *Ibid.*, p. 61.

83. *Ibid.*, pp. 243-4.

84. *Ibid.*, pp. 231, 236. Descartes has now become the hero because our perpetual time-server has become violently nationalistic, deplores the English predominance which is still defiling French science and wants to give the initiative to the French. The work pretends to be an answer to Napoleon's question to the *Académie* on the progress of French sciences since 1789.

85. *O.S.S.E.*, XV, pp. 71, 77.

86. *O.S.S.E.*, XV, p. 112.

87. *Ibid.*, p. 217: "l'idée de Dieu n'est pas autre chose que l'idée de l'intelligence humaine généralisée."

88. See W. Sombart, *Sozialismus und Soziale Bewegung*, 7th ed., 1919, p. 54.

89. *O.S.S.E.*, XV, pp. 42, 53-56.

90. *O.S.S.E.*, XL, p. 39.

91. *Ibid.*, p. 17.

92. *Ibid.*, pp. 25, 186.

93. *Ibid.*, p. 29.

94. *Ibid.*, pp. 161, 186.

95. *Ibid.*, p. 17.

96. *Ibid.*, pp. 247, 310.

97. *Ibid.*, p. 265.

98. *Ibid.*, p. 172.

99. *Ibid.*, p. 161.

100. *O.S.S.E.*, XL, p. 287.

101. *De la réorganisation de la société européenne ou de la nécessité et des moyens de rassembler les peuples de l'europe en un seul corps politique en conservant à chacun son indépendance nationale*, par H. C. Saint-Simon et A. Thierry, son élève, *O.S.S.E.*, Vol. XV, pp. 153-248, also in a new edition by A. Pereire, Paris, 1925.

102. For a discussion of the significance of the work of Thierry, Mignet, and Guizot in this connection see G. Plechanow, "Ueber die Anfänge der Lehre vom Klassenkampf," *Die Neue Zeit*, Vol. 21, 1902. Cf. also C. Seignobos, *La Méthode historique*, 2ᵐᵉ ed. 1909, p. 261: "c'est lui [Saint-Simon] qui a fourni a Augustin Thierry ses idées fondamentales."

103. *O.S.S.E.*, XV, p. 247. In the form of "L'âge d'or, qu'une aveugle tradition a placé jusq'ici dans le passé, est devant nous" the phrase appears first in 1825 as the motto of Saint-Simon's *Opinions littéraires et philosophiques*, and later as the motto of the Saint-Simonian *Producteur*.

104. See M. Leroy, *Vie de Saint-Simon*, pp. 262, 277, and Hippolyte Carnot, "Mémoire sur le Saint-Simonism," *Séances et travaux de l'Académie des Sciences Morales et Politiques*, 47° année, 1887, p. 128, where H. Carnot reports the following characterisation of Saint-Simon by his father: "J'ai connu M. de Saint-Simon; c'est un singulier homme. Il a tort de se croire un savant, mais personne n'a des idées aussi neuves et aussi hardies." The only other scholars who seem ever to have given Saint-Simon any encouragement appear to have been the astronomer Hallé and, characteristically, Cuvier.

105. *L'Industrie ou discussions politiques, morales et philosophiques dans l'intérêt de tous les hommes livrés à des travaux indépendants.* In *O.S.S.E.*, Vol. XVIII.

106. For a comparison of Saint-Simon's views of this period with those of his liberal contemporaries see E. Halévy, *L'ère des tyrannies*, 1938, pp. 33–41.

107. *O.S.S.E.*, Vol. XVIII, p. 165.

108. *Ibid.*, pp. 186, 188, 189. Cf. also Vol. XIX, p. 126.

109. See A. Augustin Thierry, *Augustin Thierry (1795–1856) d'après sa correspondance et ses papiers de famille*, Paris, 1922, p. 36.

110. See A. Comte, *Early Essays on Social Philosophy*, translated by H. D. Hutton, "New Universal Library," London (1911), p. 23; and *Système de politique positive*, 1851–54, Vol. III, p. 16.

111. See H. Gouhier, *La jeunesse d'Auguste Comte*, Vol. I, 1933, ch. 6. As the third volume of this excellent work had not yet appeared at the time this essay was written, the following exposition relies for Comte's biography after 1817 largely on the same author's brief *Vie d'Auguste Comte*, Paris, 1931.

112. A. Pereire, *Autour de Saint-Simon*, Paris, 1912, p. 25.

113. *Œuvres de Saint-Simon et d'Enfantin* (2nd ed. 1865–78) [*O.S.S.E.*], XIX, pp. 37-8.

114. *Ibid.*, p. 27: "La grande supériorité de l'époque actuelle . . . consiste en ce qu'il nous est possible de savoir ce que nous faisons; . . . Ayant la conscience de notre état, nous avons celle de ce qu'il nous convient à faire."

115. *Ibid.*, p. 23.

116. *L'Industrie*, Vol. III, 2ᵐᵉ cahier: "Il ne s'agit plus de disserter à perte de vue pour savoir quel est le meilleur des gouvernements: il n'y a rien de bon, il n'y a rien de mauvais, absolument parlant. Tout est relatif, voilà la seule chose absolue."

117. *O.S.S.E.*, XIX, p. 13.

118. *Ibid.*, pp. 82-3, 89.

119. *Ibid.*, p. 83.

120. Incidentally, and as a justification of this view, Comte develops for the first time the theory that the present constitution of property in France derives from the conquest of Gaul by the Franks. His statement (*ibid.*, p. 87) that the successors of the victors are still the proprietors while the descendants of the vanquished are today the farmers provides the basic idea for the racial theories of history of Thierry and his school. It is on this that Saint-Simon two years later based his claim of priority vis-à-vis Guizot (see *O.S.S.E.*, XXI, p. 192).

121. A. Pereire, *l.c.*, pp. 25-28.

122. *Lettres d'Auguste Comte à M. Valat*, Paris, 1870, pp. 51, 53. See also pp. 36-7; (letter dated April 17, 1818): "Je puis te dire que jamais je n'ai connu de jeune homme aussi ardent ni aussi généreux que lui: c'est un être original sous tous les rapports. J'ai appris, par cette liaison de travail et d'amitié avec un des hommes qui voient le plus loin en politique philosophique, j'ai appris une foule de choses que j'aurais en vain

cherchées dans les livres, et mon esprit a fait plus de chemin depuis six mois que dure notre liaison qu'il n'en aurait fait entrois ans si j'avais été seul. Ainsi cette besogne m'a formé le jugement sur les sciences politiques, et, par contre-coup, elle a agrandi mes idées sur toutes les autres sciences, de sorte que je me trouve avoir acquis plus de philosophie dans la tête, un coup d'oeil plus juste, plus élevé." M. Leroy, in quoting this passage (*la vie véritable du comte Henri de Saint-Simon, 1925*, p. 293), inserts after the first sentence "Saint-Simon est un accoucheur d'idées." Although this sentence is probably not by Comte, we have taken the title of section II from it.

123. A. Pereire, *l.c.*, p. 60.

124. The term journal and similar expressions in connection with Saint-Simon's works must not be taken too literally. They all appeared in irregular sequence, often out of numerical order and in different formats and in various editions. This is true of the *Organisateur* even more than of his other works.

125. *O.S.S.E.*, XX, pp. 17-26.

126. *Ibid.*, pp. 50-58.

127. *Ibid.*, XX, pp. 50-58.

128. The idea of the *chambre d'invention* is probably borrowed from Bacon's *New Atlantis*.

129. *O.S.S.E.*, XX, p. 59.

130. *Ibid.*, p. 63.

131. *Ibid.*, pp. 69-72.

132. *Ibid.*, p. 74.

133. *Ibid.*, p. 67.

134. In the Appendix to the *Système de politique positive*, 1854, later reprinted under the title *Opuscules de philosophie sociale 1819–1828*, Paris, 1883. An English translation of the latter by H. D. Hutton with an introduction by F. Harrison is available in Routledge's "New Universal Library" under the title *Early Essays on Social Philosophy*. The references added in

brackets to those of the *O.S.S.E* refer to this English edition.

135. *O.S.S.E.*, XX, pp. 118-9 (56-7).

136. *Ibid.*, p. 85 (35).

137. *Ibid.*, pp. 137-9 (68-71).

138. *Ibid.*, p. 106 (49).

139. *Ibid.*, p. 142 (72); for Comte's considerations on the same subject a few years later see also (272-4). The fear that his proposals might one day lead to a "despotism founded on science," Comte describes as "a ridiculous and absurd chimera which could only arise in minds entirely foreign to positive ideas." *Ibid.*, p. 158 (82).

140. *Ibid.*, p. 161 (85).

141. *Ibid.*, p. 150 (77).

142. *Ibid.*, pp. 144-5 (73): "Le peuple n'a plus besoin d'être gouverné, c'est-à-dire commandé. Il suffit, pour le maintien de l'ordre, que les affaires d'un intérêt commun soient administrées."

143. *Ibid.*, XX, p. 193. Cf. also the passage in Saint-Simon's later *Organisation sociale, ibid.*, Vol. XXXIX, p. 136, and Comte's remarks on the same subject in his contribution to the *Catéchisme des Industriels* in *Early Essays*, p. 172.

144. *Ibid.*, XX, p. 194.

145. *Ibid.*, pp. 194-5.

146. *Ibid.*, XX, pp. 199-200.

147. *Ibid.*, pp. 218, 226.

148. *Ibid.*, p. 220.

149. *Ibid.*, pp. 236-7.

150. *Ibid.*, pp. 240-242.

151. *Ibid.*, Vols. XXI, XXII.

152. *Ibid.*, Vol. XXI, p. 16. The phrasing of these passages is so clearly Comtian that there can be little doubt that they were written by Comte.

153. *Systéme industriel* (original edition) pp. xiii-xiv.

154. *O.S.S.E.*, XXI, p. 83. See also XXII, p. 179.

155. *Ibid.*, XXI, p. 14; XXII, p. 184.

156. *Des Bourbons et des Stuarts*

(1825) in *Œuvres Choisies*, Vol. II, p. 447.

157. *O.S.S.E.*, XXII, p. 248. See also p. 258, and XXI, pp. 14 and 80, and XXXVII, p. 179, where his disgust with the lack of organization in England finds expression in the characteristic outburst that "Cent volumes *in-folio*, du caractère le plus fin, ne suffiraient pas pour rendre compte de toutes les inconséquences organiques qui existent en Angleterre."

158. *O.S.S.E.*, XXII, p. 188.

159. *Ibid.*, p. 148.

160. *Ibid.*, XXI, p. 20.

161. *Ibid.*, XXXVII-XXXIX.

162. *Ibid.*, XXII, p. 82. See also XXI, pp. 131-2.

163. *Ibid.*, XXI, p. 47.

164. *Ibid.*, XXI, p. 161.

165. *Ibid.*, XXI, p. 107.

166. *Ibid.*, XXII, pp. 80, 185.

167. *Ibid.*, XXXVII, p. 87. See also XXI, p. 151. The formula seems to have been originally Comte's (see above, p. 133) and was later taken over by the Saint-Simonians (see particularly *Exposition*, ed. Bouglé and Halévy, p. 162), in whose publications it occurs once in the form "Il s'agit pour lui (le travailleur) non seulement *d'administrer* des choses, mais de gouverner des hommes, œuvre difficile, immense, œuvre saint" (*Globe*, April 4th, 1831). Engel's use of the expression in the *Anti-Dühring* (*Herrn Eugen Dühring's Umwälzung der Wissenschaft*, 3rd ed., 1894, p. 302) runs in the original: "An die Stelle der Regierung über Personen tritt die Verwaltung von Sachen. Der Staat wird nicht 'abgeschafft,' *er stirbt ab.*"

168. *O.S.S.E.*, XXXVII, p. 8.

169. *Ibid.*, XXII, pp. 257-8.

170. Later included under the original title in the *Early Essays on Social Philosophy*, pp. 88-217.

171. *Early Essays*, Author's Preface, p. 24.

172. Leaving it open as to how much of this "Saint-Simonian" doctrine may not be due to Comte's earlier contributions.

173. *Early Essays*, pp. 96, 98.

174. *Ibid.*, p. 97. This has now of course become orthodox Marxist doctrine. Cf. Lenin, "What is to be done?" (in *Little Lenin Library*), p. 14: "Those who are really convinced that they have advanced science, would demand not freedom for the new views to continue side by side with the old, but the substitution of the old views by the new ones."

175. *Early Essays*, pp. 130, 136, 107.

176. *Ibid.*, pp. 200-1.

177. *Ibid.*, pp. 131-2.

178. *Ibid.*, pp. 147-9, 157.

179. *Ibid.*, pp. 144, 133.

180. *Ibid.*, pp. 144, 149.

181. *Early Essays*, pp. 191, 180.

182. *Ibid.*, p. 165. Compare for a use of the same terms by Engels in his exposition of the materialist interpretation of history his *Herrn Eugen Dühring's Umwälzung der Wissenschaft* (English ed., *Herrn Eugen Dühring's Revolution in Science*, p. 300, trans. by E. Burns, where he says that the means by which the existing abuses can be got rid of "are not to be *invented* by the mind, but *discovered* by means of the mind in the existing factors of production."

183. *Ibid.*, pp. 154, 165, 167, 170.

184. Although the influence of Saint-Simonian doctrine on the birth of the materialist interpretation of history has often been pointed out (see particularly F. Muckle, *Henri de Saint-Simon*, Jena, 1908, and W. Sulzbach, *Die Anfänge der materialistischen Geschichtsauffassung*, Karlsruhe, 1911), these authors appear to have all overlooked that the crucial passages occur nearly always in works which are known to have been written by Comte.

185. *Producteur*, Vol. I, 1825, pp.

289, 596; Vol. II, 1825, pp. 314, 348; and Vol. III, 1826, p. 450. These essays have been included by Comte in the collection of *Early Essays* in the appendix to the *Politique positive* and will be found in the English edition (pp. 217-275 and 276-332) under the titles "Philosophical Considerations of the Sciences and Men of Science" and "Considerations on the Spiritual Power."

186. *Early Essays*, p. 229.

187. In a review of F. J. V. Broussais, *De l'irritation et de la folie*, 1828, published in the same year and also included in the *Early Essays*. See particularly p. 339.

188. *Ibid.*, p. 219.

189. *Ibid.*, pp. 295, 281.

190. *Ibid.*, p. 250.

191. *Ibid.*, pp. 306, 320-324.

192. *Ibid.*, p. 282.

193. *Ibid.*, p. 281. The curious similarity of this statement to certain thoughts of Hegel, which will occupy us later, will not escape the reader.

194. *Ibid.*, p. 307.

195. *Ibid.*, pp. 319-20: "Every doctrine presupposes a founder."

196. *Ibid.*, p. 301.

197. J. S. Mill, *Autobiography*, 1873, p. 213.

198. *O.S.S.E.*, XXIII, p. 99.

199. *Ibid.*, p. 152.

200. *Ibid., Vol.* XV, p. 82.

201. H. Gouhier, *La jeunesse d'Auguste Comte*, Vol. II, p. 3.

202. Quoted by G. Pinet, *Écrivains et Penseurs Polytechnicians*, 2nd ed., Paris, 1898, p. 180, from the *Livre nouveau, Résumé des conférences faites à Ménilmontant*.

203. On Enfantin and the Saint-Simonians generally see S. Charléty, *Histoire du Saint-Simonisme*, Paris, 1896 (new ed., 1931), still the best exposition of the Saint-Simonian movement. It is rather surprising that En-

fantin himself has not yet been made the subject of a monograph. S. Charléty, *Enfantin*, Paris, 1930, is merely a useful collection of texts with a brief introduction.

204. S. Charléty, *Enfantin*, p. 2.

205. Cf. H. Grossmann, "The Evolutionist Revolt against Classical Economics," *Journal of Political Economy*, October 1943, who contends that in this exposition I have overrated the originality of the Saint-Simonians at the expense of Saint-Simon himself. I am quite ready to agree that nearly all the elements of their system can be found in works that appeared during Saint-Simon's life and under his name (though partly written by Comte and probably others); but they are there so mixed up with other and in part contradictory ideas that I should rate the achievement of something like a coherent system by his disciples considerably higher than Dr. Grossmann does.

206. "Le travail de M. A. Comte . . . a servi à plusieurs entre nous d'introduction à la doctrine de Saint-Simon." *Doctrine de Saint-Simon, Exposition, Première Année*, ed. Bouglé and E. Halévy, Paris, 1924, p. 443. Comte (in a letter to G. d'Eichthal, Dec. 11, 1829) claims even more influence on the Saint-Simonians: "Vous savez fort bien que je les ai vus naître, si je ne les ai formés (ce dont je serais du reste fort loin de me glorifier) . . . ; les prétendues pensées de ces messieurs ne sont autre chose qu'une dérivation ou plutôt une mauvaise transformation de conceptions que j'ai presentées et qu'ils ont gatées en y mettant les conceptions hétérogènes dues à . . . Saint-Simon." E. Littré, *Auguste Comte et la philosophie positive*, Paris, 1863, pp. 173-4.

207. *Producteur*, Vol. I, 1825, Introduction.

208. On Bazard see W. Spühler, *Der Saint-Simonismus. Lehre und Leben*

von Saint-Amand Bazard (Zürcher Volkswirtschaftliche Forschungen, hg. v. M. Saitzew, No. 7) Zürich, 1926.

209. See Louis Reybaud, *Etudes sur les réformateurs contemporians ou socialistes modernes*, Brussels, 1841, p. 61: "M. Enfantin trouvait la pensée, M. Bazard la formulait." Compare also: C. Gide and C. Rist, *Histoire des doctrines économiques*, 4th ed., 1922, p. 251.

210. *Producteur*, Vol. I, p. 83.

211. *Producteur*, Vol. I, pp. 399 *et seq;* Vol. III, pp. 110 and 526 *et seq.* Bazard's articles were the immediate occasion for one of Benjamin Constant's most eloquent essays in defence of liberty.

212. *Producteur*, Vol. III, p. 74.

213. *Producteur*, Vol. IV, p. 86.

214. *O.S.S.E.*, Vol. XXIV, p. 86. In a letter to Fournel of June, 1832 (quoted by G. Pinet, "L'Ecole Polytechnique et les Saint-Simoniens," *Revue de Paris*, May 15, 1894, p. 85), Enfantin describes the Ecole Polytechnique as "la source précieuse ou notre famille nouvelle, germe de l'humanité future, a puisé la vie. Or, le prolétaire et le savant aiment et respectent cette glorieuse Ecole."

215. See Ch. Pellarin, *Jules Lechevalier et Abel Transom*, Paris, 1877, which, however, deals largely with the part the two men played later in the Fourierist movement. Lechevalier, after studying German philosophy in France, actually spent a year in Berlin in 1829–30 to attend Hegel's lectures.

216. See *Sadi Carnot, Biographie et manuscrit* publiés sous les auspices de l'Académie des sciences avec une préface de M. Emile Picard, Paris, 1927, p. 17-20. Cf. also G. Mouret, *Sadi Carnot et la science de l'énergie*, Paris, 1892. The *Réflexions sur la puissance motrice du feu* appeared in 1824, al-

though their importance was recognised only much later.

217. See H. Carnot, "Sur le Saint-Simonisme," *Séances et travaux de l'Académie de sciences morales at politiques*, 47ᵉ année, nouvelle série tome XXVIII, 1887, p. 132.

218. See H. Carnot, "Sur le Saint-Simonisme," *Séances et travaux de l'Académie de sciences morales et politiques*, 47ᵉ année, nouvelle série tome XXVIII, 1887, p. 129.

219. *Doctrine de Saint-Simon, Exposition, Première Année*, 1829, Paris, 1830. *Deuxième Année, 1829–30*, Paris, 1831. An excellent edition with a valuable introduction and instructive notes by C. Bouglé and E. Halévy was published in the *Collection des Economistes et Réformateurs Français*, Paris, 1924. It is to this edition that all the page references below refer.

220. C. Bouglé in his Introduction to E. Halévy, *L'Ere des Tyrannies*, Paris, 1938, p. 9.

221. [Abel Transon], *De la religion Saint-Simonienne. Aux Elèves de l'Ecole Polytechnique.* First published in the (second) *Organisateur*, July-Sept., 1829, and reprinted separately, Paris, 1830, and Brussels, 1831, and at the end of the second edition of the *Exposition, Deuxième Année, 1829–30.* A German translation appeared at Göttingen in 1832.

222. *Exposition*, ed. Bouglé and Halévy, p. 127.

223. *Ibid.*, pp. 131, 160.

224. *Ibid.*, p. 89.

225. *Ibid.*, p. 27.

226. *Ibid.*, p. 162.

227. *Ibid.*, p. 206.

228. *Ibid.*, pp. 139, 89.

229. *Ibid.*, pp. 73, 124, 153.

230. *Ibid.*, pp. 203, 206, 234, 253.

231. *Ibid.*, pp. 236, 350.

232. *Ibid.*, pp. 208-9.

233. *Exposition*, ed. Bouglé and Halévy, pp. 214-216, 238.

234. *Ibid.,* p. 225.

235. *Ibid.,* pp. 239, 307.

236. *De la religion Saint-Simonienne,* Paris, 1830, pp. 48-9.

237. *Exposition,* ed. Bouglé and Halévy, p. 243.

238. *Exposition,* ed. Bouglé and Halévy, p. 244.

239. *Ibid.,* pp. 253-4.

240. *Ibid.,* p. 255.

241. The French word "fonction" of course also means "office."

242. *Exposition,* ed. Bouglé and Halévy, p. 257.

243. In a letter to Channing in 1831 he admitted "I have shown the defects of the system of free competition, I have demolished, but I lack the strength to reconstruct." J. C. L. Simonde de Sismondi, *Fragments de son journal et de sa correspondance,* Genève-Paris, 1857, p. 130. On the general influence of Sismondi which can here not be adequately discussed see J. R. de Salis, *Sismondi,* Paris, 1932.

244. *Exposition,* p. 258.

245. *Ibid.,* pp. 258-9.

246. *Ibid.,* p. 261.

247. *Exposition,* pp. 272-3. It may be noted that this seems to be the first occurrence of the term "central bank."

248. The following passage from the *Exposition, Deuxième Année* (Première Séance, Résumé de l'exposition de la première année, ed. 1854, pp. 338-9), deserves, however, to be quoted: "Pour que cette *association industrielle* soit réalisée et produise tous ses fruits, il faut qu'elle constitue une hiérarchie, il faut qu'une vue générale préside à ses travaux et les harmonise . . . il faut absolument que l'Etat soit en possession de tous les instruments de travail qui forment aujourd'hui le fonds de la propriété individuelle, et que les directeurs de la société industrielle soient chargés de la distribution de ces instruments, fonction que remplissent aujourd'hui d'une manière si

aveugle et à si grands frais les *propriétaires* et *capitalistes* . . . alors seulement on verra cesser la scandale de la concurrence illimitée, cette grande négation critique dans l'ordre industriel, et qui, considérée sous son respect le plus saillant, n'est autre chose qu'une guerre acharnée et meurtrière, sous une forme nouvelle, que continuent se faire entre eux les individus et les nations." The opening of the passage shows clearly that at this stage they were using the term "association," in precisely the sense in which two years later they introduced the term "socialism."

249. See below, part III.

250. *Exposition,* p. 377. See, however, A. Comte in *Lettres à Valat,* pp. 164-5, for an informal use of the term in a letter dated March 30, 1825.

251. *Ibid.,* p. 275. "Industrialism" was coined by Saint-Simon himself to describe the opposite of Liberalism. See *O.S.S.E.,* XXXVII, pp. 178, 195.

252. *Ibid.,* pp. 487, 183.

253. *Ibid.,* pp. 139, 98.

254. Strictly speaking both the terms "socialist" and "socialism" had already been used in Italian (by G. Guiliani) in 1803, but had been forgotten. Independently of this, "socialist" occurs once in the Owenite *Co-operative Magazine* for November, 1827, and "socialism" (although in a different sense) in a French Catholic journal in November, 1831. But it was only with its appearance in the *Globe* that it was immediately taken up and frequently used, particularly by Leroux and Reybaud. See C. Grünberg, "Der Ursprung der Worte 'Sozialismus' und 'Sozialist,'" *Archiv für die Geschichte des Sozialismus und der Arbeiterbewegung,* Vol. II, 1912, p. 378. Cf. also *Exposition,* ed. Bouglé and Halévy, p. 205, note.

255. *Le Globe,* February 2, 1832. The word occurs in an article by H.

Joncières and the context in which it occurs is so significant that the whole sentence may be quoted: "Nous ne voulons pas sacrifier la personalité aux socialisme, pas plus que ce dernier à la personalité."

256. Some of the articles of Enfantin in the *Globe* which have been collected in a separate volume under the title *Economie politique et Politique* (Paris, 1832) deserve, however, to be specially mentioned.

257. A curious account of the motif for this is given by Eduard Gans, "Paris in Jahre 1830," in *Rückblicke auf Personen und Zustände*, Berlin 1836, p. 92: "Benjamin Constant erzählte mir, dass, als die St.-Simonisten ihn vor etwa einem Jahr um Rath gefragt hätten, wie sie ihre Grundsätze verbreiten könnten, er ihnen gesagt habe: macht eine Religion daraus."

258. See H. R. d'Allemagne, *Les Saint-Simoniens 1827–1837*, Paris, 1931.

259. See G. Pinet, *Ecrivains et penseurs polytechniciens*, 2nd ed., Paris, 1898, p. 176, and S. Charléty, *Histoire du Saint-Simonisme*, 1931, p. 29.

260. See G. Weill, "Le Saint-Simonisme hors de France," *Revue d'histoire économique et sociale*, Vol. IX, 1921, p. 105. A Saint-Simonian mission consisting of P. Leroux, H. Carnot and others had visited Brussels in February, 1831; and although, apart from the remarks of Weill just quoted, there is no direct evidence for the influence of the Saint-Simonians on Quetelet, it is remarkable how precisely from this date his ideas developed in a direction very similar to Comte's. On this see J. Lottin, *Quetelet, statisticien et sociologue*, Louvain and Paris, 1912, pp. 123, 356-367, also 10 and 21.

261. *L'Organisateur*, Vol. II, pp. 202, 213, quoted by C. Charléty, *Histoire du Saint-Simonisme*, 1931, p. 83.

262. *Globe*, June 3 and 8, 1831, quoted by Charléty, l.c., p. 110.

263. Karl Gutzkow, *Briefe eines Narren an eine Närrin*, 1832, quoted by E. M. Butler, *The Saint-Simonian Religion in Germany*, Cambridge, 1926, p. 263.

264. Duveyrier, e.g., one of the oldest members, wrote in the *Globe* of January 12, 1832: "On verrait sur la terre ce qu'on n'a jamais vu. On verrait des hommes et des femmes unis par un amour sans example et sans nom, puisqu'il ne connaîtrait ni le refroidissement, ni la jalousie; des hommes et des femmes se donneraient à plusieurs sans jamais cesser d'être l'un à l'autre et dont l'amour serait au contraire comme un divin banquet augmentant en magnificence en raison du nombre et du choix des convives."

265. Apparently the expression *chercher' a femme* derives from this.

266. See J. Lajard de Puyjalon, *L'Influence des Saint-Simoniens sur la réalisation de l'Isthme de Suez*, Paris, 1926.

267. See M. Wallon, *Les Saint-Simoniens et les chemins de fer*, Paris, 1908, and H. R. d'Allemagne, *Prosper Enfantin et les grandes entreprises du XIX siècle*, Paris, 1935.

268. On this and the following see M. Thibert, *Le Rôle social de l'art d'après les Saint-Simoniens*, Paris, 1927, H. J. Hunt, *Le Socialisme et le Romantisme en France, Etude de la Presse Socialiste de 1830 à 1848*, Oxford, 1935, and J.-M. Gros, *Le Mouvement Litteraire Socialiste Depuis 1830*, Paris, 1904.

269. For the development of the Saint-Simonian theory of art, see particularly E. Barrault, *Aux Artistes du Passé et de l'Avenir des Beaux Arts*, 1830.

270. See R. Curtius, *Balzac*, 1923.

271. See D. B. Cofer, *Saint-Simonism in the Radicalism of T. Carlyle*,

College Station (Texas) 1931; F. Muckle, *Henri de Saint Simon*, Jena, 1908, pp. 345-380; E. d'Eichthal, "Carlyle et le Saint-Simonisme," *Revue Historique*, vol. 82-3, 1903 (English translation in the *New Quarterly*, vol. II, London, April 1909); E. E. Neff, *Carlyle and Mill*, New York, 1926, p. 210; Hill Shine, *Carlyle and the Saint-Simonians. The Concept of Historical Periodicity.* Baltimore, Johns Hopkins University Press, 1941; and the same author's note in *Notes & Queries*, CLXXI, 1936, pp. 290-293. Why in the case of Carlyle, as with so many others, the influence of the Saint-Simonians blended so readily with that of the German philosophers will become clearer later. An interesting contrast to Carlyle's sympathetic reception of Saint-Simonian ideas is the exceedingly hostile reaction of R. Southey, who contributed to the *Quarterly Review* (Vol. XLV, July, 1831, pp. 407-450) under the heading "New Distribution of Property" a very full and intelligent account of the *Doctrine de Saint-Simon.* See also his letter of June 31, 1831 in E. Hodder, *The Life and Work of the 7th Earl of Shaftesbury,* London 1886, vol. I, p. 126. Tennyson, in a letter written in 1832, still says that "reform and St. Simonism are, and will continue to be, subjects of the highest interest . . . . the existence of the sect of St. Simonists is at once a proof of the immense mass of evil that is extant in the nineteenth century, and a focus which gathers all its rays. This sect is rapidly spreading in France, Germany, and Italy, and they have missionaries in London." (*Alfred Lord Tennyson, A Memoir* by his son, London, 1897, vol. I., p. 99.) It is a striking fact that the social novel begins in England with Disraeli just at the time when one would expect Saint-Simonian influences to work in this direction; but there is, as far as I am aware, no evidence of any influence of the Saint-Simonians on Disraeli.

272. See C. G. Higginson, *Auguste Comte, An Address on his Life and Work,* London, 1892 p. 6, and M. Quinn, *Memoirs of a Positivist,* London, 1924, p. 38.

273. J. S. Mill, *Autobiography,* 1873, pp. 163-167. See also *ibid.,* p. 61, where Mill describes how in 1821, at the age of fifteen, he had met in J. B. Say's house Saint-Simon himself, "not yet the founder of either a philosophy or a religion, and considered only as a clever original."

274. G. d'Eichthal and C. Duveyrier came in 1831 to London on an official Saint-Simonian mission. See the *Address to the British Public by the Saint-Simonian Missionaries,* London, 1832, and S. Charléty, *Histoire du Saint-Simonisme,* Paris, 1931, p. 93. See also *St. Simonism in London,* by Fontana, Chief, and Prati, Preacher of the St. Simonian Religion in England, London, 1834, reviewed by J. S. Mill in *The Examiner,* February 2, 1834.

275. *The Letters of John Stuart Mill,* ed. by H. S. R. Elliot, 1910, Vol. I, p. 20. See also J. S. Mill, *Correspondance inédite avec Gustave d'Eichthal,* 1828–1842, 1864–1871, ed. by E. d'Eichthal, Paris, 1898, and also, in part in the original English, in *Cosmopolis,* London, 1897-8, especially Vol. V, pp. 356 and 359-60.

276. The *Globe* of March 16th, 1832, already reports that "nul pays n'a consacré une attention plus profonde au Saint-Simonisme" than Germany.

277. See H. Fournel. *Bibliographie Saint-Simonienne,* Paris, 1933, p. 22.

278. See P. Lafitte. "Matériaux pour la Biographie d'Auguste Comte. I. Relations d'Auguste Comte avec l'Allemagne." *Revue Occidentale,* Vol. VIII, 1882, premier semestre, p. 227, and "Correspondance d'Auguste Comte et

Gustave d'Eichthal," *ibid.*, Second série, Vol. XII, 1891, premier semestre, pp. 186-276.

279. *Ibid.*, p. 228 and pp. 223 *et seq.*, where the review, dated Sept. 27th, 1824, is reprinted. It gives among other things an adequate account of the "law of three stages."

280. *Neue Monatsschrift für Deutschland*, Vol. XXI, 1821 (three articles) and Vol. XXII, 1827 (three articles); see also Vols. XXXIV and XXXV for later articles on the same subject. On Friedrich Buchholz, who for a period earlier in the century had been one of the most influential political writers of Prussia, and who in 1802 had published a *Darstellung eines neuen Gravitationsgestzes füer die moralische Welt*, see K. Bahrs, *Friedrich Buchholz, ein preussischer Publizist 1768–1843*, Berlin, 1907, and on d'Eichthal's relations to him particularly, "Correspondance d'Auguste Comte et Gustave d'Eichthal," *Revue Occidentale*, Vol. XII, premier semestre, Paris, 1891, pp. 186-276.

281. See the list of some fifty publications on Saint-Simonism which appeared in Germany between 1830 and 1832, given by E. M. Butler, *The Saint-Simonian Religion in Germany*, Cambridge, 1926, pp. 52-59, which is, however, by no means complete. On this see R. Palgen's review of this book in *Revue de Littérature Comparée*, Vol. IX, 1929; also W. Suhge, *Der Saint-Simonismus und das junge Deutschland*, Berlin, 1935.

282. See [Abel Transon], *Die Saint-Simonistische Religion. Fünf Reden an die Zöglinge der polytechnischen Schule, nebst einem Vorbericht ueber das Leben und den Charakter Saint-Simons*, Göttingen, 1832.

283. Quoted by Butler, *l.c.*, from *Briefe*, Weimarer Ausgabe, Vol. XLII, p. 300, letter dated October 17th, 1830.

284. See Eckermann, *Gespräche*

mit Goethe, under October 20th, 1830, and Goethe's *Tagebücher,* under October 31st, 1830, and May 30th, 1831.

285. *Rahel. Ein Buch des Andenkens für ihre Freunde*, Berlin, 1834, under the date of April 25th, 1832.

286. See Butler, *l.c.*, p. 70.

287. K. Grün, *Die soziale Bewegung in Frankreich und in Belgien*, Darmstadt, 1845, p. 90.

288. See Margaret A. Clarke, *Heine et la monarchie de juillet*, Paris 1927, especially Appendix II. Butler, *l.c.*, p. 71. It seems that some over-enthusiastic German admirers of Saint-Simon even compared him to Goethe, which induced Metternich (in a letter to Prince Wittgenstein, dated Nov. 30th, 1835) to make the tart comment that Saint-Simon, whom he had known personally, "had been as complete a cynical fool as Goethe was a great poet." See O. Draeger, *Theodor Mundt und seine Beziehungen zum jungen Deutschland*, Marburg, 1909, p. 156.

289. *Ibid*, p. 430. Cf., in addition to the book by Suhge already quoted also F. Gerathewohl, *Saint-Simonistische Ideen in der deutschen Literatur, Ein Beitrag zur Vorgeschichte des Sozialismus*, Munich, 1920; H. v. Kleinmayr, *Welt- und Kunstanschauung des jungen Deutschlands*, Vienna, 1930, and J. Dresch, *Gutzkow et la Jeune Allemagne*, Paris, 1904, on another German poet G. Buechner, who was not a member of the Young German group, but seems also to have been influenced by Saint-Simonian ideas. It is perhaps worth mentioning that he was the elder brother of L. Buechner, author of *Kraft und Stoff* (1855), and one of the main representatives of extreme materialism in Germany. On G. Buechner, cf., also G. Adler, *Geschichte der ersten sozialpolitischen Arbeiterbewegung in Deutschland*, Dresden, 1885, pp. 8 *et seq.*, which should also be consulted for some other early German

socialists, particularly Ludwig Gall and later Georg Kuhlmann and Julius Treichler, whose relations to Saint-Simonism need investigation. (*Ibid.*, pp. 6, 67, 72).

290. An interesting testimony to the extent of Saint-Simonian influence in Germany is a circular directed against it by the Archbishop of Trier, dated February 13, 1832. See the *Allgemeine Kirchenzeitung*, Darmstadt, March 8, 1832.

291. See B. Croce, *History of Europe in the 19th century*, 1934, p. 147.

292. Of the young Germans. T. Mundt and G. Kuehne were both Hegelian University lecturers of philosophy, and the same is true of the authors of most of the books reporting on the philosophical aspects of Saint-Simonism, particularly M. Veit, *Saint-Simon und der Saint-Simonismus*, Leipzig, 1834; F. W. Carové, *Der Saint-Simonismus und die neure französische Philosophie*, Leipzig, 1831. I have been unable to procure another work of the same period, S. R. Schneider, *Das Problem der Zeit und dessen Lösung durch die Association*, Gotha, 1834, which judging from its title seems to contain an account of the socialist aspects of Saint-Simonism.

293. Cf. B. Groethuysen, "Les jeunes Hégéliens et les Origines du Socialisme en Allemagne," *Revue Philosophique*, Vol. 95, no. 5/6, 1923, particularly p. 379.

294. In a review of his friend Mundt's *Lebenswirren*, quoted by W. Grupe, *Mundts und Kuehnes Verhältnis zu Hegel und seinen Gegnern*, Halle, 1928, p. 76.

295. In 1831, when the German Saint-Simonian movement began, Ruge was 29, Feuerbach 27, Rodbertus 26, Strauss 23, Hess 19, and Karl Marx 12 years of age. The corresponding ages of the leading Young Germans were

Laube 25, Kuehne 25, Mundt 23 and Gutzkow 20.

296. See T. Zlocisti, *Moses Hess*, Berlin, 1920, p. 13.

297. M. Hess. *Die heilige Geschichte der Menschheit*, Stuttgart, 1837.

298. See A. Kohut, *L. Feuerbach*, Leipzig, 1909, p. 77; and *Ausgewählte Briefe von und an Feuerbach*, ed. by W. Bolin, Leipzig, 1904, Vol. I, p. 256, where in a letter to his brother, dated Frankfurt, March 12th, 1832, Feuerbach explains that "Paris ist ein Ort, an den ich längst hinstrebe, für den ich mich schon längst in einem unwillkürlichen Drange, indem ich das Französische schon früher und besonders seither betrieb, vorbereitet, ein Ort, der ganz zu meiner Individualität, zu meiner Philosophie passt, an dem sich daher meine Kräfte entwickeln und selbst solche, die ich noch nicht kenne, hervortreten koennen."

299. See T. G. Masaryk, *Die philosophischen und soziologischen Grundlagen des Marxismus*, Vienna, 1899, p. 35.

300. Cf. G. Adler, *Die Geschichte der ersten sozialpolitischen Arbeiterbewegung in Deutschland*, Leipzig, 1885, und K. Mielcke, *Deutscher Frühsozialismus*, Stuttgart, 1931, pp. 185-189.

301. Lorenz von Stein, *Der Sozialismus und Kommunismus des heutigen Frankreich*, Leipzig, 1842, and K. Grün, *Die soziale Bewegung in Frankreich und Belgien*, Darmstadt, 1845. On the latter compare K. Marx and F. Engels, *The German Ideology* (Marxist Leninist Library), London, 1938, pp. 118-179.

302. Cf. B. Foeldes, "Bemerkungen zu dem Problem Lorenz von Stein—Karl Marx," *Jahrbücher für Nationalökonomie und Statistik*, Vol. 102, 1914, and H. Nitschke, *Die Geschichtsphilosophie Lorenz von Steins* (Beiheft No.

26, *Historische Zeitschrift*), München, 1932.

303. See Maxim Kowalewski in: *Karl Marx, Eine Sammlung von Erinnerungen und Aufsätzen*, herausgegeben von V. Adoratskij, Zürich, 1934, p. 223. Judging from a remark by W. Sulzbach in *Die Anfänge der materialistischen Geschichtsauffassung*, Stuttgart, 1911, p. 3, there seems to be also other independent evidence of Marx having studied Saint-Simonian writings while still at school. But I have been unable to trace it.

304. Apart from various earlier works by Muckle, Eckstein, Cunow and Sulzbach, see particularly Kurt Breysig, *Vom historischen Werden*, Vol. II, pp. 64 *et seq.* and 84 and W. Heider, *Die Geschichtslehre von Karl Marx*, "Forschungen" etc. ed. by K. Breysig, No. 3, 1931, p. 19. These suggestions have been confirmed by the careful investigation by V. Volgin, "Ueber die historische Stellung Saint-Simons," *Marx-Engels Archiv*, Vol. I/1, Frankfurt a. M., 1926, pp. 82-118.

305. Cf. G. Mayer, *Friedrich Engels, Eine Biographie*, Berlin, 1920. Vol. I, pp. 40 and 108.

306. See H. Dietzel, *Rodbertus*, 1888, Vol. I, p. 5, Vol. II, pp. 40, 44, 51, 66, 132 *et seq.*, 184-189; Ch. Andler, *Les origines du socialisme d'état en Allemagne*, Paris, 1897, pp. 107, 111; Ch. Gide and Ch. Rist, *Histoire des doctrines économiques*, Paris, 1909, pp. 481, 484, 488, 490.; F. Muckle, *Die grossen Sozialisten*, Leipzig, 1920, Vol. II, p. 77; W. Eucken, "Zur Würdigung Saint-Simons," *Jahrbuch für Volkswirtschaft und Gesetzgebung*, Vol. 45, 1921, p. 1052. The objections which have recently been raised against this contention by E. Thier, *Rodbertus, Lassalle, Adolf Wagner, Zur Geschichte des deutschen Staatssozialismus*, Jena, 1930, pp. 15-16, seem to be due to an inadequate knowledge of the Saint-Simonian writings.

307. See F. Mehring, *Geschichte der deutschen Sozialdemokratie*, 4th ed., 1909, Vol. II, p. 180.

308. See Ch. Andler, *l.c.*, p. 101.

309. Another curious and yet completely unexplored case where Saint-Simonian influence on German thought seems to have been at work is that of the economist Friedrich List. There is at least evidence of his direct contact with Saint-Simonian circles. List came to Paris, which he had already visited in 1823-4, on his return from America in December, 1830. On his earlier visit he had already made the acquaintance of the first editor of the *Revue Encyclopædique*, which during his second visit came into the hands of the Saint-Simonians and from August, 1831, onwards was edited by H. Carnot. List's interest, as that of the Saint-Simonians, was largely in railway projects and any attempt to make contact with people of similar interests during his visit must have led him straight to the Saint-Simonians. We know that List met Chevalier early and that he at least tried to make the acquaintance of d'Eichthal. (See his *Schriften, Reden, Briefe*, ed, by the Friedrich List Gesellschaft, Vol. IV, p 8.) Two of his articles on railways appeared in the *Revue Encyclopædique*. I have not been able to ascertain whether the *Globe*, from which he quotes in one of these articles (a passage for which the unsuspecting editor of the *Schriften* searched in vain in the English *Globe and Traveller*,) was not, as seems much more likely, the Saint-Simonian Journal of that name. (*See Schriften*, Vol. V., 1928, pp. 62 and 554.) Some years later List translated Louis Napoleon's *Idées Napoléoniennes*, the Saint-Simonian tendencies of which we shall yet have to note. As it is now known that he wrote the first version of his

chief work, the *Nationale System der Politischen Oekonomie,* during a third much more extended stay in Paris in the 'thirties as a prize essay and that in that essay he felt himself compelled to defend himself against any suspicion of "Saint-Simonism" in the sense of communism in which it was then generally understood (*Schriften,* Vol. IV, p. 294), there can be little doubt that any marked resemblance to Saint-Simonian ideas we find in his later work are likely to be due to that source. And such similarities are indeed not wanting. Particularly List's conception of "natural laws of historical development," according to which social evolution necessarily pass through definite stages, an idea readily accepted by the historical school of German economists, is most likely of Saint-Simonian origin. How strong in general the French influence on List was, of this his declamations against "ideology" bear witness. —That the other German author from whom the historical school of German economists derived its preoccupation with the discovery of definite stages of economic development, B. Hildebrandt, derived his ideas from the Saint-Simonians has been pointed out by J. Plenge, *Stammformen der vergleichenden Wirtschaftstheorie,* Essen, 1919, p. 15.

310. See H. Louvancour, *De Henri Saint-Simon à Charles Fourier,* Chartres, 1913, and H. Bourgin, *Fourier, Contribution à l'étude du socialisme Français,* 1905, particularly pp. 415 *et seq.*

311. See M. Dommanget, *Victor Considérant, Sa Vie, Son Oeuvre,* Paris, 1929.

312. On the Saint-Simonian elements in Proudon's doctrine see particularly K. Diehl. *Proudbon,* 1888–1896, Vol. III, pp. 159, 176, 280.

313. There may even have been a direct influence on early English social-

ism. At least one of T. Hodgskin's letters, written in 1820 soon after his return from France, shows fairly definite traces of Saint-Simonian ideas. See E. Halévy, *Thomas Hodgskin,* Paris, 1903, pp. 58-9. I owe this reference to Dr. W. Stark.

314. Mazzini was in the years between 1830 and 1835, particularly during his exile in France, in intimate contact with the Saint-Simonians P. Lerroux and J. Reynaud, and the effect of this can be traced throughout his work. See on this G. Salvemini, *Mazzini* (in G. d'Acandia, *La Giovine Europa*), Rome, 1915, *passim,* O. Vossler, *Mazzini's politisches Denken und Wollen* (Beiheft No. 11 *Historische, Zeitung*) München, 1927, pp. 42-52, and B. Croce, *History of Europe,* pp. 118, 142. On Mazzini's later critical attitude toward Saint-Simonism see his "thoughts on Democracy" in *Joseph Mazzini,* A Memoir by E. A. V[enturi], London, 1875, particularly pp. 205-217.

315. See G. Weill, "Le Saint-Simonisme hors de France," *Revue d'histoire économique et sociale,* Vol. IX, 1921, p. 109, and O. Vossler, l.c., p. 44.

316. See N. Mehlin, "Auguste Strindberg," *Revue de Paris,* Vol. XIX, Oct. 15th, 1912, p. 857.

317. See A. Herzen, *Le monde Russe et la révolution,* Paris, 1860–62, Vol. VI, pp. 195 *et seq.*

318. See G. Weill, *l.c.,* and J. F. Normano, Saint-Simonian America, *Social Forces,* Vol. IX, October, 1932.

319. See Ernest Solvay, *A propos de Saint-Simonisme* (Principes libéro-socialistes d'action sociale). Projet de lettre au journal *Le Peuple,* 1903 (printed 1916). Cf. P. Héger and C. Lefebure, *Vie d'Ernest Solvay,* Brussels, 1929, pp. 77, 150.

320. The post-war *Producteur* was published in Paris from 1919 by a group which included G. Darquet, G. Gros, H. Clouard, M. Leroy and F.

Delaisi. See on this M. Bourbonnais, *Les Néo-Saint-Simoniens et la vie sociale d'aujourd'hui,* Paris, 1923.

321. Cf. also G. J. Gignoux, "L'Industrialisme de Saint-Simon à Walter Rathenau," *Revue d'histoire des doctrines économiques et sociales,* 1923, and G. Salomon, Die Saint-Simonisten, *Zeitschrift für die gesamte Staatswissenschaft,* Vol. 82, 1927, pp. 550-576. On the influence Saint-Simonian ideas had in the conception of the corporativist theories of Fascism see Hans Reupke, *Unternehmer und Arbeiter in der fascistischen Wirtschaftsidee,* Berlin 1931, pp. 14, 18, 22, 29-30, 40.

322. See Johann Plenge, *Gründung und Geschichte des Crédit Mobilier,* Tübingen, 1903, particularly pp. 79 *et seq.,* and the passage quoted there on p. 139 from the Annual Report of the Crédit Mobilier for 1854: "Quand nous touchons à une branche de l'industrie, nous désirons surtout obtenir son développement non par la voie de la concurrence, mais par voie *d'association et de fusion,* par l'emploi le plus économique des forces et non par leur opposition et leur déstruction réciproque."

There is no space here for the discussion of the Saint-Simonian theories of credit in the hands of the Pereires and we must refer in this respect to J. B. Vergeot, *Le Crédit comme stimulant et régulateur de l'industrie, La conception Saint-Simonienne, ses réalisations,* etc., Paris, 1918, and K. Moldenhauer, *Kreditpolitik und Gesellschaftsreform,* Jena, 1932. But it may just be mentioned that the Pereires, after acquiring the *Banque de Savoy* with its note issuing privilege, in order to be in a position to put their theories into practice, became ardent advocates of "free banking" and the cause of the great controversy between the "free banking" and the "central banking" school which raged in France in and

after 1864. On this see V. C. Smith, *The Rationale of Central Banking,* London, 1936, pp. 33 *et seq.*

323. See J. Hansen, *G. v. Mevissen,* Berlin, 1906, Vol. I, pp. 60, 606, 644-6, 655, and W. Daebritz, *Gründung und Anfänge der Discontogesellschaft,* Berlin, Muenchen, 1931, pp. 34-36.

324. See H. M. Hirschfeld, "Le Saint-Simonisme dans les Pays-Bas. Le Crédit Mobilier Néerlandais": *Revue d'Economie Politique,* 1923, pp. 364-374.

325. See F. G. Steiner, *Die Entwicklung des Mobilbankwesens in Oesterreich von den Anfängen bis zur Krise von 1873,* Wien, 1913, pp. 38-78.

326. See H. M. Hirschfeld, Der Crédit-Mobilier Gedanke mit besonderer Berücksichtigung seines Einflusses in den Niederlanden. *Zeitschrift für Volkswirtschaft und Sozialpolitik,* N.F., Vol. III, 1923, pp. 438-465.

327. See G. v. Schulze-Gaevernitz, *Die deutsche Kreditbank (Grundriss der Sozialökonomik* V/2) 1915, p. 146.

328. See M. Wallon, *Les Saint-Simoniens et les Chemins de Fer,* Paris, 1908, and H. R. d'Allemagne, *Prosper Enfantin et les grandes entreprises du XIX siècle,* Paris, 1935.

329. See the *Vues politiques et pratiques sur les travaux publiques en France,* published in 1832 by the four Saint-Simonian engineers, G. Lamé, B. P. E. Clapeyron and S. and E. Flachat.

330. Quoted by G. Pinet, *Ecrivains et penseurs polytechniciens,* Paris, 1887, p. 165.

331. See C. Pecqueur, *Economie sociale: des intérêts du commerce, de l'industrie et de l'agriculture, et de la civilisation en général, sous l'influence des applications de la vapeur,* Paris, 1838.

332. Particularly Jourdan, an intimate friend of Enfantin, and Guérault. On the latter compare Saint-Beuve, *Nouveaux Lundis,* IV; and on Saint-

Beuve's own relations to Saint-Simonism M. Leroy, "Le Saint-Simonisme de Saint-Beuve," *Zeitschrift für Sozialwissenschaft*, vol. VII, 1938, pp. 132-147.

333. See A. Guerard, *Napoleon III*, Harvard University Press 1943, p. 215, where this description of Napoleon III. is called "strikingly accurate"; and H. N. Boon, *Rêve et réalité dans l'oeuvre économique et sociale*, The Hague 1936.

334. *Des Idées Napoléoniennes*, 1839, *L'idée Napoléonienne*, 1840, and *De l'extinction du paupérisme*, 1844.

335. On this whole phase of their activities see G. Weill, "Les Saint-Simoniens sous Napoleon III," *Revue des études Napoléoniennes*, May 1931, pp. 391-406.

336. Cf. E. Halévy, "La doctrine économique Saint-Simonienne," in *L'Ère des Tyrannies*, Paris, 1938, p. 91.

337. See L. Brentano, "Die gewerbliche Arbeiterfrage," in Schönberg's *Handbuch der politischen Oekonomie*, 1st ed., 1882, p. 935 *et seq.*

338. K. Grün, *Die soziale Bewegung in Frankreich und Belgien*, 1845, p. 182. It is interesting to compare this statement with a manuscript note by Lord Acton (Cambridge University Library, Acton 5487) in which, *a propos* Bazard, Acton says: "A system is shut in. It is the broken fragments of it, dissolved, that fructify."—*Cf.* also J. S. Mill, *Principles of Political Economy*, 2nd ed., 1849, vol. I, p. 250: St. Simonism, "during the few years of its public promulgation, sowed the seeds of nearly all socialist tendencies which have since spread so widely in France"; and W. Roscher, *Geschichte der Nationalökonomik in Deutschland*, 1874, p. 845: "Und es lässt sich nicht leugnen, wie diese Schriftsteller [Bazard, Enfantin, Comte, Considerant] an praktischem Enfluss auf ihre Zeit mit den heutigen Socialistenführern gar nicht verglichen werden können, ebenso sehr

überragen sie die letzteren an wissenschaftlicher Bedeutung. Es kommen in der neuesten socialistischen Literatur sehr wenig erhebliche Gedanken vor, die nicht bereits von jenen Franzosen ausgesprochen wären, noch dazu meist in einer viel würdigern, geistreichen Form."

339. Originally published in 1822 under the title *Prospectus des travaux nécessaires pour réorganiser la société* and republished under the above title only in 1824.

340. Page references to the *Cours* will be to the second edition, edited by E. Littré, Paris, 1864, the pagination of which is identical with the third and fourth, but not with the first and fifth editions. English quotations in the text will be taken, wherever practicable, from the admirable condensed English version by Miss Martineau (*The Positive Philosophy of Auguste Comte*. Freely translated and condensed by Harriet Martineau. Third edition in two volumes. London, 1893. In references to this edition the title will be abbreviated as *P.P.* as distinguished from the French original referred to as *Cours*).

Although the coincidence of the exact date is no more than an accident, it is perhaps worth pointing out that the year 1842, in which the concluding volume of the *Cours* appeared and which for our purposes thus marks the conclusion of the "French phase" of the strand of thought with which we are here concerned, is also the year which more than any other may be regarded as the beginning of the "German phase" of the same development, with which we hope to deal on another occasion. In 1842 Lorenz von Stein's *Sozialismus und Communismus im beutigen Frankreich* and J. K. Rodbertus' first work *Zur Erkenntnis unserer staatswirtschaftlichen Zustände* appeared and Karl Marx sent his first essays to the publisher. In the preceding year Friedrich List had published his *Nationale System der Politischen Oekonomie,* and L. Feuerbach his *Wesen des Christentums.* In the following year there appeared W. Roscher's *Grundriss zu Vorlesungen über die Staatswirtschaft nach historischer Methode.* The special significance of this date in German intellectual history is well brought out by H. Freund, *Soziologie und Sozialismus. Ein Beitrag zur Geschichte der deutschen Sozialtheorie um 1842.* Würzburg, 1934.

341. *Cours,* II, p. 438.

342. The essential unity of Comte's thought, which had always had its defenders, has since G. Dumas' investigations (*Psychologie de deux Messies positivistes,* Paris, 1905) been accepted by practically all French scholars concerned with these questions. See on this the recent survey of the discussion in H. Gouhier, *La jeunesse d'Auguste Comte,* Vol. I, Paris, 1933, pp. 18-29, and the two works by P. Ducassé, *Méthode et intuition chez Auguste Comte* and *Essai sur l'origine intuitive du positivisme,* both Paris, 1939.

343. Cf. the interesting confession by Mr. H. G. Wells in his *Experiment in Autobiography,* London, 1934, p. 658: "Probably I am unjust to Comte and grudge to acknowledge a sort of priority he had in sketching the modern outlook. But for him, as for Marx, I have a real personal dislike."

344. Cf. *Cours,* I, p. 9: "L'état métaphysique, qui n'est au fond qu'une simple modification général du premier." Also IV, p. 213.

345. Cf. L. Lévy-Bruhl, *La philosophie d'Auguste Comte,* 4th ed., Paris, 1921, p. 42, and *Cours,* V, p. 25.

346. *Cours,* II, p. 312, and IV, p. 469.

347. *Cours,* III, pp. 188-9: Le véritable esprit général de toute philosophie théologique ou métaphysique consiste à prendre pour principe, dans

l'explication des phénomènes du monde extérieur, notre sentiment immédiat des phénomènes humains; tandis que, au contraire, la philosophie positive est toujours caractérisée, non moins profondément, par la subordination nécessaire et rationelle de la conception de l'homme à celle du monde. Quelle que soit l'incompatibilité fondamentale manifestée, à tant de titres, entre ces deux philosophies, par l'ensemble de leur développement successif, elle n'a point, en effet, d'autre origine essentielle, ni d'autre base permanente, que cette simple différence d'ordre entre ces deux notions également indispensables. En faisant prédominer, comme l'esprit humain a dû, de toute nécessité, le faire primitivement, la considération de l'homme sur celle du monde, on est inévitablement conduit à attribuer tous les phénomènes à des *volontés* correspondantes, d'abord naturelles, et ensuite extra-naturelles, ce qui constitue le système théologique. L'étude directe du monde extérieur a pu seule, au contraire, produire et développer la grande notion des lois de la nature, fondement indispensable de toute philosophie positive, et qui, par suite de son extension graduelle et continue à des phénomènes de moins en moins réguliers, a dû être enfin appliquée à l'étude même de l'homme et de la société, dernier terme de son entière généralisation. . . . L'étude positive n'a pas de caractère plus tranché que sa tendance spontanée et invariable à baser l'étude réelle de l'homme sur la connaissance préalable du monde extérieur." *Cf.* also IV, pp. 468-9.

348. *Cours,* IV, p. 256.

349. *Cours,* I, p. 16, cf. also II, p. 312, IV, p. 230.

350. *Cours,* I, p. 12.

351. *Cours,* VI, p. 600. Cf. *Early Essays on Social Philosophy,* translated from the French of Auguste Comte by H. D. Hutton, London (Routledge's

New Universal Library), 1911, p. 223. As it is of some interest that nearly all the basic ideas were already clearly stated in Comte's *Early Essays*, references to the corresponding passages in these will occasionally be added to the references to the *Cours*.

352. Cf. L. Grunicke, *Der Begriff der Tatsache in der positivistischen Philosophie des 19. Jabrhunderts*, Halle, 1930.

353. *Cours*, VI, pp. 402-3, cf. also I, pp. 30-32: "L'organe observé et l'organe observateur étant, dans ce cas, identique, comment l'observation pourrait-elle avoir lieu?", and III, pp. 538-541. *P.P.* II, 385, and I, 9-10, 381-2.

354. *Cours*, I, p. 30.

355. *Cours*, III, p. 535.

356. *Cours*, III, p. 540.

357. *Cours*, III, pp. 533, 563, 570.

358. *Cours*, III, pp. 429-30, and 494, *P.P.* I. p. 354.

359. *Cours*, III, pp. 336-7, cf. also III, pp. 216-7 and *Early Essays*, p. 219. It is interesting to note that while the passage in the early work states simply: "L'action personelle de l'homme sur les autres êtres est la seule dont il comprenne le mode, par le sentiment qu'il en a" (A. Comte, *Opuscules de la philosophie sociale, 1819–1828*, Paris, 1883, p. 182), this becomes in the corresponding passage of the *Cours* (IV. p. 468): "Ses propres actes, les seuls dont il *puisse jamais croire comprendre* le mode essentiel de production." (Italics ours.)

360. *Cours*, I, pp. 10, 44.

361. *Cours*, VI, p. 601.

362. Cf. C. Menger, *Untersuchungen über die Methode der Sozialwissenschaften*, Leipzig, 1883, p. 15 note, where he argues that in the exact social sciences "sind die menschlichen *Individuen* und *Bestrebungen*, die letzten Elemente unserer Analyse, empirischer Natur und die exakten theoretischen Sozialwissenschaften somit in grossem

Vorteil gegenüber den Naturwissenschaften. Die 'Grenzen des Naturerkennens' und die hieraus für das theoretische Verständnis der Naturphänomene sich ergebenden Schwierigkeiten bestehen in Wahrheit nicht für die exakte Forschung auf dem Gebiete der Sozialerscheinungen. Wenn A. Comte die 'Gesellschaften' als reale Organismen, und zwar als Organismen komplizierterer Art, denn die natürlichen, auffasst und ihre theoretische Interpretation als das unvergleichlich kompliziertere und schwierigere wissenschaftliche Problem bezeichnet, so befindet er sich somit in einem schweren Irrtum. Seine Theorie wäre nur gegenüber Sozialforschern richtig, welche den, mit Rücksicht auf den heutigen Zustand der theoretischen Naturwissenschaften, geradezu wahnwitzigen Gedanken fassen würden, die Gesellschaftsphänomene nicht spezifisch sozialwissenschaftlich, sondern in naturwissenschaftlich atomistischer Weise interpretieren zu wollen."

363. *Cours*, IV, pp. 356-7, *P.P.* II, p. 97.

364. *Cours*, VI, p. 599.

365. *Cours*, I, p. 122, III, p. 295.

366. *Cours*, III, p. 29.

367. *Cours*, III, p. 291.

368. *Cours*, IV, pp. 365-7. *Early Essays*, pp. 193-198.

369. *Cours*, III,[40e] leçon, VI, p. 671.

370. *Cours*, III, pp. 321-2.

371. *Cours*, IV, p. 258, cf. *Early Essays*, p. 239.

372. This has often been noted and commented upon. See particularly E. Bernheim, *Geschichtsforschung und Geschichtsphilosophie*, Göttingen, 1880, p. 48, and *Lehrbuch der historischen Methode*, 5th ed., 1908, Index *s. v.* "sozialistisch-naturwissenschaftliche oder kollektivistische Geschichtsauffassung."

373. There is one vague reference to this aspect in *Cours*, IV, pp. 270-1.

374. See below, pp. 316-17.

375. *Cours*, IV, p. 15, footnote.

376. Defourny, *La Philosophie positiviste. Auguste Comte*, Paris, 1902, p. 57.

377. *Sociologie* is introduced in *Cours*, IV, p. 185, *lois sociologiques* appears first a few pages earlier, IV, p. 180.

378. *Cours*, I, p. 29, IV, pp. 230-1.

379. The *Cours* is dedicated to Fourier and De Blainville, the two men among these four who were still alive at the time of its publication.

380. It may however be mentioned, since it does not seem to have been noticed before, that the distinction between *Gemeinschaft* and *Gesellschaft*, popularized by the German sociologist F. Toennies, already appears in Comte, who stresses the fact that "domestic relations do not constitute an association but a *union*." (*Cours*, IV, p. 419, *P.P.*, II, 116.)

381. Smith's influence appears in a clear and rather surprising form when Comte asks: "peut-on réellement concevoir, dans l'ensemble des phénomènes naturels, un plus merveilleux spectacle que cette convergence régulière et continue d'une immensité d'individus, doués chacun d'une existence pleinement distincte et, à un certain degré, indépendante, et néanmoins tous disposés sans cesse malgré les différences plus ou moins discordantes de leur talents et sourtout de leurs caractères, à concourir spontanément, par une multitude de moyens divers, à un même développement général, sans s'être d'ordinaire nullement concertés, et le plus souvent à l'insu de la plupart d'entre eux, qui ne croient obéir qu'à leurs impulsions personelles?" *Cours*, IV, pp. 417-8.

382. *Cours*, IV, p. 436, *P.P.*, II, p. 121.

383. *Lettres d'Auguste Comte à M. Valat*, 1815-1844, Paris, 1870, pp.

138-9. (Letter dated September 8th, 1824.)

384. *Cours*, I, p. 51, II, p. 20, VI, p. 618, *Early Essays*, p. 191.

385. Cours, V, 14, cf. also V, p. 188, where it is explained that "ces dénominations de grec et romain ne désignent point ici essentiellement des sociétés accidentelles et particulières; elles se rapportent surtout à des situations nécessaries et générales, qu'on ne pourrait qualifier abstraitement que par des locutions trop compliquées."

386. *Cours*, I, p. 65.

387. Cf. *Cours*, VI, pp. 620, 622.

388. Cf. the concluding sentences in Professor Morris Ginsberg's recent *Sociology* (Home University Library, 1934, p. 244): "The conception of a self-directing humanity is new and as yet vague in the extreme. To work out its full theoretical implications, and, with the aid of the other sciences, to inquire into the possibilities of its realization, may be said to be the ultimate object of sociology."

389. This was, perhaps, even more true of the Continent, where it was generally known that the various "sociological societies" consisted almost exclusively of socialists.

390. *Cours*, VI, p. 670.

391. *Cours*, VI, p. 671.

392. See above p. 198.

393. The "grammarians are even more absurd than the logicians." *Système de politique positive*, II, pp. 250-1.

394. R. Mauduit, *Auguste Comte et la science économique*, Paris, 1929, particularly pp. 48-69. A full reply to Comte's strictures on political economy has been given by J. E. Cairnes in an essay on "M. Comte and Political Economy," first published in the *Fortnightly Review*, May, 1870, and reprinted in *Essays on Political Economy*, 1873, pp. 265-311.

395. *Cours*, IV, p. 196.

396. *Cours,* IV, p. 194, *P.P.,* II, p. 51.

397. *Cours,* I, p. 84, IV, pp. 144-5, 257, 306, 361.

398. *Cours,* VI, p. 547, *P.P.,* II, p. 412.

399. *Cours,* IV, pp. 197-8, 255.

400. *Cours,* IV, p. 195.

401. *Cours,* IV, p. 197.

402. *Cours,* IV, p. 203, *P.P.,* II, p. 54.

403. *Cours,* IV, pp. 200-1.

404. *Cours,* IV, p. 203, *P.P.,* II, p. 54.

405. Cf. *Lettres à Valat,* p. 99 (letter dated September 28th, 1819): "J'ai une souveraine aversion pour les travaux scientifiques dont je n'aperçois l'utilité soit directe, soit eloignée."

406. *Cours,* I, p. 42.

407. *Cours,* IV, p. 139.

408. J. S. Mill, *Auguste Comte and Positive Philosophy,* Second edition, London, 1866, p. 141.

409. *Ibid.,* p. 196.

410. *Cours,* I, p. 15. Cf. *Early Essays,* p. 132.

411. *Cours,* IV, p. 43.

412. *Cours,* IV, p. 43, *P.P.,* II, p. 12.

413. *Cours,* IV, p. 48.

414. *Cours,* IV, p. 147, *P.P.,* II, p. 39.

415. *Cours,* VI, p. 495.

416. *Cours,* VI, p. 511.

417. *Système de politique positive,* I, p. 156.

418. *Cours,* VI, p. 454, *Système de politique positive,* I, pp. 151, 361-3, II, p. 87.

419. *Cours,* VI, pp. 482-485.

420. *Cours,* VI, p. 484.

421. *Cours,* IV, p. 437, *P.P.,* II, p. 122.

422. This applies particularly to the writings of O. Spengler and W. Sombart.

423. *Cours,* VI, p. 590. *Discours sur l'esprit positif,* ed. 1918, p. 118.

424. *Cours,* IV, p. 51.

425. The fullest account of Quetelet's life and work is that by J. Lottin, *Quetelet, Statisticien et Sociologue,* Louvain-Paris, 1912.

426. On the reputed influence of the Saint-Simonians on Quetelet compare above, p. 153 and note 260.

427. The English translation of the above passage is taken from H. M. Walker, *Studies in the History of Statistical Method,* Baltimore, 1929, p. 40.

428. H. M. Walker, *Studies in the History of Statistical Method,* Baltimore, 1929, p. 29.

429. Cf. L. Dimier, *Les maîtres de la contre-révolution,* Paris, 1917, pp. 215-235.

430. J. S. Mill, *Auguste Comte and Positivism,* p. 2.

431. For a full account of English Positivism see R. Metz, *A Hundred Years of British Philosophy,* London, 1936, pp. 171-234, and J. E. McGee, *A Crusade for Humanity—The History of Organized Positivism in England,* London, 1931. On Comte's influence in the United States see the two studies by R. L. Hawkins, *Auguste Comte and the United States (1816–1853),* 1936, and *Positivism in the United States (1853–1861),* 1938 (both Harvard University Press).

432. This penetration of Comtian positivism into Germany through the medium of English authors is a curious reversal of the earlier process when English seventeenth and eighteenth century thought had become known to Germany largely through the instrumentality of French writers, from Montesquieu and Rousseau down to J. B. Say. This fact explains to a large extent the belief, widely held in Germany, that there exists a fundamental contrast between "Western" naturalist and German idealist thought. In fact, if such a contrast can at all be drawn, there is a much more continuous difference between English thought, as repre-

sented, say, by Locke, Mandeville, Hume, Smith, Burke, Bentham and the classical economists and, on the other hand, Continental thought as represented by the two parallel and very similar developments which went from Montesquieu, through Turgot, Condorcet, down to Saint-Simon and Comte, and from Herder through Kant, Fichte, Schelling and Hegel down to the later Hegelians. The French school of thought which indeed was closely related to English thought, that of Condillac and the "ideologues," had disappeared by the time with which we are now concerned.

433. The infiltration of positivist thought into the social sciences in Germany is a story by itself which cannot be told here. Among its most influential representatives were the two founders of *Völkerpsychologie*, M. Lazarus and H. Steinthal (the former important because of his influence on W. Dilthey), E. du Bois-Reymond (see particularly his lecture *Kulturgeschichte und Naturwissenschaft*, 1877), the Viennese circle of T. Gomperz and W. Scherer, later W. Wundt, H. Vaihinger, W. Oswalt and K. Lamprecht. See on this E. Rothacker, *Einleitung in die Geisteswissenschaften*, Tübingen, 1920, pp.

200-206, 253 *et seq.*, C. Misch, *Der junge Dilthey*, Leipzig, 1933, E. Bernheim, *Geschichtsforschung und Geschichtsphilosophie*, Göttingen, 1880, and the same authors' *Lehrbuch der historischen Methode*, 5th and 6th ed., Leipzig, 1908, pp. 699-716, and for the influence on some of the members of the younger historical school of German economists particularly H. Waentig, *August Comte und seine Bedeutung für die Entwicklung der Socialwissenschaft*, Leipzig, 1894, pp. 279 *et seq.*

434. Cf. S. Deploige, *Le conflit de la morale et de la sociologie*, Louvain, 1911, particularly chapter VI on the genesis of Durckheim's system.

435. The direct influence of Comte on Charles Maurras should perhaps also be mentioned here.

436. Cf. W. Jaffé, *Les théories économiques et sociales de T. Veblen*, Paris, 1924, p. 35, and R. V. Teggart, *Thorstein Veblen, A Chapter in American Economic Thought*, Berkeley, 1932, pp. 15, 43, 49-53.

437. Cf. F. S. Marvin, *Comte* (in the series "Modern Sociologists"), London, 1936, p. 183.

438. Cf. E. Bernheim, *Lehrbuch der historischen Methode*, pp. 710 *et seq.*

Part Three

1. Bernard Bosanquet, *The Meeting of Extremes in Contemporary Philosophy*, London, 1921, p. 100.

2. See Hutchinson Stirling, "Why the Philosophy of History Ends with Hegel and Not with Comte," in "Supplementary Note" to A. Schwegler's *Handbook of the History of Philosophy*, and John Tulloch, *Edinburgh Review*, CCLX 1868. E. Troeltsch,

Der Historismus und seine Probleme (*Gesammelte Schriften III*) Tübingen, 1922, p. 24, is inclined to ascribe even Comte's celebrated law of the three stages to the influence of Hegel's dialectics, although it derives in fact from Turgot. Cf. also R. Levin, *Der Geschichtsbegriff des Positivismus*, Leipzig, 1935, p. 20.

3. First published in 1822 in H. de

Saint-Simon's *Catéchisme des industrielles* as *Plan for the Scientific Operations Necessary for Reorganizing Society* and two years later republished separately as *System of Positive Polity* —"a title premature indeed, but rightly indicating the scope" of his labors, as Comte wrote much later when he reprinted his early works as an Appendix to his *Système de politique positive*. A translation of this appendix by D. H. Hutton was published in 1911 under the title *Early Essays in Social Philosophy* in Routledge's "New Universal Library," and it is from this little volume that the above English titles and the later quotations are taken.

4. On Comte's early history and his relation to Saint-Simon see the comprehensive account in H. Gouhier, *La jeunesse d'Auguste Comte et la Formation du Positivisme*, 3 vols.; Paris, 1933–40.

5. Gustave d'Eichthal to Auguste Comte, November 18, 1824, and January 12, 1825. P. Lafitte, "Matériaux pour servir à la Biographie d'Auguste Comte: Correspondance, d'Auguste Comte avec Gustave d'Eichthal," *La Revue Occidentale*, second series, XII 19 année, 1891, Part II, pp. 186 ff.

6. *Lettres d'Auguste Comte à Divers*, Paris, 1905, II, p. 86 (April 11, 1825).

7. R. Flint, *Philosophy of History in Europe*, I, 1874, pp. 262, 267, 281.

8. J. T. Merz, *History of European Thought*, IV (1914), pp. 186, 481 ff., 501-3.

9. A. Fouillée, *Le mouvement positiviste*, 1896, pp. 268, 366.

10. E. Meyerson, *L'explication dans les sciences*, 1921, II, pp. 122-38.

11. T. Wittaker, *Reason: A Philosophical Essay with Historical Illustrations*, Cambridge, 1934, pp. 7-9.

12. Troeltsch, *op. cit.*, p. 408.

13. E. Spranger, "Die Kulturzyklentheorie und das Problem des Kulturver-falles," *Sitzungsberichte der Preussischen Akademie der Wissenschaften*. Philosophisch-Historische Klasse, 1926, pp. xlii ff.

14. W. Ashley, *Introduction to English Economic History and Theory*, 3d ed.; 1914, I, ix-xi. A. W. Benn, *History of British Rationalism*, 1906, I, 412, 449; II, 82. E. Caird, *The Social Philosophy and Religion of Comte*, 2d ed.; 1893, p. 51. M. R. Cohen, "Causation and its Application to History," *Journal of the History of Ideas*, III, 1942, 12. R. Eucken, "Zur Würdigung Comte's und des Posivitismus," in *Philosophische Aufsätze Eduard Zeller gewidmet*, Leipzig, 1887, p. 67, and also in *Geistige Strömungen der Gegenwart*, 1904, p. 164. K. R. Geijer, "Hegelianism och Positivism," *Lunds Universitets Arsskrift*, XVIII, 1883. G. Gourvitch, *L'idée du droit social*, 1932, pp. 271, 297. H. Hoeffding, *Der menschliche Gedanke*, 1911, p. 41. M. Mandelbaum, *The Problem of Historical Knowledge*, New York, 1938, pp. 312 ff. G. Mehlis, "Die Geschichtsphilosophie Hegels und Comtes," *Jahrbuch für Soziologie*, III, 1927. J. Rambaud, *Histoire des Doctrines Economiques*, 1899, pp. 485, 542. E. Rothacker, *Einleitung in die Geisteswissenschaften*, 1920, pp. 190, 287. A. Salomon, "Tocqueville's Philosophy of Freedom," *Review of Politics*, I, 1939, 400. M. Schinz, *Geschichte der französischen Philosophie*, 1914, I, 2. W. Windelband, *Lehrbuch der Geschichte der Philosophie*, new ed.; 1935, pp. 554 f. An article by G. Salomon-Delatour, "Hegel ou Comte," in the *Revue Positiviste Internationale*, LII, 1935, and LIII, 1936, became available to me only after the present essay was in the hands of the printer.

15. F. Dittmann, "Die Geschichtsphilosophie Comtes und Hegels," *Vierteljahrsschrift für wissenschaftliche*

Philosophie und Soziologie, XXXVIII (1914), XXXIX (1915).

16. The list of additional names, which could be extended almost indefinitely, would include, among others, such ones as Eugen Dühring, Arnold Ruge, J. P. Proudhon, V. Pareto, L. T. Hobhouse, E. Troeltsch, W. Dilthey, Karl Lamprecht, and Kurt Breysig.

17. Quoted by K. R. Popper, *The Open Society and Its Enemies,* London, 1945, II, 25.

18. J. S. Mill to A. Bain, November 4, 1867, *The Letters of John Stuart Mill,* ed. H. S. R. Elliot, London, 1910, II, 93.

19. Meyerson, *op. cit.,* esp. chap. xiii.

20. Meyerson, *op. cit.,* II, 50.

21. J. Laporte, *Le Rationalisme de Descartes,* new ed.; Paris, 1950.

22. E. Buss, "Montesquieu und Cartesius," *Philosophische Monatshefte,* IV (1869), 1-37, and H. Trescher, "Montesquieu's Einfluss auf die philosophischen Grundlagen der Staatslehre Hegels," *Schmollers Jahrbuch,* XLII (1918).

23. Cf. Schinz, *op. cit.,* and G. Misch, "Zur Entstehung des französischen Positivismus," *Archiv für Geschichte der Philosophie,* XIV (1901).

24. In a letter of August 5, 1824, Comte writes of Herder as "prédécesseur du Condorcet, mon prédécesseur immediat." See *Lettres d'Auguste Comte à Divers,* Paris, 1905, II, 56.

25. Comte, *Cours de Philosophie Positive,* 5th ed. (identical with the 1st); Paris, 1893, IV, 253; see also *Early Essays,* p. 150.

26. For a systematic analysis and criticism of these ideas see part I of this volume.

27. Cf. K. R. Popper, "The Poverty of Historicism," *Economica* (N.S.), XI (1944), 94.

28. *Cours,* IV, 286: "l'ensemble du sujet est certainement alors beaucoup mieux connu et plus immédiatement abordable que les diverses parties qu'on distinguera ultérieurement."

29. *Cours,* IV, 291.

30. *Cours,* IV, 526.

31. See, for example, E. de Roberty, *Philosophie du siècle,* Paris, 1891, p. 29, and Schinz, *op. cit.,* p. 255.

32. Salomon, *op. cit.,* p. 400.

33. *Cours,* VI, 590; *Discours sur l'esprit positive* (1918 ed.), p. 118.

34. Cf., for example, Dittmann, *op. cit.,* XXXVIII, 310, and Merz, *op. cit.,* p. 500.

35. Cf. Popper, *Open Society,* and Karl Löwith, *Von Hegel zu Nietzsche,* Zürich, 1941, p. 302.

36. This long-standing confusion has been accentuated recently by the fact that so distinguished a historian as Friedrich Meinecke devoted his great work, *Die Entstehung des Historismus,* München, 1936, entirely to that earlier historical school, in contradistinction to which the term *historicism* was coined during the second half of the nineteenth century. See also W. Eucken, "Die Ueberwindung des Historismus," *Schmollers Jahrbuch,* LXIII (1938).

37. Quoted by G. Bryson, *Man and Society,* Princeton, 1945, p. 78.

38. Quoted by Troeltsch, *op. cit.,* pp. 189-90, note.

39. Popper, "The Poverty of Historicism," as quoted above.

40. On Comte's influence on the growth of the younger historical school in German economics compare particularly F. Raab, *Die Fortschrittsidee bei Gustav Schmoller,* Freiburg, 1934, p. 72, and H. Waentig, *August Comte und seine Bedeutung für die Entwicklung der Sozialwissenschaft,* Leipzig, 1894.

41. Most clearly seen in the person of Wilhelm Scherer. See also Rothacker, *op. cit.,* pp. 190-250.

42. *Early Essays,* p. 15.

43. *Cours,* IV, 298.

44. *Cours,* IV, 157: "Car la vraie liberté ne peut consister, sans doute, qu'en une soumission rationelle a la seule prépondérance, convenablement constatée, des lois fondamentales de la nature."

45. *Philosophie der Geschichte,* ed. Reclam, p. 77: "Notwendig ist das Vernünftige als das Substantielle, und frei sind wir, indem wir es als Gesetz anerkennen und ihm als Substanz unseres eigenen Wesens folgen: der objektive und der subjektive Wille sind dann ausgesöhnt und ein und dasselbe ungetrübte Ganze."

46. *Cours,* IV, 144; cf. *Early Essays,* p. 132.

47. For references see Meyerson, *L'explication,* II, 130, and cf. Popper, *Open Society,* II, 40.

48. J. S. Mill to Harriet Mill, Rome, January 15, 1855: "Almost all the projects of social reformers of these days are really *liberticide*—Comte's particularly so" (F. A. Hayek, *John Stuart Mill and Harriet Taylor,* Chicago, 1951, p. 216). For a fuller statement of Comte's political conclusions, whose antiliberal tendencies go far beyond anything Hegel ever said, see above pp. 183-184.

49. In Comte's "Positivist Calendar" the "Month of Modern Statesmanship" is given the name of Frederick the Great!

50. Cf. H. Preller, "Rationalismus und Historismus," *Historische Zeitschrift,* CXXVI (1922).

51. *Grundlinien der Philosophie des Rechts,* Preface ("Philosophische Bibliothek," Leipzig, Felix Meiner, 1911), p. 14.

52. *Système de Politique Positive* (1854), I, 356: "La supériorité nécessaire de la moral démontrée sur la morale revelée."

53. *L'industrie,* ed. H. de Saint-Simon, Vol. III, 2ᵐᵉ cahier.

54. A. Thiers, *Histoire de la révolution française* (1823-27).

55. T. Carlyle to J. S. Mill, January 12, 1833, in *Letters of Thomas Carlyle to John Stuart Mill, John Sterling and Robert Browning,* ed. Alexander Carlyle, London, 1910.

56. J. S. Mill to T. Carlyle, February 2, 1833 (unpublished letter in the National Library of Scotland).

57. On Hegel's legal positivism see particularly H. Heller, *Hegel und der nationale Machstaatsgedanke in Deutschland,* Leipzig and Berlin, 1921, p. 166, and Popper, *The Open Society,* II, 39. For Comte see *Cours,* IV, 266 ff.

58. Cf. above pp. 88-93.

59. Cf. my *Individualism and Economic Order,* Chicago, 1948, p. 7.

60. Cf. above p. 168 *et seq.*

61. Engels, *Ludwig Feuerbach and the Outcome of Classical German Philosophy,* New York, 1941, p. 18.

62. On Feuerbach see S. Rawidowicz, *Ludwig Feuerbachs Philosophie,* Berlin, 1931; K. Löwith, *Von Hegel bis Nietzsche,* Zürich, 1941; A. Lévy, *La philosophie du Feuerbach,* Paris, 1904, and F. Lombardi, *L. Feuerbach,* Florence, 1935. A recent English study of Feuerbach by W. B. Chamberlain, *Heaven Wasn't His Destination,* London, 1941, is unfortunately quite inadequate. For the widespread positivistic tendencies among the Young Hegelians see particularly D. Koigen, *Zur Vorgeschichte des modernen philosophischen Sozialismus in Deutschland,* Bern, 1901.

63. L. Feuerbach to W. Bolin, Oct. 20, 1860, *Ausgewählte Briefe von und an Feuerbach,* ed. W. Bolin, Leipzig, 1904, II, 246-47.

64. Lorenz Stein, *Der Socialismus und Communismus im heutigen Frankreich,* Leipzig, 1842.

65. See Heinz Nitschke, "Die Geschichtsphilosophie Lorenz von Steins,"

Historische Zeitschrift, Supplement XXVI, 1932, especially p. 136 for the earlier literature on the subject; and T. G. Masaryk, *Die philosophischen und soziologischen Grundlagen des Marxismus,* Vienna, 1899, p. 34.

66. On Jules Lechevalier see H. Ahrens, *Naturrecht,* 6th ed.; Vienna, 1870, I, 204; Charles Pelarin, *Notice sur Jules Lechevalier et Abel Transon,* Paris, 1877; A. V. Wenckstern, *Marx,* Leipzig, 1896, pp. 205 f.; and S. Bauer, "Henri de Saint-Simon nach hundert Jahren," *Archiv für die Geschichte des Sozialismus,* XII (1926), 172.

67. A careful analysis of the positivist influence on Marx and Engels would require a separate investigation. A direct influence extending to surprising verbal similarities could be shown in the writing of Engels, while the influence on Marx is probably more indirect. Some material for such a study will be found in T. G. Masaryk, *op. cit.,* p. 35, and Lucie Prenant, "Marx et Comte," in *A la Lumière de Marxisme,* Paris, Cercle de la Russie Neuve, 1937, Vol. II, Part I. In a late letter to Engels (July 7, 1866), Marx who was then reading Comte, apparently for the first time consciously (as distinguished from his probable acquaintance with Comte's Saint-Simonian writing), describes him as "lamentable" compared to Hegel.

68. Friedrich List, *Nationales System der politischen Oekonomie,* 1841.

69. Wilhelm Roscher, *Grundriss zu Vorlesungen über die staatswirtschaft nach historischer Methode,* 1843.

70. The special significance of the year 1842 in this connection is well brought out by D. Koigen, *op. cit.,* pp. 236 ff., and by Hans Freund, *Soziologie und Sozialismus,* Würzburg, 1934. Particularly instructive on the influence of positivism on the German historians

of the period are the letters of J. G. Droysen. See particularly his letter of February 2, 1851, to T. v. Schön, in which he writes: "Die Philosophie ist durch Hegel und seine Schüler für geraume Zeit nicht nur diskreditiert sondern in ihrem eigensten Leben zerrüttet. Die Götzendienerei mit dem konstruierénden, ja schöpferischen Denken hat, indem alles ihm vindiziert wurde, zu dem Feuerbachschen Wahnwitz getrieben, der methodisch und ethisch jener polytechnischen Richtung ganz entspricht"; and the letter of July 17, 1852, to M. Duncker, which contains the following passage: "Weh uns und unserem deutschen Denken, wenn die polytechnische Misère, an der Frankreich seit 1789 verdorrt und verfault, diese babylonische Mengerei von Rechnerei und Lüderlichkeit, in das schon entartete Geschlecht noch tiefer einreisst. Jener bunte Positivismus, den man in Berlin betreibt, setzt diese Revolution des geistigen Lebens ins Treibhaus." (J. G. Droysen, *Briefwechsel,* ed. R. Hübner, Leipzig, 1929, II, 48, 120.)

71. Cf. D. D. Rosca, *L'influence de Hegel sur Taine,* Paris, 1928, and O. Engel, *Der Einfluss Hegels auf die Bildung der Gedankenwelt Taines,* Stuttgart, 1920.

72. See S. Deploige, *The Conflict between Ethics and Sociology,* St. Louis, 1938, chap. iv.

73. See P. Barth, *Die Philosophie der Geschichte als Soziologie,* 1925.

74. See E. Grünwald, *Das Problem der Soziologie des Wissens,* Vienna, 1934.

75. C. Bouglé, *Chez les Prophètes socialistes,* 1918, chap. iii.

76. That Comte's ideas influenced Veblen seems fairly clear. See W. Jaffé, *Les théories économiques et sociales de T. Veblen,* Paris, 1924, p. 35.

INDEX

FREE PRESS PAPERBACKS

A *NEW SERIES* OF PAPERBOUND BOOKS
IN THE SOCIAL AND NATURAL SCIENCES, PHILOSOPHY, AND THE HUMANITIES

These books, chosen for their intellectual importance and editorial excellence, are printed on good quality book paper, from the large and readable type of the cloth bound edition, and are Smyth-sewn for enduring use. *Free Press Paperbacks* conform in every significant way to the high editorial and production standards maintained in the higher-priced, case-bound books published by *The Free Press of Glencoe*

.8523

For information address:

THE FREE PRESS OF GLENCOE
A Division of the Macmillan Company, 60 Fifth Avenue, New York, N.Y. 10011

PB 20552